DEVELOPMENT and LEARNING:

Conflict or Congruence?

The Jean Piaget Symposium Series
Available from LEA

SIGEL I. E., BRODZINSKY, D. M., & GOLINKOFF, R. M. (Eds.) • New Directions in Piagetian Theory and Practice

OVERTON, W. F. (Ed.) • Relationships Between Social and Cognitive Development

LIBEN, L. S. (Ed.) • Piaget and the Foundations of Knowledge

SCHOLNICK, E. K. (Ed.) • New Trends in Conceptual Representation: Challenges to Piaget's Theory?

NEIMARK, E. D., De LISI, R., & NEWMAN, J. L. (Eds.) • Moderators of Competence

BEARISON, D. J., & ZIMILES, H. (Eds.) • Thought and Emotion: Developmental Perspectives

LIBEN, L. S. (Ed.) • Development and Learning: Conflict or Congruence?

DEVELOPMENT and LEARNING:

Conflict or Congruence?

edited by
Lynn S. Liben
The Pennsylvania State University

LAWRENCE ERLBAUM ASSOCIATES, PUBLISHERS
1987   Hillsdale, New Jersey   Hove and London

Development and learning

Lawrence Erlbaum Associates, Inc., Publishers
365 Broadway
Hillsdale, New Jersey 07642

Library of Congress Cataloging-in-Publication Data
Development and learning.
    (The Jean Piaget Symposium series)
    Bibliography: p.
    Includes index.
    1. Educational psychology—Congresses. 2. Child
development—Congresses. 3. Learning, Psychology of—
Congresses. 4. Piaget, Jean, 1896–   —Congresses.
I. Liben, Lynn S. II. Series.
LB1051.D468 1987   370.15   87-5424
ISBN 0-8058-0009-3

Printed in the United States of America
10 9 8 7 6 5 4 3 2 1

Contents

List of Contributors

Ann L. Brown—*University of Illinois*
David Henry Feldman—*Tufts University*
Lynn S. Liben—*The Pennsylvania State University*
Frank B. Murray—*University of Delaware*
Robert A. Reeve—*University of Illinois*
Lauren B. Resnick—*University of Pittsburgh*
Robert S. Siegler—*Carnegie Mellon University*
Hermine Sinclair—*University of Geneva*
Christopher Shipley—*Carnegie Mellon University*
Sidney Strauss—*Tel-Aviv University*
Robert H. Wozniak—*Bryn Mawr College*

Preface: Development and Learning—Questions

The members of the Board of Directors of the Jean Piaget Society hold a diverse set of opinions about developmental epistemology. However, probably all share a commitment to the Piagetian view that conflict, and the disequilibrium it provokes, act as powerful forces in motivating cognitive progression—not only for the developing child, but also for the mature academician. As a result, scholars invited as Plenary Speakers at the Annual Symposia of the Society are only occasionally those who would be readily labeled as *Piagetians*. Far more commonly, invited speakers are scholars who offer alternative approaches to the study of developmental phenomena.

These alternatives are sometimes couched in terms of challenges to Piagetian theory, in which the fundamental question is whether Piagetian theory can maintain its integrity in the face of critiques (as in a recent Symposium focused on new theories of concepts, see Scholnick, 1983). Sometimes the alternatives are couched in terms of content domains that received relatively little attention from Piaget, in which the central question is whether Piagetian theory can assimilate those domains (as in a Symposia focused on various aspects of emotional development, see Overton, 1983; Bearison & Zimiles, 1986; or as in one focused on constructivism and computers, see Forman & Pufall, in preparation). Sometimes—as in the Symposium on which the present volume is based—the alternatives are drawn from research programs addressed to contents similar to those studied by Piaget, but couched within a different language and employing different empirical paradigms. Here, the fundamental question is whether these alternatives are fundamentally compatible with Piagetian theory, offering progressive refinements of that theory, or instead, are fundamentally distinct, "competing" approaches.

One of the most pervasive contemporary approaches to cognitive development, often viewed as a "rival" to Piagetian theory, is information processing. In information processing, the focus is on the way that individuals acquire and process material in specific domains such as mathematics. It has been suggested that information processing has changed the basic paradigm of psychological research during the last 10–15 years.

> Psychologists like Thorndike were primarily interested in extending established principles of psychology to the learning of academic subjects. Today the tables have turned. Research within specific content domains is being used to provide a window on basic cognitive processes. Researchers are carefully analyzing the way in which knowledge is structured within a content domain, and they are using this analysis to help explain how a wide variety of individuals ranging from novices to experts organize knowledge and solve problems within that domain. (Carpenter, 1982, p. 969)

Carpenter contrasts general principles to specific content domains. The former might, of course, be principles derived from any one of a number of theoretical orientations—from Hull to Piaget. The latter might involve acquisition of principles, strategies, or information, but is clearly focused on what most people would agree is *learning*. A fundamental question then becomes whether the acquisition of knowledge in specific domains (learning) can account for what appear to be changes in broader strategies, changes that when age-linked are typically labeled *developmental*.

Piaget, of course, saw development as primary. In his view it is within the general structures of thought that the learning of specifics is embedded. A view in which learning is primary might thus provide a true alternative to Piaget. The purpose of the Symposium on which the present volume is based was to provide a forum to consider this development/learning issue. In the letters of invitation, speakers were specifically asked to address the concepts of development and learning, with particular attention to how "questions generated within the framework of structural cognitive-developmental theories such as Piaget's have been analyzed from the perspective of a task analytic, information-processing approach."

The particular selection of speakers was guided by an interest in including a number of different theoretical approaches, a variety of content domains, and a diversity in the learning environments examined. To set the context for the discussions within Piagetian theory, the Board invited Hermine Sinclair to deliver the Keynote Address. This address provided the opportunity to discuss the development/learning issue from the perspective of traditional Piagetian theory, and in addition, from the perspective of more recent Genevan work focused explicitly on learning (e.g., *Learning and the Development of Cognition*, Inhelder, Sinclair, & Bovet, 1974). These discussions form the core of the first chapter in the present volume.

Alternative approaches were provided by scholars who are strongly associated with the information-processing approach. Lauren Resnick and Robert Siegler were invited as representatives of this tradition, not only because they have been concerned with age-linked changes in information-processing mechanisms, but also because they have focused on a content domain—mathematics—that has been a central focus of Genevan theory and research as well. Resnick (chapter 2) and Siegler and Christopher Shipley (chapter 4) address some basic issues in the relationship between development and learning, and illustrate these issues by their empirical work on children's developing arithmetic skills.

Another approach to the development/learning issue is represented in the contribution by Sidney Strauss (chapter 6). Whereas Resnick and Siegler and Shipley are primarily (although not exclusively) focused on learning as it occurs as a consequence of exposure to mathematics curricula in the schools, Strauss considers how developmental theories (especially those of Piaget and Vygotsky) and educational psychology may be combined to develop, implement, and evaluate new classroom curricula. Strauss' contribution emphasizes the synergistic combination of basic cognitive–developmental theory and classroom learning.

Ann Brown was invited as a Plenary Speaker both because her empirical work is highly relevant and because she has specifically addressed the issue of development and learning in past writings. Her previous analyses have been concerned particularly with whether children might be best viewed as universal novices who have not yet learned as much as their older counterparts, and with whether learning as a concept has been given short shrift in the developmental literature (e.g., Brown, 1982). In this volume, Brown and Robert Reeve (chapter 8) draw from both Piaget's and Vygotsky's theories to argue that "contexts create learning and development." They illustrate this argument by reference to research on instruction in formal classroom settings as well as in everyday family and cultural contexts.

In keeping with the commitment of the Jean Piaget Society to use these Symposia as an opportunity to challenge and extend Piagetian theory, each of the Plenary Speakers' addresses was followed by a discussant who was asked to react to the Plenary presentation from the perspective of Piagetian theory. Four chapters in this volume are expanded versions of these discussions.

In reaction to Resnick's chapter, Frank Murray (chapter 3) considers the development of arithmetic skills as constructions or inventions rooted in the child's developing logical system. In addition, he reviews work from his program of research concerning the development of children's understanding of the necessity of arithmetic outcomes. My own discussion of Siegler and Shipley's contribution (chapter 5) considers whether Siegler's information-processing approach should be interpreted as a "tight" formulation of a portion of Piagetian theory, or as a radically different interpretation of cognitive development.

In response to the chapter by Strauss, David Feldman (chapter 7) argues that—in contrast to much of the traditional work in educational psychology that is derived from laboratory experimental psychology—Strauss' use of Piaget's and Vygotsky's theories to inform educational practice is a successful endeavor. In addition, Feldman discusses an alternative (but compatible) "middle-ground" approach, stressing the importance of examining mastery of *both* universal and non-universal domains.

Finally, Robert Wozniak (chapter 9) considers relationships among a number of theoretical positions relevant to the themes and data presented in the chapter by Brown and Reeve. In particular, he discusses relationships among Piaget, Vygotsky, and Gibson, culminating in the question: "To what extent does it or does it not make sense to attempt to combine the ecological approach of Gibson with the constructivism of Piaget, or, for that matter, to combine the constructivism of Piaget with the socio-historicism of Vygotsky?" He concludes that Piaget is less similar to Vygotsky and more similar to Gibson than is commonly assumed.

In short, the chapters serve not only to highlight and critique the contents of the Plenary Speakers' contributions, but also to set them within broader theoretical, metatheoretical, and empirical contexts.

Introductory comments entitled "Development and Learning: Questions" almost beg for closing comments entitled "Development and Learning: Answers." Readers should be warned that the Epilogue does not provide this symmetry: It is not possible to merge the diverse set of positions concerning development and learning into a neat package of answers. Nor would it necessarily be better if such a merger were possible. As a Society, we endorse the statement made by Piaget (1974, cited in T. Brown, 1980), that "All knowledge consists in bringing up new problems at the same time that it resolves preceding ones" (p. xii). The reader may be assured that even if the volume fails to resolve old problems, it undeniably succeeds at raising new ones!

ACKNOWLEDGMENTS

Many individuals deserve credit for the production of this volume. First, of course, are the authors of the chapters themselves. They have expended much effort, not only in writing their chapters, but also in serving as Plenary Speakers and Discussants at the 14th Annual Symposium of the Jean Piaget Society from which this book is drawn.

David Henry Feldman also played a central role in this volume. His own work has demonstrated the advances that may be made by probing the relationship between development and learning, and by combining developmental theory and educational practice. Further, he was involved in the planning and implementation of the 14th JPS Symposium. He was unable to co-edit the book only because it needed to be done precisely at the same time that he was completing (with

Lynn Goldsmith) another major project—*Nature's Gambit* (Basic Books, 1986). His conceptual contributions and personal support have been invaluable.

Robbie Case, Howard Gardner, and Sheldon White participated in the Symposium as special invited speakers. Although their involvement did not include written chapters, their presentations added significantly to the excitement of the meetings themselves, and undoubtedly influenced the written contributions of others.

A competent and dedicated group of developmental graduate students at Temple University, working with Willis Overton, Local Arrangements Chairperson, performed the innumerable tasks that allowed this (and every other JPS) Symposium to function. James Byrnes deserves special recognition for taking on extra duties as the student member of the Board of Directors during this Symposium.

The production of the volume itself was aided immeasurably by the expert secretarial assistance of Sandy Ranio, the professional drafting of Roger Downs, and the efficient editorial work of Robin Marks Weisberg and the rest of the staff at Lawrence Erlbaum Associates.

On behalf of the Jean Piaget Society, I express sincere appreciation to all these individuals for their hard and generous work, and add my personal thanks for making my job a rewarding and manageable one.

Lynn S. Liben

REFERENCES

Bearison, D. J., & Zimiles, H. (Eds.). (1986). *Thought and emotion.* Hillsdale, NJ: Lawrence Erlbaum Associates.

Brown, A. L. (1982). Learning and development: The problem of compatibility, access, and induction. *Human Development, 25,* 89–115.

Brown, T. A. (1980). Foreword. In J. Piaget *Experiments in contradiction* (pp. vii–xii). Chicago: University of Chicago Press.

Carpenter, T. P. (1982). Toward a new psychology of cognitive learning. *Contemporary Psychology, 27,* 969–970.

Forman, G., & Pufall, P. (Eds.). (in preparation). *Constructivism in the computer age.* Hillsdale, NJ: Lawrence Erlbaum Associates.

Inhelder, A. B., Sinclair, H., & Bovet, M. (1974). *Learning and the development of cognition.* Cambridge, MA: Harvard University Press.

Overton, W. F. (Ed.). (1983). *The relationship between social and cognitive development.* Hillsdale, NJ: Lawrence Erlbaum Associates.

Piaget, J. (1974). *L'equilibration des structures cognitives.* Paris: Presses Universitaires de France.

Scholnick, E. K. (Ed.). (1983). *New trends in conceptual representation: Challenges to Piaget's theory?* Hillsdale, NJ: Lawrence Erlbaum Associates.

1 Conflict and Congruence in Development and Learning

Hermine Sinclair
University of Geneva

When the theme, "Conflict and Congruence," was first suggested to me as the focus of my presentation and chapter, I wondered whether I was being asked to address conflict and congruence in theories of cognitive development (because I took for granted that cognitive development was to be the general theme) or conflict and congruence in the mind of the developing child. When I asked for clarification on this point, the Board of Directors of the Piaget Society suggested I address both, no doubt realizing that in the case of Piaget's theory at least, it is impossible not to do so! Indeed, as I saw only later, *conflict* and *congruence* can almost be seen as synonyms for disequilibrium and equilibration—the most general mechanisms of the construction of knowledge according to Piaget. Thus, my chapter presents a mixture of theories and descriptions of children's behavior, although the latter is used mainly to provide illustrations of theoretical points.

FUNDAMENTAL PROBLEMS AND SOURCES OF CONFLICT

In the numerous and often passionate discussions on cognitive psychology, certain fundamental problems make their appearance time and time again. One of these problems concerns methodology: What is considered to be scientific methodology, leading to scientific psychology, and what instead belongs to the realm of philosophy or speculation? Another problem concerns the relation between psychologists and the object of their studies: the thinking and feeling human being. Yet another problem (in fact, the most ancient and the most essential)

1

concerns the nature of knowledge: What is the relation between the knowing subject and the object of his knowledge (i.e., the world of people, animals, plants, and other things in which he lives)?

Gréco (1967) makes the following rather ironic, but profound remark: "The psychologist is never sure that what he does is 'science.' And if what he does is 'science' he is never sure that it is psychology" (p. 937). I imagine that most psychologists often feel caught in this dilemma. Partly, the dilemma has to do with method. Historically, certain psychological experiments combine an adulation of method for its own sake with a total disregard of what psychological problem the experiment is supposed to elucidate. More recently, however, controversy about methodology has become less dogmatic than before: Virtually everybody now admits that methods are to be judged in light of the questions asked; and the latter are obviously linked to the particular epistemological positions espoused. Certain questions of perception and memory, for example, can be perfectly well treated in a strict stimulus-response situation. Other problems in human learning and the behavior of human groups cannot be treated by this experimental method. Should they therefore be relegated to the field of nonscientific or philosophical psychology? Most of us, I think, would answer no, if only because methods and their underlying theories change. For example, Skinner's strict stimulus-response, input–output schema changed considerably with the introduction of operant conditioning or instrumental learning. The organism under study and its spontaneous behavior became, in a way, included both in the input and in the output, and the strict schema was no longer as clear-cut as before. Similarly, the introduction of intervening variables modified the initial opposition to interpretation or explanation of behavior. The information-processing approach to psychological questions goes even further along these lines, without, however, giving up the stimulus-response schema. In the words of one author (Massaro, 1975), "The central assumption of our information-processing model is that a number of processing stages occur between the stimulus and the response" (p. 599). The author presents information processing as the current state of the art in experimental psychology, and explicitly excludes social and developmental psychology. In my opinion, this approach constitutes an important extension of stimulus-response methodology. The author emphasizes the essential aspects of the different processing stages that occur between the stimulus and the response, and the fact that the operations of a particular stage transform the information processed in the previous stage. In spite of these modifications of the former stimulus-response schema, the information-processing approach continues, in my opinion, to share some of the most basic tenets of stimulus-response learning theory.

The status of certain methods may also be changed by technology. Observational methods, in either a natural or a laboratory setting, are changing under the impact of new technology. Audiovisual recording and the computer treatment of data, for example, render observational, that is, non-experimental data, more readily measurable and therefore more acceptable to the scientific community.

Another method, long known in the history of psychology, but, I think, more frequently used thanks to advancing technology, is the establishment of analogical models or simulations of human cognitive activities. This approach must certainly be counted among the scientific methods that promise to further our understanding of cognition. Piaget himself had great hopes of cybernetics or artificial intelligence as a source of interdisciplinary models of mechanisms that are at the same time preprogrammed and self-regulatory.

Methods thus no longer seem to be a source of conflict by themselves. They are discussed instead with a view to their adequacy for the study of particular problems, not with respect to whether they have a particular value in themselves. A certain agreement appears thus to have been reached, even if only in the form of admitting the necessity of diversity.

Similarly, there no longer seems to be any controversy about whether psychologists should only give a description of the behavior they have observed, or whether they may and indeed should offer interpretations and explanations. All or almost all agree that psychologists are legitimately interested in interpreting and explaining, as well as describing the behavior of their subjects. There may, however, be controversy about what kind of experimental or observational data lend themselves to interpretative or explanatory theories and to what degree interpretations and explanations can be generalized. I think that on this point, too, psychologists have come to agree with Piaget (1970) who argued that as long as specific fields of study do not produce imperialistic and reductionist theories, "the results obtained in one field can explain those in another but are simultaneously enriched by properties that were undiscovered until then, though necessary in order to establish a link between the two fields" (p. 372).

The second problem, that is, the relation between the psychologist, a thinking and feeling subject himself, and the human being (or animals) that are the object of his studies, is certainly also a factor in Gréco's dilemma. On this point also, however, we seem to have reached agreement, if only in the form of resignation. The observer–observed relation is a question that arises in almost all scientific endeavors. We should be aware of it, but there is no way of circumventing it. Perhaps it can even serve as an encouragement for psychologists. Gréco (1967) himself pointed out: "It may not be such a bad thing for the psychologist to have chosen for the object of his studies a subject in his own image" (p. 988). Despite all the danger inherent in introspection, it may also give us some precious insights.

There remains, then, the last and fundamental problem that continues to divide cognitive psychologists into different camps, that is, the age-old problem of the relation between the subject and the world he or she lives in, and the nature and value of the knowledge that results from this relation.

According to a venerable tradition, going back to the pre-Socratics, the contact between the subject and his or her world is provided by the subject's senses. The senses transmit information from which the subject can construct a correct representation of the "real" world. However, this view of knowledge as essentially a copy-type knowledge derived from sensory experience suffers from the fact that we can never compare it to the real world. Plato's solution was to enclose the subject in the world of ideas and to deny the existence of reality.

Pure copy theories of knowledge based on this radical division between subject and the world around him seem no longer to be in favor. As we have seen, the organism has been interposed between the stimulus and the response of stimulus-response theories. In the neurosciences, subjects are seen as computing a representation, according to models of the functioning of neurons; and in the information-processing approach, the subject transforms the information obtained by a first phase of processing in later phases. Almost everywhere, the subject is seen as active and as interacting with his or her environment. Piaget's solution is, however, more radical and has certain important consequences.

According to Piaget, the essential way of knowing the real world is not directly through our senses, but first and foremost through our actions. In this context, action has to be understood as all behavior by which we bring about a change in the world around us, or by which we change our own situation in relation to the world. In other words, it is behavior that changes the knower–known relationship. From the baby who laboriously pushes two objects together or who attracts his or her mother's attention by crying, to the scientist who invents new ways of making elementary particles react, to the child or adult who tries to convince his or her friends of his or her opinions, new knowledge is constructed from the changes or transformations the subject introduces in the knower–known relationship.

The quality of the knowledge gathered in this way is partly determined by its correspondence to the knowledge other people have constructed and partly by the ways in which reality reacts to our interventions. As von Glasersfeld (1983), who may be an even more radical constructivist than Piaget, puts it:

> From an explorer who is condemned to seek 'structural properties' of an inaccessible reality, the experiencing organism now turns into a builder of cognitive structures intended to solve such problems as the organism perceives or conceives. . . . What determines the value of the conceptual structure is their experimental adequacy, their goodness of *fit* with experience, their *viability* as a means for the solving of problems. (pp. 50–51)

This does not mean that the knowing subjects are forever living in a world of their own making, but it does mean that they can never get absolute knowledge of reality as it is. As Piaget (1980), who saw himself as a realist of a rather special kind, expresses it: "With every step forward in knowledge that brings the subject nearer to his object, the latter retreats . . . so that the successive models elaborated by the subject are no more than approximations that despite improvements can never reach . . . the object itself, which continues to possess unknown properties" (pp. 221–222). This, according to Piaget, is applicable to children as well as to adult scientists and to science as a social enterprise.

The fundamental constructivist view thus postulates changes in the relation between subject and object, and the movement toward better, although never perfect, knowledge of the object has as its concomitant another movement whereby the subject obtains better knowledge of his or her own actions or thought processes. There may not be perfect synchronicity, but sooner or later every new conquest of the world of objects will lead the subject to restructure his or her action- or thought-operations system, just as new deductions and inferences derived from the internal system will lead to new interrogations of reality.

This view of the knower–known relation, which, I think, is particular to Piaget's epistemology, relativizes the division between subject and object, just as it avoids the choice between idealism and empiricism. It introduces two partly distinct ways of knowing. In one, the subject constructs new knowledge from his or her own actions or mental operations by which he or she organizes the object. In the other, through the subject's interventions, the subject constructs new knowledge from hitherto and undiscovered properties of the objects.

This epistemological view is already present in Piaget's early works. In *La naissance de l'intelligence* and *La construction du réel chez l'enfant* taken together, he shows through an analysis of the same observations how infants construct their reality by constructing their intelligence. Subsequently, he and his collaborators, principally Bärbel Inhelder, studied the cognitive structures of different levels of development, already then supposing that these structures are subject to equilibration processes. Only later did Piaget (1974) begin to study the mechanisms of disequilibrium (taken for granted until then) and equilibration. This new orientation led to a series of works that are, in a certain sense, more "psychological" because they deal with mechanisms or processes that lead to the construction of new knowledge. These processes should all be seen in the light of the particular knower–known relationship as postulated by Piaget. Taken outside that context, many of them resemble processes discussed by authors of different epistemological persuasion. Consciousness, abstraction, generalization, contradictions are all concepts that are familiar to developmental psychologists as factors to be invoked for the interpretation and/or explanation of certain behaviors. But in the context of dialectical constructivism they have specific epistemological meanings. In particular, it is conflicts—the clash between action modes or conceptual systems which worked and new experiential apprehensions—that is a source of progress. In other cases, the success of certain action modes is tested against experiential situations and consolidated so as to form the basis for the opening up of new possibilities.

THREE EXAMPLES OF CONFLICT AND PROGRESS
OR CONSOLIDATION IN CHILDREN'S THINKING

Presented here are three examples (taken from many) that may clarify some of the basic principles of constructivism: conflict, disequilibrium, progress, consolidation, and equilibration. These examples also illustrate the differences between the two types of knowledge just enumerated.

The first example concerns object permanence. Piaget (1937, obs. 52) describes how his nephew, at 13 months, when playing with a ball, sees it disappear under an armchair and retrieves it. A little later the ball rolls under a sofa. The child sees it disappear, looks under the sofa, but cannot see the ball, and goes back to the armchair and feels around for the ball in the place where he found it the first time. This observation led Piaget to construct a series of experimental situations (1937) used in certain developmental assessment scales (e.g., Uzgiris & Hunt, 1975).

The gradual construction of object permanence confers a new status to the objects that children manipulate. The objects become units that can enter into different kinds of relations (spatial and causal relations, relations of belonging to collections, etc.). Object permanence is accordingly considered to be an important aspect of cognitive development.

My example shows a child spontaneously creating problem situations that exhibit an astonishing resemblance to several of Piaget's experimental situations. The example, reported in detail by Rayna (1984), is taken from an extensive study concerning infants' behavior with several collections of objects using a longitudinal as well as a cross-sectional method (Sinclair, Stambak, Lezine, Rayna, & Verba, 1982). In this study, one of the collections children were given consisted of about 30 objects with no familiar function (unlike the usual cups, spoons, combs or sponges, for example). The objects were partly transformable and included raw spaghetti, little paper balls, sticks, a piece of paper, a piece of cloth, a length of string, and an elastic band. The children were filmed during 30 minutes of spontaneous play. The longitudinal group was filmed in principle once a month. Nicolas, the child referred to in the example, was observed at 19, 21, and 22 months.

During the first session, Nicolas explores the bit of cloth, then holding it in one hand puts a ball of clay inside it; he turns his hand over so the ball is no longer visible. He lifts up a corner of the cloth and finds the ball is visible again! He pursues his hiding and discovering actions in various ways during the total observation time: cloth in hand, ball on top, covers ball by pulling cloth over it; ball on table, cloth on top, picks up the covered ball, turns it over, and so on.

Two months later, the very first thing Nicolas does is to take the ball in one hand and to wrap it in the cloth. To our great surprise, Nicolas seems to pick up the problem where he left it 2 months earlier (he has not seen the collection of objects in the meantime, although he has, of course, seen and handled other similar objects). During this session, Nicolas explores the possibilities of using other objects, either as covers or as objects to be covered. He starts by placing the ball of clay on a piece of paper that he folds around it; then he places a piece of cotton carefully inside the paper. From time to time he opens the paper a bit as if to verify that indeed the objects are still inside it.

At the third session, a month later, Nicolas once again immediately continues working on his problem. He puts the paper flat on the floor and the ball on top of it, and wraps the paper around it. He repeats these actions several times, and at one point, he turns to another child and shows his package. A little later, he wraps the ball in the cloth, turns to the observer, shows her the package, opens up the cloth a bit, shows the ball and says: "a caché" ('s hidden). This, too, is repeated several times. Sometimes the ball rolls away, sometimes Nicolas folds the paper around the ball and when he picks it up, the ball remains behind. The empty paper (which keeps the shape of what is inside) is then carefully explored. Nicolas continues to hide various small objects under or inside other objects, saying "caché" over and over to himself, and at the end of the observation session he makes a package and gives it to another child.

This sequence of spontaneous actions (nothing is suggested by the observer; the objects are put down pell-mell) presents several astonishing aspects:

1. During three half-hour observation sessions with intervals of respectively 2 and 1 months, the child works exclusively on his problem of hiding and retrieving. The presence of the collection of objects (one would really have to stretch one's imagination to regard it as a "stimulus") activates the child's problem as he had worked it out previously ("working memory"?) and each time the problem is elaborated further.

2. At the last observation session, when Nicolas seems to have mastered the various problems he had raised for himself, two interesting behaviors appear. In the first place, he shows his construction to someone else, as if he wanted to share his new knowledge or, maybe, as if he wanted to verify the inter-subjectivity of the information he has created. Secondly, he names his discovery, first for someone else, then, many times, for himself ("caché"). To quote Piaget (1937): "Why, at a certain moment in his mental evolution does the subject try to represent spatial relationships to himself instead of simply acting on them? Obviously in order to communicate to someone else or to obtain from someone else some information on a fact concerning space. Outside of this social relation there is no apparent reason why pure representation should follow action. The existence of multiple perspectives relating to various individuals is therefore already involved in the child's effort to represent space to himself."

Nicolas is well on the way to full-blown object permanence: What he is exploring is the exchangeability of objects under spatial and causal constraints of size (smaller inside bigger objects), of pliability (cloth or paper vs. ball or beads), and of number (two objects can be retrieved just as a single one can). He creates small surprises for himself, but basically is busy consolidating and extending his understanding of object permanence and spatial relations such as inside, outside, around, under, and on.

A second example concerns number. Number concepts (which are very difficult to define, so I do not attempt to do so) are generally admitted by psychologists to be important in cognition. Many mathematicians, philosophers, and psychologists have theorized about number.

In the course of an observational study of free play with some toy animals among 3- to 5-year-olds, one little girl (4 years, 9 months old) gave an astonishing demonstration of Piaget's theoretical hypothesis concerning the construction of number and even a sort of reproduction of Piaget and Szeminska's well known conservation-of-numerosity task. Katya starts off, like most other children between 3 and 5, by introducing various orders into her materials. She puts the animals into horizontal, vertical, or oblique lines in front of her on the table. The celluloid animals are four identical swans, one duck, and three identical fish. By chance, the duck has the same length as a swan, although it differs in form and color. When aligned head to tail, the three fish form a line of the same length as the four swans similarly aligned.

Katya makes various arrangements, shifting between groupings that are collections of identical animals: alignments of three fish and four swans, with the duck either at the end or in the middle, and numerical divisions: three fish, three swans, and a swan plus the duck.

Finally, she makes two vertical lines: one of the three fish, one of the four swans and the duck, and she counts out loud: ". . . five . . . three." In this arrangement, the line of swans plus duck goes beyond that of the three fish. She then takes away the duck (the element that goes beyond the line of the fish) and counts again: ". . . four . . . three." Because this time the two lines coincide in length, she is confronted with a problem of her own making. (This is of course a Piagetian interpretation.) Her behavior is very much in accord with this interpretation. She appears surprised and disappointed, spends a long time looking at the two alignments, and then takes away one of the four swans. Now the line of the fish goes well beyond that of the swans. She says, with great satisfaction: "three and three". She then goes on to make other groupings (see Fig. 1.1).

The sequence of manipulations I have sketched is satisfactorily explained in the framework of Piagetian theory. Katya is involved in constructing new knowledge from her own actions by which she introduces organization into the toys. She is, at this point, not experimenting on the objects themselves. Her putting-together actions make her ideas about classifying things clear to the observer and to her. She struggles with the fact that the material, by chance, does not lend itself to forming collections that are both "logical" and "numerical": That is, she does not have four swans, four fishes and four ducks. Nor does the material

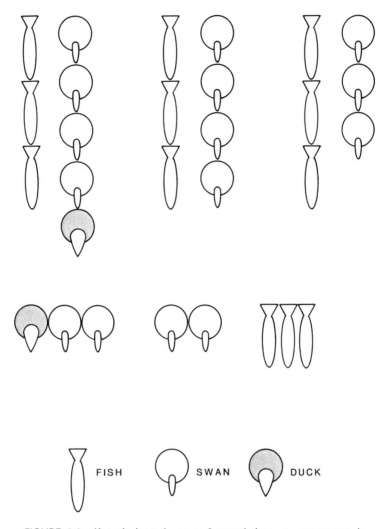

FIGURE 1.1. Katya's (age 4 years; 9 months) toy arrangements in mastering logical and numerical collections.

lend itself to numerical groups of the same length of alignment, because the three fish make a longer line than the three swans. Each of Katya's new arrangements raises a new problem which she proceeds to work on. In the end, to all appearances, she has successfully dissociated logical class, equality or inequality of number, and the space taken up (Robert, Cellérier, & Sinclair, 1972).

Obviously, this short developmental sequence in perfectly spontaneous behavior was preceded by many other experiences and developments. Among other things, Katya was taught to count in the sense that she has learned the counting words from other people. In addition, in the course of playing with other children, she has probably had experience in the distribution of toys with the aim of numerical or qualitative fairness. We can also think of subitizing, a peculiar capacity that seems to have neurological bases and that has also been studied in animals. The experiential and cognitive backgrounds for Katya's activity in this particular sequence are no doubt very varied. But her actions and her few words exemplify what Piaget means by problems and knowledge derived mainly from one's own organizing actions.

My third example is different in many ways. It concerns adolescents, it is placed in an experimental setting, and especially, it deals with the type of knowledge where the properties of objects are important.

This example concerns the well-known experiment on the dissociation between weight and volume. Generally speaking, 11- to 12-year-olds are immediately convinced that weight does not matter if one wants to calculate the rise of the water level when different objects are immersed in a glass container. If they are not convinced in the beginning, they come to this conclusion very rapidly. Bovet, Baranzini, Kamii, and Sinclair (1975) interviewed high-school students between 12 and 15 year olds. The adolescents usually start off by affirming that of course the water level should always go up to the same place, as long as the volume of the different objects is the same: Never mind if the clay has been broken up into little bits, or if the two cylinders do not have the same weight. However, they ask many questions and propose manipulations to verify what they themselves call *hypotheses*. They want to understand the possible effects of weight or of the pressure an object exerts on the water around it, and of the speed with which it will sink, and they consider the possibility that air or water could get into the clay. All of these different considerations, that is, new problems younger children do not think of, often make them hesitate and give non-conservation answers. Typical remarks are: "It *should* go up the same amount, because the volume is the same, but . . ." "*Logically,* one would say, the bigger the volume, the higher the water will rise, but . . . " Many factors are invoked: "I would like to know whether the little bits of clay float. . ." "Maybe some water could get in (irregular surface of the ball of clay) but you say that the clay does not absorb the water. . ." "The heavy cylinder exerts all the same more pressure on the water than the lighter one . . . that should play a role. . . ."

In other words, the 12- to 15-year-olds think of new properties of the objects they are experimenting with, they look for explanations, they propose little experiments to "see whether I was wrong", and most of them resolve the conflicts and return to conservation-of-volume answers. However, the concept is now enriched. They have thought of many properties of the objects that could influence the rise of the water but discard them, often experimentally.

These three examples, in my opinion, illustrate several of the important principles of Piaget's theory: the transformations subjects introduce in their interactions with objects, the different types of knowledge, the importance of conflicts, and the mechanism of equilibration, which in favorable cases results in a re-conceptualization at a higher level. By contrast, I fail to see how learning theory or the information processing approach (if the latter is seen as a theory of cognition rather than as a technique that can elucidate particular phenomena) can account for the examples I have cited. In both of these theories, *information* or *object properties* are considered to exist in the outside world for the subject to react to or to process. Katya's activities cannot be explained by some process of choosing what to attend to, what information to select, and what to discard.

In the case of what Piaget calls *logico-mathematical knowledge,* exemplified by the example of Katya, there is no such thing as information to be processed before Katya herself invents different ways of organizing the objects in space. Nothing in the objects themselves has a property such as numerical equivalence or non-equivalence.

With respect to the example of Nicolas, the concept of the gradual elaboration of object permanence runs counter to a theory that presupposes units and rules to be ''out there'' and the subject's activity to consist in computations. The whole point of object permanence is that during the first 6 months of life there are no such things as discrete objects. Instead, action and object are inextricably entwined and the gradual construction of discrete units (things, as we know them) and some aspects of space (different spots the things can be moved to and from) proceed synchronously with the gradual dissociation between the subject's actions and the objects he acts upon. I cannot see how an information processing view of cognition can deal with the construction of units, proceeding in step with the construction of space in terms of structure of displacements.

My last example probably appears to be more amenable to an analysis in terms of information or learning. After all, objects do have properties that can be observed under certain circumstances such as floating or sinking in water, taking up a certain space, exerting pressure, and so forth. However, without a deductive and inductive framework within which the subject can construct the situations that allow pertinent observations, no progress can be made. What changes between the solution found at the age of 11–12 and at the age of 14–15 is the capacity to create new observable phenomena that become facts to be accounted for in a new conceptual framework.[1]

SOME LACUNAE IN PIAGET'S WORK

Although the basic elements of the theory (of which I have tried to sketch those I see as the most important) are well-established, Piaget himself was well aware of what he called ''lacunae'' in the body of his work. One of the things missing is a detailed study of the interaction of the knowing subject with the world of people.

---

[1]For similar objections against information-processing theory, see Kolers and Smythe, 1984.

It is certainly true that interaction with people has received little attention as a factor in the construction of knowledge in Piaget's research, with the exception of his work on moral development. However, to quote Damon (1979):

> A quirk of scientific history has made Piaget's theory representative . . . of a model that presents the child working out concepts in relative isolation. . . On a theoretical level, his writings yield to no one in their recognition of the two-way relations between individual cognitive growth and cultural heritage. Yet it is also true that the predominant Genevan experimental paradigm over the last 40 years has been the testing of the young child-as-a-scientist, in solitary reflexion, wrestling with problems of mathematics or science. (p. 209)

Only fairly recently have psychologists that subscribe to the Piagetian epistemological theory begun to carry out research that bears on the interpersonal interaction and its importance for cognitive development.

Piaget himself considered social interaction as a necessary condition of cognitive development. However, in several writings he emphasizes that not all social interaction leads to cognitive development (1932, 1976). Piaget characterizes interaction leading to this development as *cooperative relations,* which he defines as follows: "all relations between two or n individuals that are equal or consider themselves as such; in other words, all social relations in which elements of authority or prestige do not intervene. (p. 67)" This, of course, does not mean that children could not learn from adults; it does mean, however, that they do not make genuine cognitive progress if the adults impose their ways of thinking on them. Adults, be they parents, psychologists, or teachers, can propose things to be thought about, and can create situations that bring about cognitive growth. Social-learning experiments, and learning experiments in general are not in contradiction with Piaget's theory, as long as the imposition of certain ways of thinking is avoided and as long as the constructivist principle is maintained. On the contrary, such studies can give us important insights into the course of cognitive growth (see, for example, Inhelder, Sinclair, & Bovet, 1974).

When Piaget and his collaborators devised their well known conservation tasks, their main concern was the formulation of cognitive structures underlying children's and adolescents' ways of thinking about problems that incorporate certain epistemologically important concepts. The mechanisms by which the structures change did not become a topic of research and theorizing until much later. The original experiments show that the various conservation concepts have to be constructed, but not how children come to change the ways in which they apprehend the problems. Clearly, as we have already remarked with reference to Katya's behavior sequence, their different "theories" are the results of many varied experiences in everyday life that confirmed or infirmed the "viability" (to use von Glasersfeld's term) of their ideas. It is obviously impossible to follow a child during all of his or her waking hours every day over several years in order to discover how his or her multifarious encounters with people, animals, plants, and objects lead to inferences and theories. Fortunately, the results of the original Piagetian experiments are very consistent and thus may provide insight into the theories that children seem to apply to a great number of different situations.

The training procedures devised by Inhelder et al. (1974) were constructed on the basis of some of the principles that children often apply to problems of conservation (e.g., one-to-one correspondences and spatial congruence). In addition, the procedures were aimed at testing the hypothesis that in many cases disequilibrium (i.e., awareness of discrepancies in one's own reasoning) is a powerful factor in cognitive progress. It was hoped that by presenting children with specially constructed situations designed to create conflict it would be possible to compress into a few weeks' experiences and in a "purified" form what in everyday life would take much longer.

For example, with respect to ideas of measurement, young children may have two different ways of judging whether lines composed of elements are of equal length: they may either use a one-to-one correspondence (or count) or they may base their judgment on the spatial congruence of extremities. If the child is asked to make a straight road directly underneath and just as long as a model straight road, he or she will try to make the extremities coincide (which is obviously correct) and will not bother about the number of elements, even if the child's road has to be made out of elements of a different size than those of the model road. When the child is asked to make the road elsewhere on the table, he or she will, being unable to compare the extremities, count the elements (which is a correct approach provided the elements are all of the same size). When next the model road is made in a zigzag and the child is asked to make a straight road just as long directly underneath, a conflict arises if the child thinks that both approaches are valid: if he or she simply makes the extremities coincide, the number of elements is no longer the same, and if the number of elements is the same, the child's road will go beyond the model road. That such situations indeed induce conflict was particularly clear in certain curious compromise solutions: some children would break the elements in two, or even in three, in order to have a road that did not go beyond the model road but that still had the same number of elements.

Most of the training procedures were designed, like the road problem, to present children with situations that appealed to several possible but incompatible approaches. When the children could be made aware of the incompatibility, they would often reconstruct their various ideas and coordinate them into a new, more powerful, principle that "worked" in all the situations presented. Some children remained impervious to the discrepancies in their different solutions, but many progressed. Indeed, considerable progress was made by many subjects at ages much younger than observed in the original cross-sectional experiments. Conflict, therefore, appears as an important factor in the progress of knowledge; moreover, progress is clearly not simply a result of maturation, but also of encounters with particular situations, which can be especially engineered.

Although the authors did not hesitate to call their learning sessions "training procedures," the design of these sessions and the way they were carried out have little in common with traditional learning studies. The experimenters did not try to eliminate inadequate reasoning, and the experimental features of the situation were not imposed as unavoidable facts to be dealt with. For example, if a child saw no discrepancy in constructing one road of five elements and another of seven, all elements being equal and both constructions being supposed to be equal in length to a model road, the child was not obliged to make a choice between his or her solutions. The experimenter might have drawn the child's attention to the difference in the number of elements, but some children did not think that that mattered: Sometimes one has to count, but sometimes it's better not to count.

Inhelder and her collaborators made no effort to assess different training methods. Their aim was not to compare pre- and posttests, and to establish a certain proportion of successes, but to follow closely what happened when progress occurred. Because it occurred frequently, it was indeed possible in many cases to observe how children changed their ways of reasoning. Other types of learning studies can, of course, also yield interesting results, especially if the method allows detailed analyses of the individual subject's ways of reasoning.

Another area in which one could suppose there were gaps in the theory is that of physiological or neurological concomitants of psychological phenomena. Once again, Piaget warns us against reductionist or imperialistic theories. Organic concomitants should not be seen as the only reality and the direct explanation of psychological phenomena, just as learning in the traditional sense should not be seen as the only explanation of cognitive development. However, Piaget (1970) applauds what he calls "the dialectical trend," which leads to a distinction between phenomena belonging to different scales (physiological, neurological, and behavioral) and "to the discovery of feedbacks or interactions in general between these different processes. . . [Once the processes are regarded in this way,] there is no longer any question of reducing superior phenomena to inferior ones, but ever closer connexions can be established" (p. 154).

Certainly, the neurosciences will raise many new questions and provide many new answers. According to the epistemological tenets of the researchers, the interpretation of the results will be either compatible or contradictory to Piaget's general theory. Like social and other learning studies, studies in the neurosciences may well bring about momentary conflicts, which in the most favorable cases will result in new and higher level equilibria.

FINAL REMARKS

Gardner (1978) argues that in contrast to what happened during the first half of the century "psychologists have become suspicious of grand theories" (p. 470). Psychologists, indeed, appear far readier to accept different interpretations or approaches (either methodological or theoretical) in various fields. In Piagetian terms, they *center* on different aspects of development, and feel that the outcomes of their research are not necessarily contradictory with the results of other research. As Gardner puts it "What is notable is that a host of nontheoretical approaches are currently valued by developmental psychologists" (p. 470), though "overarching theories" as those of Piaget and Freud remain influential. According to Gardner, however, the appeal of these theories lies not "in the pretension to an overall grand system"; rather "the features of Piaget's and Freud's work that command the most interest are the isolated concepts (like operations or the unconscious) and compelling phenomena (like conservation and/or identification)" (p. 470). Similarly, programs such as that of Hull, which aimed at a stimulus-response theory that could explain all details of human behavior, are now considered unworkable.

I think that, up to a point, Gardner correctly depicts the rather eclectic state of developmental cognitive psychology today. However, I am not sure if this is a happy state of affairs.

In my opinion, there is a real conflict between constructivist theories of the development of knowledge, in the child as well as in science in general, and other theories. To put the difference in simple terms, Piaget sees the child as a problem raiser who, on the basis of his already existing knowledge, finds ever new ways of asking questions and provoking reality, as he has seen it until now, to provide him with new observations. The progress of knowledge lies in the fact that the child, the scientist, and society as a whole ask new questions, and this capacity stems from already existing knowledge that was also obtained by asking new questions, and by looking at things in a different way.

As Garcia (1983) expresses it, with reference to the situation of science in the 17th century: "The core of the scientific revolution was not a revolutionary change in the methodology of science but rather a change in the kind of questions people asked about nature" (p. 7).

By contrast, other theories view the development of knowledge in a different way. Problems, like reality itself, somehow exist by themselves. Either the child encounters them through experience with objects and people, or, as happens more often, adults and older children ask the child to solve a problem. Starting with simple problems, little by little the child will be able to solve more and more complex problems in what is accepted as the correct way. The child's knowledge expands gradually, without there ever being a genuine change in his or her way of looking at things. Piaget sees the child as a theory-builder and problem-constructor; many other theorists see the child as a problem solver.

This is a profound difference. However, it does not mean that constructivist psychologists see all progress in knowledge as a construction that leads to new perspectives and new questions. Obviously, other types of learning, implying other mechanisms, exist; but the constructivist epistemologist regards them as accessory, not as essential.

If it is true that progress in knowledge stems from disequilibria of which contradictions (and, in the interpersonal domain, argumentation amongst peers in a situation of collaboration, as Piaget himself adds) are an essential mechanism, then we should look for profound oppositions rather than for eclectic conciliations. Thus, as collaborators in a common cause, we should look for and highlight our differences; our agreements and common principles will look after themselves.

ACKNOWLEDGMENTS

The author wishes to acknowledge the support of the *Fonds national suisse de la recherche scientifique,* Grant No. 1.769-0.83.

REFERENCES

Bovet, M., Baranzini, C., Kamii, C., Sinclair, H. (1975). Prénotions physiques chez l'enfant. *Archives de Psychologie, 43,* 47–81.

Damon, W. (1979). Why study social-cognitive development? *Human Development, 22,* 209.

Garcia, R. (1983). Psychogenesis and history of science. In *Histoire des sciences et psychogenèse, Actes du 4e cours avancé organisé par la Fondation Archives Piaget.* Genève: Fondation Archives Piaget.

Gardner, H. (1978). *Developmental psychology.* Boston and Toronto: Little, Brown.

Glaserfeld (von), E. (1983) Learning as a constructive activity. In J. Bergeron & N. Herscovics (Eds.), *Proceedings of the 5th Annual Meeting of the North American Chapter of the International Group for the Psychology of Mathematics Education* (pp. 41–70) Montreáal.

Gréco, P. (1967). Logique et connaissance. In J. Piaget (Ed.), *Encyclopédie de la Pléiade* (pp. 927–992).

Inhelder, B., Sinclair, H., & Bovet, M. (1974). *L'apprentissage des structures cognitives,* Paris: PUF. (Transl.: *Learning and the development of cognition.*) Cambridge MA: Harvard University Press.

Kolers, P. A., & Smythe, W. E. (1984). Symbol manipulation: Alternatives to the computational view of mind. *Journal of Verbal Learning and Verbal Behavior, 23,* 289–314.

Massaro, D. W. (1975). *Experimental psychology and information processing.* Chicago: Rand McNally.

Piaget, J. (1932). *Le jugement moral chez l'enfant.* Paris: Alcan. (Transl.: *The moral judgment of the child.*) London: Routledge & Kegan, Paul, 1968.

Piaget, J. (1937). *La construction du réel chez l'enfant.* Neuchâtel: Delachaux et Niestlé. (Transl.: *The construction of reality in the child.*) London: Routledge & Kegan, Paul, 1955.

Piaget, J. (1967). *Encyclopédie de la Pléiade.* Paris: Gallimard.

Piaget, J. (1970). *Epistémologie des sciences de l'homme.* Paris: UNESCO.

Piaget, J. (1974). *La prise de conscience.* Paris: PUF. (Transl.: *The grasp of consciousness: Action and concept in the young child.*) London: Routledge & Kegan, Paul, 1977.

Piaget, J. (1976). Logique génétique et sociologie. *Revue européenne des sciences sociales, XVI.*

Piaget, J. (1980). *Les formes élémentaires de la dialectique.* Paris: Gallimard.

Rayna. S. (1984). A propos de la permanence de l'objet. *Archives de psychologie, 52*(201), 73–83.

Robert, M., Cellerier, G., & Sinclair, H. (1972). Une observation de la genése du nombre. *Archives de psychologie 164,* 289–299.

Sinclair, H., Stambak, M., Lezine, I., Rayna, S., & Verba, M. (1982) *Les bébés et les choses ou la créativité du développement cognitif.* Paris: PUF.

Uzgiris, I. C. & Hunt, J.McV. (1975). *Assessment in infancy: Ordinal scales of psychological development.* Urbana IL: University of Illinois Press.

2 CONSTRUCTING KNOWLEDGE IN SCHOOL

Lauren B. Resnick
Learning Research and Development Center,
University of Pittsburgh

We are in the midst of a major convergence of psychological theories. Functionalists and structuralists, learning theorists and developmental psychologists, information-processing psychologists and Piagetians are finding common ground in today's research on cognition. One of the most striking aspects of this convergence is the centrality given in almost all current cognitive theories to individual construction and invention of knowledge. *Constructivism,* a central tenet of Piagetian theory, in the past sharply divided Piagetians from learning theorists. Today, cognitive scientists generally share the assumption that knowledge is constructed by learners.

The major current theories of natural language understanding, for example, assume that even the simplest language exchange requires the listener to supply some of the information necessary to make the message sensible. Understanding a message is a matter of using the message to construct for oneself a representation of the situation to which the message refers, and perhaps also of the speaker's or writer's intentions and emotions in producing the message. According to these theories, the representation that one builds in understanding a communication is simultaneously selective and elaborative with respect to the communication itself. The skillful listener or reader adds to the representation elements that are necessary to make it coherent and sensible and omits elements that do not seem central to its main argument. All natural communications are incomplete in that they do not explicitly state everything that is necessary for building a fully coherent representation. The speaker or writer relies on the natural tendency and ability of listeners and readers to supply some of these elements. In building a coherent representation, the listener or reader uses knowledge of the rules of the

19

language and the topic of the communication to infer the main arguments and to supply the missing propositions.

Information-processing research on skill acquisition also supports the view that human learning involves individual construction of knowledge (see Anderson, 1981). This research suggests that even when all that is apparently happening is rehearsal and practice of a performance, people are actually engaged in a process of transforming their knowledge. Skilled performers do not do exactly what they have been taught. Instead they construct new procedural forms in the course of practicing. An intriguing example of knowledge construction in the course of procedural practice lies in the arithmetic shortcuts that young children invent. Experiments in several countries have shown that 6-year-old children who are asked to add two numbers often use a procedure in which they set a "mental counter" to the larger of the two numbers stated, and then count in the smaller number by ones. Thus, to add 3 plus 5, they will say, "Five . . . six, seven, eight." This procedure, although mathematically correct, is not systematically taught in school. Indeed, preschool children who are taught a simpler to learn but less efficient procedure (count out three objects, count out five objects, then count the combined set of objects) and then are given practice in addition over a number of weeks without further instruction have been shown to invent the more efficient procedure (Groen & Resnick, 1977). Neches (1981; Resnick & Neches, 1984) has constructed an artificial intelligence program that at the outset has only the inefficient algorithm of counting all the objects, but in the course of performing this algorithm transforms its procedure into the more efficient one. The program does this by inspecting its own performance on trial after trial and applying a small set of procedure-modifying heuristics. The program serves as one theory of how humans might be "learning" the efficient procedure.

These are but a few examples suggesting that invention and construction are pervasive both in human cognition and in current cognitive science theory. This, however, is not to argue that all inventions and constructions are equivalent and to be celebrated equally by those of us interested in improving the quality of human thought. One of the negative legacies of the long period in which the various psychological theories were arrayed against each other has been a tendency among some educators and psychologists to argue that construction and invention necessarily lead to understanding, while direct instruction and drill necessarily produce "mindlessness" and failure to understand. Echoing and exaggerating debates among psychologists, educational theory often poses sharp dichotomies: construction versus recording of knowledge, understanding versus rule-following, discovery versus drill-and-practice. It is supposed that when people construct their knowledge they understand it and that discovery-oriented methods of teaching promote this construction and understanding. By contrast, it is imagined that knowledge that is taken in verbatim produces rule-following and that drill-oriented forms of instruction foster this kind of learning.

Piaget has, probably unintentionally, fostered this dichotomous way of thinking with his equation of understanding and invention. He argued, in what may be his most important statement on education (Piaget, 1948/1973), that the words parroted back or procedures rehearsed to perfection that we often take as evidence of learning in school may not reflect any new levels of "real knowledge" or understanding—for real knowledge needs to be constructed and will not be an exact reflection of what was told or taught. Piaget was not the only one to argue this. The Gestaltist, Wertheimer (1945/1959), distinguished "beautiful" from "ugly" forms of thinking. Beautiful thinking depended on apprehending the underlying structure of the thing being studied; ugly thinking involved following rules without reference to their rationales or justifications. This distinction was carried into educational theory by Katona (1940/1967) and others as a championing of learning by discovery. Studies were done to demonstrate that discovery methods of teaching were more likely to produce beautiful, structurally based knowledge and understanding than were drill and memorization methods.

I argue in this chapter that the implied correlation between invention and understanding does not exist. Although Piaget was correct in arguing that to understand one must invent, we cannot conclude the converse, that is, to invent one must understand. Using relatively simple school mathematics as my example domain, I show that children are constructing mathematical knowledge all the time, that their constructions are based on whatever knowledge they have available that seems to them relevant to the task at hand, and that only some of their constructions reflect what we might be willing to call mathematical understanding. It is not just that the children are making errors. Errors are, in fact, a hallmark of the knowledge construction process. They are just as often present in cases of invention that appear to involve understanding as in those that do not. However, when we inspect errors closely, some appear to be based on a partial understanding that is enroute to deep comprehension, while others seem to involve very shallow interpretations that are not promising as routes to comprehension.

I explore here the fundamental differences between errors that appear to be in route to understanding and those that do not. To do this, I describe and analyze some examples of errorful knowledge construction. My cases are from topics in the elementary and middle-school mathematics curriculum: (a) multidigit subtraction involving borrowing, (b) decimal fractions, and (c) interpretation of simple three-term numeric and algebraic expressions. The errors I describe and analyze are characteristic errors—that is, errors that typify significant proportions of school children—rather than idiosyncratic ones. These characteristic errors are quite different from each other in the extent to which they appear to reflect understanding—and therein lies their value to a theory of knowledge construction in school. By examining these errors in detail, we can begin to distinguish what is common to all construction and invention processes and what discriminates the inventions that reflect understanding from those that do not. To anticipate the argument, I conclude that the same *processes* are involved in errors that reflect understanding and those that do not, but that the two classes of errors are based on different *representations* of the problems to be solved. This broad statement has implications for the nature of understanding in procedural domains such as mathematics, and for the relationship between symbols and their referents in domains where artificial symbol systems constitute a central part of the knowledge that is to be acquired. At the end of the chapter, I turn to these questions and consider their implications for the relations between learning, development, and schooling.

BUGGY SUBTRACTION ALGORITHMS

A recurrent finding in research on mathematics learning is that children who are having difficulty with arithmetic often use systematic routines that produce wrong answers. This observation has been made repeatedly over the years by investigators concerned with mathematics education, and a number of studies have attempted to describe the most common errors. Most recently, investigation of "buggy algorithms" by cognitive scientists has yielded automated diagnostic programs capable of reliably detecting the particular errorful algorithms used by a child on the basis of response to a very small but carefully selected set of problems. Formal theories of the reasoning processes by which children invent incorrect procedures have also been constructed. Although systematic procedural errors have been documented for many parts of school arithmetic, the domain that has received the most careful analysis up to now is written subtraction with borrowing. Brown and Burton (1978; Burton, 1982), for example, have constructed an extensive catalog of incorrect procedures used by children doing written multidigit subtraction. These wrong procedures are variants of the correct ones. They are analogous to computer algorithms with bugs in them—hence the name, "buggy algorithms." A finite number of bugs, which in various combinations make up several dozen buggy algorithms, have been identified for subtraction. Figure 2.1 shows a few of the most common buggy algorithms that have been identified in studies of elementary school children.

Inspection of these examples shows that the results of buggy calculations tend to "look right" and to obey a large number of the important rules for manipulating symbols in written calculation: There is only a single digit per column, all of the columns are filled, there are increment marks in some columns with (usually) decrements to their left, and so forth. The buggy algorithms seem to be orderly and reasonable responses to problem situations. This sense is further confirmed when we examine the details of a computer program that was designed to invent the same buggy algorithm that children are known to invent, but not the many other logically possible bugs that have not been observed in children (Brown & VanLehn, 1982). Because the program's performance largely matches that of

1. **Smaller-From-Larger.** The student subtracts the smaller digit in a column from the larger digit regardless of which one is on top.

$$
\begin{array}{r} 3\,2\,6 \\ -\,1\,1\,7 \\ \hline 2\;\;1\;\;1 \end{array}
\qquad
\begin{array}{r} 5\,4\,2 \\ -\,3\,8\,9 \\ \hline 2\,4\,7 \end{array}
$$

2. **Borrow-From-Zero.** When borrowing from a column whose top digit is 0, the student writes 9 but does not continue borrowing from the column to the left of the 0.

$$
\begin{array}{r} 6\,\cancel{0},2 \\ -\,4\,3\,7 \\ \hline 2\,6\,5 \end{array}
\qquad
\begin{array}{r} 8\,\cancel{0},2 \\ -\,3\,9\,6 \\ \hline 5\,0\,6 \end{array}
$$

3. **Borrow-Across-Zero.** When the student needs to borrow from a column whose top digit is 0, he skips that column and borrows from the next one. (Note: This bug must be combined with either bug 5 or bug 6.)

$$
\begin{array}{r} \cancel{6}\,0,2 \\ -\,3\,2\,7 \\ \hline 2\,2\,5 \end{array}
\qquad
\begin{array}{r} \overset{7}{\cancel{8}}\,0,4 \\ -\,4\,5\,6 \\ \hline 3\,0\,8 \end{array}
$$

4. **Stops-Borrow-At-Zero.** The student fails to decrement 0, although he adds 10 correctly to the top digit of the active column. (Note: This bug must be combined with either bug 5 or bug 6.)

$$
\begin{array}{r} 7\,0,3 \\ -\,6\,7\,8 \\ \hline 1\,7\,5 \end{array}
\qquad
\begin{array}{r} 6\,0,4 \\ -\,3\,8\,7 \\ \hline 3\,0\,7 \end{array}
$$

5. **0 − N = N.** Whenever there is 0 on top, the digit on the bottom is written as the answer.

$$
\begin{array}{r} 7\,0\,9 \\ -\,3\,5\,2 \\ \hline 4\,5\,7 \end{array}
\qquad
\begin{array}{r} 6\,0\,0\,8 \\ -\;\;3\,2\,7 \\ \hline 6\,3\,2\,1 \end{array}
$$

6. **0 − N = 0.** Whenever there is 0 on top, 0 is written as the answer.

$$
\begin{array}{r} 8\,0\,4 \\ -\,4\,6\,2 \\ \hline 4\,0\,2 \end{array}
\qquad
\begin{array}{r} 3\,0\,5\,0 \\ -\;\;6\,2\,1 \\ \hline 3\,0\,3\,0 \end{array}
$$

7. **N − 0 = 0.** Whenever there is 0 on the bottom, 0 is written as the answer.

$$
\begin{array}{r} 9\,7\,6 \\ -\,3\,0\,2 \\ \hline 6\,0\,4 \end{array}
\qquad
\begin{array}{r} 8\,\cancel{5},6 \\ -\,4\,0\,9 \\ \hline 4\,0\,7 \end{array}
$$

8. **Don't-Decrement-Zero.** When borrowing from a column in which the top digit is 0, the student rewrites the 0 as 10, but does not change the 10 to 9 when incrementing the active column.

$$
\begin{array}{r} \overset{6}{\cancel{7}}\,0,2 \\ -\,3\,6\,8 \\ \hline 3\,4\,4 \end{array}
\qquad
\begin{array}{r} \overset{1}{\cancel{2}},0,5 \\ -\;\;\;\;9 \\ \hline 1\,1\,0\,6 \end{array}
$$

9. **Zero-Instead-Of-Borrow.** The student writes 0 as the answer in any column in which the bottom digit is larger than the top.

$$
\begin{array}{r} 3\,2\,6 \\ -\,1\,1\,7 \\ \hline 2\,1\,0 \end{array}
\qquad
\begin{array}{r} 5\,4\,2 \\ -\,3\,8\,9 \\ \hline 2\,0\,0 \end{array}
$$

10. **Borrow-From-Bottom-Instead-Of-Zero.** If the top digit in the column being borrowed from is 0, the student borrows from the bottom digit instead. (Note: This bug must be combined with either bug 5 or bug 6.)

$$
\begin{array}{r} 7\,0,2 \\ -\,3\,\cancel{6}\,8 \\ \hline 4\,5\,4 \end{array}
\qquad
\begin{array}{r} 5\,0,8 \\ -\,4\,\overset{7}{\cancel{8}}\,9 \\ \hline 1\,0\,9 \end{array}
$$

FIGURE 2.1. Descriptions and examples of Brown and Burton's (1978) common subtraction bugs. (Adapted from Resnick, 1982. Reprinted by permission.)

children, we can use its processes and knowledge as a theory of what children probably do and know that leads them to buggy inventions.

The Brown and VanLehn program creates bugs by a process of patching and repairing the incomplete algorithms with which it begins; it is thus commonly known as the *repair theory* for buggy subtraction algorithms. According to repair theory, buggy algorithms arise when a subtraction problem is encountered for which the child's current algorithms are incomplete or inappropriate (either because certain steps have been forgotten, or because they have never been learned). The child, trying to respond, eventually reaches an impasse, a situation for which no action is available in the current algorithm. At this point, the child calls on a list of actions to try when the standard action cannot be used. The repair list includes strategies such as performing the action in a different column, skipping the action, swapping top and bottom numbers in a column, and substituting an operation (such as incrementing for decrementing). The outcome of this repair process is then tested against a set of "critics." The critics inspect the resulting solution for conformity to some basic criteria, such as no empty columns, only one digit per column in the answer, only one decrement per column, and the like. If the outcome passes the critics' tests, the repaired algorithm is retained; if not, a new repair is tried.

The repair theory program is a "generate and test" problem-solving routine of the kind that produces successful performances in many other domains (cf. Newell & Simon, 1972; Simon, 1976). It engages in perfectly intelligent reasoning within the limits of its knowledge. The bugs are sensible constructions to deal with situations for which a known procedure is inadequate—as long as we define what is "sensible" within the limits of a set of rules for operating on written numerical symbols. On the other hand, if we look beyond the symbol manipulation rules to what the symbols represent, the buggy algorithms look much less sensible. Each of the bugs in fact violates fundamental mathematical principles (Resnick, 1982). This becomes clearest when we consider some of the bugs in Fig. 2.1 individually:

Smaller-From-Larger. By inverting the numbers, this bug violates the principle of noncommutativity of subtraction. Even more fundamentally, by treating the columns as if they were a string of unrelated single-digit subtraction problems, it violates the understanding that the bottom quantity as a whole is to be subtracted from the top quantity as a whole.

Borrow-From-Zero. This bug looks reasonable at first glance, because it respects the requirement that in a borrow there must be a crossed-out and rewritten numeral to the left of the column that is incremented. It also respects the surface rules for the special case of zero, where the rewritten number is always 9. However, the bug violates the fundamental principle that the total quantity in the top number must be conserved during a borrow. Interpreted semantically—that is, in terms of quantities rather than simply as manipulations on symbols—a total of 100 has been added, 10 to the tens column and 90 to the hundreds column.

Borrow-Across-Zero. This solution respects the syntactic rules for symbol manipulation that require that a small 1 be written in the column that is incremented and that a nonzero column to the left be decremented. However, like the previous bug, it violates the principle of conservation of the top quantity. In this case 100 is removed from the hundreds column, but only 10 is returned to the units column.

Stop-Borrow-At-Zero. This bug violates both symbol manipulation rules and the conservation principle. It produces the increment part of the borrow operation—the 1 in the active column—but does not show a crossed-out number or the change of a 0 to a 9. The result is that 10 is added to the tens column with no compensating change in another column.

Don't-Decrement-Zero. The change of 0 to 10 in this bug is the proper symbolic move after borrowing from the hundreds column. But the failure to continue by changing the 10 to 9 results in a violation of the conservation principle. A total of 110 is added to the tens and units columns, but only 100 is borrowed from the hundreds column.

Zero-Instead-Of-Borrow. Like Smaller-From-Larger, this bug avoids the borrowing operation while observing all of the important symbolic rules for operating within columns, writing only one answer digit per column, and the like. This bug, however, does not violate quantity principles or the structure of decimal notation as blatantly as does the Smaller-From-Larger bug. Furthermore, the zero answer may come from an interpretation of decrementing (subtracting) that is not unreasonable in the absence of a concept of negative numbers. In this interpretation, when a large number must be taken from a smaller one, decrementing is initiated and continued until there is nothing left, yielding zero as the answer.

This brief consideration of the most frequently observed buggy subtraction algorithms reveals an interesting set of regularities. In most cases, the constraint imposed by the quantitative meaning of the symbols is dropped, but constraints derived from the rules of symbol manipulation are retained. All of the bugs thereby violate basic principles of quantity and conventions of place value notation. If children had these principles in mind as they inspected their work or as they attempted to deal with impasses during calculation, we would not expect these types of inventions to occur.

This analysis once prompted me to propose a kind of thought experiment. In this experiment the repair program would be used as a way to test the idea that if people had and applied the appropriate quantity-based principles, they would not invent buggy algorithms. To this end, I proposed to Kurt VanLehn that some additional critics be added to the repair program, critics that would reflect the basic principles of quantity. For example, it seemed sensible to add a conservation or compensation critic to the program that would check to make sure that the minuend quantity had been maintained in the regrouping process.

After considering my proposal, VanLehn (personal communication) concluded that it would not be possible simply to add semantic critics of this kind to the repair program without making much more fundamental changes. This is because the repair program represents subtraction as a system of operations on symbols rather than as a system of operations on quantities. It "knows" what symbolic marks need to be made to perform the incrementing and decrementing involved in borrowing, but it does not know that when it puts an increment mark in the tens column it is adding 10 or that when it decrements the number in the hundreds column by 1 it is really subtracting 100. This being the case, a critic that checked for whether the total quantity had been maintained in the course of a repair would have nothing to attend to. The program has no representation of either the total quantity or the quantities being transferred among columns in the course of a borrow operation. To incorporate semantic critics based on principles of quantity rather on than rules for manipulating symbols, it would be necessary to change fundamentally the way in which the program represents subtraction.

We can conclude, then, that the buggy algorithms studied in subtraction research seem to result from applying intelligent forms of reasoning (generate-and-test problem solving) to a knowledge base devoid of a representation of quantity. The reasoning processes thus cannot recognize and do not apply mathematical principles. At least in this domain, arithmetic apparently is learned by some children in a way that allows the rules of symbol manipulation to become separated from the principles that justify them. When this happens, perfectly intelligent reasoning processes applied to the procedures for symbol manipulation are likely to produce errors.

MALRULES FOR COMPARING DECIMAL FRACTIONS

Another example of intelligent invention leading to incorrect rules can be seen in children's knowledge of decimal fractions shortly after this topic is first introduced in school. Here, we are able to detect two kinds of constructions. One appears to be based, as are buggy subtraction algorithms, on a kind of syntactic interpretation of written symbols in which the reference of the decimal numbers to their fractional parts is ignored. The second kind of construction is one in which the child apparently is attempting to interpret decimals as fractions, and is in the process of building an integrated theory of place value that can encompass both whole numbers and decimal fractions.

To investigate decimal fraction knowledge, we conducted parallel research in Israel, France, and the United States (Resnick et al., in preparation).[1] In each country, 10- to 11-year-old children were individually administered an interview that required performance of a number of fixed tasks and included semistructured probes for reasons and justifications.

An initial assessment of children's rules for decimal fractions can be made by examining patterns of responses to items in which two numbers are compared.

[1]This work was funded in part by a grant from the National Science Foundation (Grant No. SED-8112453). The research was done in collaboration with Pearla Nesher, Francois Leonard, and Catherine Sackur-Grisvard, with the help of Maria Magone, Susan Omanson, and Irit Peled.

TABLE 2.1
Response Distribution on Items Discriminating Malrule Use

Item		Rule 1						Rule 2			Correct			Mixed				
A	B	12	13	14	15	16	17	5	7	11	1	2	3	4	6	8	9	10
4.8	4.63	B	B	B	B	B	B	A	A	A	A	A	A	A	A	B	A	A
0.5	0.36	B	B	B	B	B	B	A	A	A	A	A	A	A	A	A	A	A
0.25	0.100	B	B	B	B	B	B	A	A	A	A	A	A	A	A	A	A	A
4.7	4.08	B	B	B	B	B	B	A	A	A	A	A	A	A	A	B	B	A
2.621	2.068796	B	B	B	B	B	B	A	A	A	A	A	A	A	A	A	A	A
4.4502	4.45	A	A	A	A	A	A	B	B	B	A	A	A	B	B	A	A	B
0.457	4/10	A	A	A	A	A	A	B	B	B	A	A	A	A	A	A	A	B

Several malrules accounted for most of the observed errors in comparing decimals. These had been described earlier by Sackur-Grisvard and Leonard (1985) on the basis of data from a large sample of French children. The malrules are used when the numbers to be ordered have the same whole number digit (e.g., 3.214 and 3.8). Of interest here are malrule 1, choose the number with the greater number of digits in the decimal portion as the larger, and malrule 2, choose the number with the smaller number of digits in the decimal portion as the larger.[2]

Table 2.1 shows the distribution of responses on a number of items that allow us to discriminate the malrules for a sample of 17 American children. Similar data, with similar degrees of regularity in application of the malrules, exist for the Israeli and French children in our study. For the first block of items, choice of the number in column B as the larger discriminates malrule 1; choice of the number in column A as the larger can be based either on a correct rule or on malrule 2, thus it cannot be used to discriminate malrule use. For the second block of items, choice of the number in column B as the larger discriminates malrule 2; choice of the number in column A as the larger can reflect either a correct rule or malrule 1. For ease of reading and interpretation, children are grouped in the table according to their predominant malrule use. As can be seen, children showed very great regularity in their application of malrules.

Another set of items helped to confirm this categorization of the children. In

---

[2]Sackur-Grisvard and Leonard also discriminated a third malrule. This is a special variant of malrule 1 that is applied when there is a zero in the first position after the decimal point. However, we have been unable to detect any difference in underlying conceptual understanding for malrule 1 and malrule 3 children. Therefore, in this discussion the variant is ignored and children who use it are treated as if they were applying malrule 1.

TABLE 2.2
Response Distribution on Hidden Numbers Task

Hidden numbers		Students Grouped According to Rule Used															
		Rule 1						Rule 2			Experts			Mixed				
Short	Long	12	13	14	15	16	17	5	7	11	1	2	3	4	6	8	9	10
−.−	−.− − − −	L	+	L	LS	L	+	S	S	S	+	+	+	−	S	L	L	−
0.−	0.− − − −	L	L	L	+	L	+	S	S	+	+	+	+	S	L	+	S	+

Note: + = correct, L = long number, S = short number, − = no response.

these items children were shown a pair of numbers, but the digits were covered so that while the children could know the number of digits in the decimal portion, they could not know the value of each digit. Under these circumstances, the children could not actually determine the total value of the decimal. Thus, the correct response to the question, "Which is larger?" is either "I don't know" or "It's impossible to tell." Choosing one of the numbers as larger is incorrect and also discriminates between the malrules. A child applying malrule 1 would choose the number with more digits, a child applying malrule 2 would choose the number with fewer digits. Table 2.2 shows the distribution of children (grouped according to their malrule category from Table 2.1) on this set of items. The malrule classification is largely confirmed.

Derivations of Children's Malrules

Having established the existence and systematicity of the malrules, we can now investigate their origins. The malrules are inventions—but what is their conceptual base? Are they, like buggy subtraction algorithms, the result of reasoning about the symbol system without reference to the mathematical meaning of the symbols, or do they reflect an effort to understand the nature of decimal numbers as fractions and of the decimal system for notating quantities? The answers to these questions appear to be quite different for malrule 1 and malrule 2 children.

Malrule 1: Borrowing a Rule From Whole Numbers.   Our data suggest that in applying malrule 1, children recognize that things "start over" at the decimal point, but do not really cope with the special nature of the digits to the right of the point. In particular, they do not reason about the values of the digits to the right of the decimal point, and seem not to be paying attention to the fractional nature of the decimal portion of the number. These children import to the right of the decimal point a set of rules that are correct for digits on its left, and treat the decimal portion of the number as if it were an integer. Children who apply malrule 1 typically say things like, "4.63 is larger than 4.8 because 63 is more than 8,'' or ''1.067 is greater than 1.4 because 67 is greater than 4.'' They are consistent in this interpretation even when they must first translate an ordinary fraction to a decimal in order to make the comparison. For example, they are likely to say, ''0.038 is greater than 4/100 because 38 is greater than 4.''

Children who apply malrule 1, then, are doing something essentially in the spirit of buggy algorithm construction as we have seen it in the case of subtraction. They encounter an impasse—a number with a point in the middle for which they have no established interpretive rules. They know that the decimal point cannot be ignored, and they search for something they do know that might be applied to this new situation. By considering the digits after the point as a separate number, a well-established rule for comparing whole numbers can be applied. Because these children have not represented the number with all its digits as a single quantity, no constraint limits this application.

Malrule 1 children's performance on several interview items makes it clear that these children do not understand the decimal notation system as it applies to decimal fractions. For example, we showed children the numbers 1.54 and 2.45 and asked them to tell us the value of the 5s in each number. Counting as correct those children who labeled the 5 in 1.54 as tenths and the 5 in 2.45 as hundredths, we found that most malrule 1 children were incorrect, but most malrule 2 children, along with our expert and mixed-response children, were correct. Some examples from the protocols give a flavor of the difficulty malrule 1 children were having. Four of the children first said that the 5 in 2.45 was 5 ones. Another said that 5 in 2.45 was 5 tens (here she showed a common confusion between the integer term *tens* and the fractional term *tenths*) but then changed her mind and said that the 5 in 1.54 showed the tens. She also explained that the 5 was worth more in 1.54 than in 2.45 because, ''You add 10 more from the ones row to get to the second . . . to get to the tens row.'' She was correct in her choice of the 5 with the larger value, but she justified the choice in terms of whole number values rather than fractional values.

In another set of items, we had children write decimals from dictation such as ''six tenths and two hundredths,'' or ''three wholes and two hundredths.'' Most malrule 1 children had difficulty. Many of their errors suggest that they were thinking of the decimals as whole numbers. For example, for ''three hundredths,'' one subject wrote .300. When the interviewer said, ''six tenths and two hundredths,'' another child replied, ''You mean sixty and two hundredths?'' and then wrote 2.60.

It is important to note that the application of the whole number rule in comparing decimals is likely to work—that is, to produce a correct answer— much of the time. Thus, children may not need to search for a new and more powerful rule for a considerable period of time. This is because, in school and elsewhere, the decimal numbers that children encounter (e.g., money for the children in all of our samples, distance and weight measures for Israeli and French children growing up in a metric culture) almost always have a standard number of digits. The whole number rule will yield a correct answer whenever the number of digits in the decimal portion is the same in both numbers. Moreover, in most initial school instruction children work mainly with decimal numbers that have the same number of digits in the decimal portion. They are even taught a method—adding zeros at the right of the decimal portion—that they can use to convert a given number into one that has the same number of digits as another with which they want to compare it.

Malrule 2: Interpreting Decimals as Fractions Written in Place Value Notation.   In marked contrast to children who used malrule 1, the malrule 2 children from all three countries seemed to attend simultaneously to two key aspects of the semantics of decimal numbers in constructing this malrule. The two aspects are the fact that decimals represent *fractions,* that is, parts smaller than one; and the fact that place value notation assigns increasingly smaller values to columns as one moves to the right. Let us examine how these ideas could produce the malrule 2 response. Here is a possible derivation:

1. If a quantity is cut into parts, the more parts there are, the smaller each part will be; the fewer parts there are, the larger each part will be.
2. Ten parts are fewer than 100 parts, which in turn are fewer than 1,000 parts.
3. Therefore (from 1 and 2) tenths are greater than hundredths, which are greater than thousandths.
4. The number of places in a decimal fraction tells the size of the parts. Specifically, if there is one place after the decimal, the parts are tenths; if there are two places, the parts are hundredths; if there are three places, the parts are thousandths.
5. Therefore (from 3 and 4) a decimal with one place is larger than a decimal with two places, which is larger than a decimal with three places.

Careful analysis of malrule 2 children's protocols provides evidence that this derivation of malrule 2 (although of course not in formal syllogistic form) is a reasonable one to attribute to most of the children who applied that rule. First, there is evidence that malrule 2 children knew and applied the "more parts means smaller pieces" idea. In comparing ordinary fractions, for example, almost all malrule 2 children said $\frac{1}{333}$ was bigger than $\frac{1}{334}$, $\frac{1}{3}$ was bigger than $\frac{1}{4}$, and $\frac{1}{10}$ was bigger than $\frac{1}{100}$. They justified these judgments in terms of the size of pieces created by the division into parts. By contrast, most malrule 1 children tended to judge $\frac{1}{333}$ to be smaller than $\frac{1}{334}$ because, they said, 334 is greater than 333. The malrule 2 children gave further evidence of their reasoning when comparing ordinary fractions to decimal fractions and decimal fractions among themselves. For example, one child who was comparing $\frac{4}{100}$ and 0.038 said that

$\frac{4}{100}$ was bigger because, "one hundred is smaller than one thousand in the decimals. Smaller numbers make the larger pieces." Another child, comparing the value of the 5s in 1.54 and 2.45, said the first 5 was worth more "because you have more of a part. Like if you have 7 tenths and 7 hundredths, 7 tenths would be higher because you have more of a part." Still another child regularly translated decimal fractions into a money representation (so many dimes, so many pennies, so many mils) and used his knowledge that dimes are greater than pennies and pennies greater than mils to reason about the decimals. Comparing the hidden numbers, $-.----$ and $-.-$, he said that the one on the right would be bigger, because the other would "go down to tens, dimes . . . wait . . . dimes, pennies, mils, and I don't know what this [the fourth place] is. And this [on the right] will be 10 cents."

Occasionally, the malrule 2 children also explicitly said that the number of places in a decimal fraction tells the size of the parts. For example, one child (our dimes, pennies, and mils subject) when comparing $\frac{13}{100}$ and .125, picked $\frac{13}{100}$ as the larger, saying, "This is 125 thousandths and this is 13 hundredths. These is . . . this is 13 pennies right here, 13 pennies out of 100. And this one is mils. They're a little bit less than a penny." Another child, comparing 2.621 with 2.0687986, picked 2.621 as the larger and justified the choice by saying, "as you go down [the places] it sinks the value. And so this [.0687986] is a smaller portion, and so this [.621] would be closer to the . . . , you know . . . , to these real . . . , to these [whole] numbers." Explanations such as these also appeared in the protocols of children who were mostly correct in comparing decimals and fractions. However, they never appeared in the protocols of malrule 1 children.

Malrule 2 children also gave evidence of understanding the effects of zeros on the value of a number, a particularly important and difficult aspect of the understanding of place value. We asked our subjects to tell us whether and how the value of 2.35 changed when a zero was inserted in different places to produce 2.305, 02.35, 2.035, and 2.350. Having made the individual judgments, they then were asked, "In general, when does zero make a difference?" For the most part, the malrule 2 children—like those who were largely correct in their comparisons—recognized that 2.305 and 2.035 are smaller than 2.35, while 02.35 and 2.350 leave its value unchanged. The most articulate child gave explanations such as 2.35 is greater than 2.305, "because the 0 would take hundredths place, and 5 would get pushed down to thousandths."

These place value judgments and justifications are quite sophisticated, and stand in sharp contrast to those of the malrule 1 subjects. Most malrule 1 children applied the whole number rule to the decimal portion. They judged 2.305 and 2.350 to be greater than 2.35. Most of these subjects also judged 2.035 to be greater than 2.35, consonant with malrule 1 in that more digits are judged to be greater. Although a variety of interesting interpretations were given, no malrule 1 child gave any justifications in terms of place value—even in childlike language.

Finally, there is evidence that the malrule 2 subject knew—as the malrule 1 subjects did not—that digits to the right of a decimal point represent the numerator of an ordinary fraction. Children were asked to write a variety of ordinary fractions as decimals. This was difficult for almost all children and error rates were high. However, the quality of the errors reveals something about the kind of coordination between decimal fractions and ordinary fractions that the children were making. There were three main categories of incorrect translation:

1. Encode only the numerator as a decimal and ignore the denominator. For example, $\frac{3}{4}$ becomes .3 or .003, $\frac{3}{100}$ becomes .3. This translation recognizes that only the numerator of a fraction (i.e., the number of parts) is explicitly encoded in decimal notation.

2. Encode only the denominator as a decimal and ignore the numerator. For example, $\frac{1}{3}$ becomes .3, $\frac{3}{4}$ becomes .04 or .4. This translation recognizes that only one part of the fraction actually is shown in the decimal notation, but it mistakes the part.

3. Keep both the numerator and the denominator of the fraction, and put a decimal in somewhere. For example, $\frac{3}{4}$ becomes 3.4 or .34. These are syntactic translations. They produce a number that has the surface structure of a decimal, but has no sensible relation to the quantity expressed in the fraction.

Table 2.3 shows the pattern of translation responses for the American sample of children. As can be seen, the malrule 2 subjects made entirely category 1 errors—ones in which they encoded the numerator of the fraction in the decimal notation. This is the category that comes closest to the correct decimal interpretation of fractions. By contrast, the malrule 1 subjects typically either encoded only the denominator (category 2), or made (category 3) syntactic translations.

TABLE 2.3
Types of Errors on Fraction-to-Decimal Translation Task

Fraction for Translation	Students Grouped According to Rule Used																
	Rule 1						Rule 2			Correct			Mixed				
	12	13	14	15	16	17	5	7	11	1	2	3	4	6	8	9	10
3/4	−	C	C	C	C	−	A	A	−	−	−	−	A	C	C	−	B
1/5	−	C	C	A	B	−	A	A	−	B	A	−	A	C	−	−	−
3/2	−	C	C	C	B	−	A	−	−	−	−	−	−	−	−	−	−
2/3	−	−	C	C	B	−	A	−	−	−	−	−	−	−	−	−	−

Note: A = numerator encoded, B = demoninator encoded, C = syntactic, − = no response or uncodable response.

The derivation of malrule 2 that I have suggested here constitutes perfectly logical reasoning based on a true set of premises. This reasoning produces a malrule, however, because it is based on an incomplete specification of the values signified by decimal notation, and this incompleteness makes it impossible for the children to coordinate all of the information carried in the written numeral. Specifically, malrule 2 children appear to have based their judgments of the relative size of numbers entirely on the number and value of the places in the decimal, paying limited or no attention to the digits in those places. It is as if these children based their judgments entirely on the denominators of the fractions, ignoring the numerators. Everything in the derivation would be true, if the numerators of the fractions were 1 (i.e., if $\frac{1}{10}$ were compared with $\frac{1}{100}$, and $\frac{1}{100}$ with $\frac{1}{1000}$).

We have seen, however, that malrule 2 children in fact seem to know that the digits written in a decimal correspond to the numerator of an ordinary fraction. Why, then, would these children focus only on the denominator when comparing decimal fractions? The answer probably lies in the fact that the children are in the midst of working out a representation of place value for decimals that will coordinate their understanding of decimals as fractions with their understanding of the notational system. If they focused exclusively on the numerator of the decimal fraction (i.e., on the digits written), they could only apply whole number knowledge—in effect, malrule 1. However, they know that this would be incorrect because the column values must be taken into account in assigning total value to a written number. They further apply this knowledge of column values to produce malrule 2. They apparently have not yet succeeded in coordinating digits with their column values—that is, in simultaneously taking into account the explicit information about the number of parts and the implicit information about the size of the parts.

It is easy to see why children have difficulty in achieving this coordination. If one takes both a decimal fraction's *numerator* and its *denominator* into account, it is not possible to compare directly decimals that have a different number of places unless one elaborates one's representation of decimal notation. This is because a lot of small parts can cumulate to a larger total amount than just a few large parts; so, for example, lots of thousandths could be a greater quantity than just a few hundredths. To deal with this problem, the representation of place value at step (4) in the derivation on p. 30 would have to be changed from its present global form to a form reflecting the additive structure of decimal numbers. It would have to become something like:

4. The number of places in a decimal fraction tells the size of the parts. Specifically, if there is one place after the decimal, the parts are tenths; if there are two places, the parts are tenths plus hundredths; if there are three places, the parts are tenths plus hundredths plus thousandths. The digit in each place tells how many parts of that size are included.

Such a representation of decimal fractions would, in fact, constitute a mathematically correct and nearly complete[3] understanding of the place value notational system.

To summarize, we have seen in the case of decimal fractions two quite different kinds of malrule construction. The difference between them seems to lie not in fundamentally different reasoning processes, but in the different representations of decimal numbers that the two groups of subjects are using. Malrule 1 children appear to have a very impoverished representation of decimal numbers. Their representation of the place value system apparently does not include the crucial information that column values descend as one moves to the right—even across the decimal point boundary—and they do not seem to encode the decimal portion of the number as a fraction. This means that nothing in their representation contrains them from using a whole number rule to compare decimal fractions.

Malrule 2 children's representation of decimal fractions and the place value system is much more complex. Their enriched representation not only blocks application of the whole number rule, but also provides a basis for inferring a new malrule. Still, a further enrichment would be needed to provide a basis for inferring a fully correct rule for comparing decimal fractions. As we have seen, however, the enrichment needed constitutes only a local elaboration: the switch from a global specification of the relationship between number of places and sizes of parts to a specification in terms of the addition of parts of different sizes. Once this elaboration occurs, whether as a result of instruction or independently, it should not be very difficult to incorporate it into one's reasoning about decimals. This analysis shows that malrule 2 seems so much more elegant than malrule 1 because malrule 2 is based on an enriched representation that is quite close to a fully elaborated representation of decimal structure. This is also why it seems quite correct to say that malrule 2 children "almost understand" decimals, whereas we would not want to say that of malrule 1 children.

ERRORS IN INTERPRETING ALGEBRA EXPRESSIONS

Another domain in which systematic bugs and malrules can be demonstrated during the course of learning is algebra. Several investigators (e.g., Carry, Lewis, & Bernard, 1980; Greeno, 1983b) have studied the errors that students make in the early period of algebra learning (and that some people never overcome). This work has shown that there is great systematicity in which errors

---

[3]The complete understanding includes recognition of the systematic multiplicative relationship between columns, such that each column has a value *ten times* the one to its right. Decimal notation is thus based on *powers* of ten, which is what permits its direct translation to scientific notation.

appear; that is, only a small number of the logically possible algebra errors actually tend to be made. In this respect, algebra appears similar to subtraction and other domains of buggy arithmetic. However, a common finding for algebra is that subjects do not always apply the same algebra malrule, even in what appears to the experimenter to be the same situation. For this reason, a theory of algebra learning difficulties would have to attribute to the individual a state of knowledge in which several competing rules can coexist and in which rules are only weakly linked to conditions of application (so that one can do one thing this time and another the next), and at the same time account for why some malrules are invented regularly whereas others are not.

To date, the best developed theories of how algebra malrules are invented are those of Matz (1982) and Sleeman (1982). These theories, like Brown and VanLehn's (1982) theory for subtraction bugs, are expressed as computer programs that invent the malrules observed for algebra, but do not invent other logically possible bugs. According to Matz's theory, for example, people generate malrules by constructing prototype rules from which they extrapolate new rules. Although the results are malrules, both construction of prototypes and extrapolation come about through the application of intelligent learning processes. An illustration appears in Fig. 2.2. The initial rule is the distribution law as it is typically taught in the beginning algebra course. From this correct rule a prototype is created by generalizing over the operator signs. The prototype

1. **The correct rule as taught:**

$$a \times (b + c) = (a \times b) + (a \times c)$$

2. **Prototype created by generalizing over operator signs:**

$$a \square (b \triangle c) = (a \square b) \triangle (a \square c)$$

3. **Incorrect rules created from the prototype.**

$$a + (b \times c) = (a + b) \times (a + c)$$

$$\sqrt{b + c} = \sqrt{b} + \sqrt{c}$$

FIGURE 2.2. Invention of algebra malrules according to Matz's theory.

specifies not that multiplication can be distributed over addition, but that some operator can be distributed over some other operator. From this prototype, new incorrect distribution rules can be constructed by substituting specific operations for the operator placeholders in the prototype.

Although the Matz and Sleeman theories are specific to algebra, they share a key feature of Brown and VanLehn's theory of the origin of buggy subtraction algorithms: They do not attribute to learners a representation of quantities and relationships. Algebra malrules, like the buggy algorithms, are interpreted strictly as deformations of symbol manipulation rules. We wondered what the source might be of this tendency to treat algebra as a strictly symbolic domain. Did children entering algebra instruction lack the competence to reason about algebra expressions in more quantitative, principled terms, or did they simply fail to bring their knowledge of principles to bear because school instruction did not encourage them to think of algebra in other than symbolic terms?

To explore this question, we have been studying how understanding of algebra expressions develops at the very beginning of algebra learning.[4] In this research, conducted partly in France and partly in the United States, we are trying to construct useful descriptions of the psychological content of principles justifying algebra expressions and rules of transformation. We are also trying to determine the extent to which learners are able to assign meaning to algebra-like expressions and to use their prior arithmetic knowledge to justify and give sense to the symbol system. We have focused our work on a limited set of expressions that form part of children's earliest introduction to algebra. These are additive expressions of the form $a \pm b \pm c$, where a, b, and c are all positive integers and parentheses may be around either the ab or the bc portion of the expression. This domain is rich enough to pose certain complexities of semantic interpretation; at the same time it is limited enough to permit a fairly complete psychological characterization of the kinds of knowledge and processes used in reasoning.

We conducted structured interviews with students during the period of their first exposure to algebraic expression, that is, with students from about 11 to 14 years of age.[5] The interviews were designed to elicit information about students' understanding of the effects of parentheses on the value of expressions—particularly the effects of a minus sign immediately before the parentheses—and their knowledge of constraints on exchanges of signs and numbers between subexpressions in an expression. Three types of questions were used: (a) indicate whether two expressions are equivalent or not, and explain why; (b) state where parentheses can be placed in an expression without changing its value, and explain

---

[4]This research is conducted in collaboration with Evelyne Cauzinille and Jacques Mathieu.

[5]In American schools, this introduction comes as part of the prealgebra curriculum. In the French schools where we worked, algebra is gradually introduced as part of a unified mathematics curriculum, beginning when children are 11 or 12 years old.

why; and (c) state whether parentheses can be removed from an expression without changing its value, and explain why. In some cases, subjects were first asked to judge expressions with letters, then were shown numerical expressions of identical form and asked whether they would still make the same equivalence judgment.

For the domain of expressions under consideration, all transformations and equivalences can be explained and justified with reference to four basic principles of number. These are:

Order irrelevance for addition. This principle expresses the fact that it is permissible to add quantities in any order, regardless of how they are formed into subgroups (e.g., by parentheses) or their order of presentation. This principle is expressed in mathematics texts as two rules, commutativity and associativity. The subjects in our experiments more often expressed it in terms such as, "You can do things in any order if you are only adding things in." The principle justifies not only simple exchanges of terms such as $a + (b + c) = a + (c + b)$ but also exchanges of subexpressions such as $a + (b - c) = (b - c) + a$ and compound exchanges such as in $a + (b + c) = (c + b) + a$.

Order relevance for subtraction. This is expressed in textbooks as noncommutativity of subtraction. Our subjects express this principle as, "You can't change around subtraction," or, "Starting with 8 and taking away 3 isn't the same as starting with 3 and taking away 8." This principle justifies nonequivalences such as $(a - b) + c \neq (b - a) + c$ and $(a + b) - c \neq c - (a + b)$.

Order irrelevance for multiple transformations on a starting set. This principle justifies equivalences such as $a - b + c = a + c - b$. Most subjects, if they recognized this principle at all, expressed only a rule-like version of the form, "Keep the signs with their numbers." A few subjects, however, expressed this principle in terms such as, "If you are going to start with an amount and then take away something and add back something, it doesn't matter whether you do the taking away first or the adding in first."

Composition of quantity inside parentheses. This principle expresses the fact that the two terms inside parentheses are the parts of a single whole quantity. This is the principle behind the sign change rules for removing parentheses: $a - (b + c) = a - b - c$ and $a - (b - c) = a - b + c$. Our subjects had great difficulty verbalizing this principle, even when they could state and apply the sign change rule. When they did manage to verbalize it, they said things like, "In $15 - (4 + 5)$ you are starting with 15 and taking away 9, but the take-away amount is in two pieces."

These are the principles that children would be using if they were thinking about algebra expressions as descriptions of quantities, and about algebra transformation rules as formalizations of regularities in the behavior of quantities under various transformations and exchanges. However, we in fact encountered very little reasoning of this kind. Instead we observed a heavy dependence on calculation rules, often without principled justification, and on a variety of symbol manipulation rules, many of them incorrect or buggy inventions.

Priority of Calculation Rules.   A very strong finding is that most subjects showed a strong preference for reasoning in terms of rules of calculation rather than principles of number or rules of symbol manipulation. When two numerical expressions were given, virtually all subjects calculated to determine equivalence. When the interviewer pressed them to make judgments without calculating they would sometimes comply, but usually they then calculated to confirm their judgments. When literal rather than numerical expressions were to be judged, subjects frequently set the literals in an expression equal to numbers and then calculated.

On the whole, children's calculation rules were correct. In particular, virtually all had mastered the rule of first calculating within parentheses and then treating the result of the parentheses operation as if it were a single quantity. Note that this standard procedural rule for algebraic expressions in fact is a procedural expression of the composition of quantity inside parentheses principle. However, subjects rarely justified the parentheses-first calculation rule in these terms. Most typically, they said that the parentheses were to help one know what to do first, but had no idea of why it was better to do the parentheses calculation first except that the answer would otherwise come out wrong. The major exception to correct calculation was that some subjects under certain conditions inverted the numbers in subtraction, thus apparently violating the order relevance for subtraction principle.

Priority of Symbol Manipulation Rules Over Quantity Principles.   When subjects did not calculate, they usually judged equivalence on the basis of rules for transforming expressions that did not make any apparent reference to the principles of number. Their rules were often incorrect. However, it appears possible to account for most of them as systematic deformations of the correct rules that are taught in algebra instruction. A number of the most frequent incorrect rules, for example, can be interpreted as the dropping or adding of constraints on the rule that instantiates commutativity and associativity. This rule, as it is likely to have been formulated by the children, is:

> A. IF all the signs are $+$, THEN can change position of parentheses, insert or remove parentheses, change the order of numbers, invert the order of the term in parentheses and the other term.

A number of the incorrect rules our subjects formulated can be derived from this rule, through a process that looks much like Matz's prototype formation and extrapolation. For example, a very often observed incorrect rule is one that relaxes the constraint on the condition side of rule A. This produces:

B. IF all of the signs are the same, THEN can . . . [do all of the things specified in rule A].

Rule B permits the changes specified in rule A whenever all the signs are −, as well as when all are +. This rule was verbalized by a number of our subjects.

A further relaxation of constraints on rule A would in effect drop the condition side of the production altogether, thereby allowing all of the changes specified in rule A under any conditions (i.e., when one of the signs is + and the other is −, as well as when both signs are the same). Our subjects did not construct this rule, which essentially would have had them declare that all expressions that contained the same numbers were equivalent. Even when they gave no evidence of thinking about principles of quantity, they seemed to be aware that the domain of algebra expressions had certain constraints. To deal with the problem of what transformations are permissible when the signs in an expression are different, subjects typically developed constraints on the action side of the rule. This led to rules such as:

C1. IF the expression has mixed signs, THEN can change the order of numbers, but keep the parentheses and the signs in place.

C2. IF the expression has mixed signs, THEN can move the parentheses around, but keep the signs and numbers in place.

Another set of incorrect rules seems to derive from ignoring those constraints that are implied in learned rules, but are not stated explicitly. Take, for example, the rule that even when minus signs are present, inversion of numbers is possible as long as the signs are kept with their numbers. This rule is expressed by subjects as:

D. IF you invert the numbers, THEN keep each sign with its number.

There is an implied constraint in this rule, namely that the sign immediately preceding the parentheses goes with the whole quantity inside the parentheses, not just with the first number inside the parentheses. Ignoring this implied constraint produces rules such as:

E. IF the signs are kept with the numbers that immediately follow them, THEN can move numbers in and out of the parentheses.

F. IF the parentheses are removed, THEN the signs in front of each number must stay the same.

Rule E leads to incorrect equivalence statements such as $a - (b + c) = a - b + c$; rule F leads subjects to reject the correct equivalence, $a - (b + c) = a - b - c$. Both of these rules were quite frequently expressed by our subjects in the context of removing or changing the position of parentheses.

Perhaps the most surprising incorrect performance we observed was the frequent willingness of our subjects to invert the terms in a subtraction statement. They did this particularly under two conditions: (a) when the expression specified subtracting a larger number from a smaller one, and (b) when a quantity in parentheses was to be subtracted from a starting number, as in $a - (b + c)$. In the first case, subjects appeared to be looking for a way to proceed under conditions where the given expression appeared to demand an impossible calculation (larger from smaller) or an illegal response (a negative number). But why did subjects willingly contravene a rule so fundamental as the noncommutativity of subtraction, a rule that we can assume they learned some years earlier? We think the frequency of subtraction inversion in the second case suggests an answer.

Suppose that the syntactic and parsing requirements of algebra notation were incompletely learned by our subjects at the point at which we interviewed them, so that the linear notation did not imply the same order constraints for our subjects that it does for the skilled algebra performer. With respect to order of operations, many of our subjects seemed to have acquired a rule that could be expressed as:

F. IF computing an algebra-like expression, THEN go from left to right.

Let us examine a very plausible series of minor changes in this rule, each of which represents good logical reasoning, but which taken together result in an inadequately constrained rule:

G. IF there are parentheses, THEN compute inside the parentheses first.

H. IF there are parentheses on the right, THEN start at the right.

I. IF there are parentheses on the right, THEN go from right to left.

J. IF going from left to right is not appropriate, THEN go from right to left.

In early stages of learning, especially when the parentheses-first rule is taught without any principled justification, it is reasonable to imagine that learners might proceed through a reasoning chain of this kind. This would produce violations of the order relevance for subtraction principle. However, according to this analysis what is really happening is not intentional violation of order relevance. The violation occurs as a side effect of an inappropriate relaxation of a constraint on the left-to-right processing rule that allows the individual to interpret $(a - b)$ as if it meant "subtract a from b."

The main point to be made here is that these early algebra inventions look a good deal more like buggy subtraction algorithms than malrule 2 decimal inventions. They operate at a purely symbolic level. Unlike the decimal case, there is little reference to the quantities that the symbols represent and very basic principles concerning quantities, such as order relevance for subtraction that we know children do understand, are "traded away" in chains of reasoning about symbols. This same kind of constraint trading is evident in the derivation of buggy subtraction algorithms according to Brown and VanLehn's (1982) repair theory.

UNDERSTANDING PROCEDURES: CONSTRAINTS AND PERMISSIONS

What makes the decimal construction errors appear to be—using Wertheimer's term—*beautiful* even if their results are wrong, while the buggy subtraction and algebra constructions seem to be awkward and meaningless? Differences in the quality of reasoning do not appear to account for this difference, if by quality of reasoning we mean reasonable inductions and inferences properly grounded in the individual's initial knowledge. In all three domains, errors seem to result from smart and intelligent reasoning processes. Furthermore, the processes of malrule construction that we have seen in the cases of subtraction and algebra appear similar in important ways to what we know of the processes involved in very young children's acquisition of the syntactic system of their native language. In language, too, incorrect generalizations that produce systematic errors are made at certain points in the acquisition process—and these are typically taken as evidence that the child is constructing increasingly more powerful and comprehensive rule systems for language (e.g., Karmiloff-Smith & Inhelder, 1974). Thus, in a certain sense, even buggy algorithms and algebra malrules provide evidence that the child is acquiring certain important features of the mathematical system that is taught in school. However, these features appear to be largely those associated with the syntax of the formal, symbol system; the semantic referents of the symbols apparently play little, if any, role in the process.

It is useful to think of buggy algorithms and algebra malrules as resulting from incomplete knowledge of the *permissions* and *constraints* that underlie particular formal procedures. In any system of rule-governed actions, the actions that are appropriate can be justified in terms of interconnected sets of permissions and constraints. In elementary school mathematics, both derive from certain basic principles concerning the nature of quantities and the relations among quantities. I can best illustrate the ways in which permissions and constraints interact to define a rule system and the ways in which they derive from elementary principles of the nature of quantities by developing the justification for the standard subtraction-with-borrowing algorithm taught in American schools.

Constraints and Permissions in Subtraction.   In multidigit subtraction the goal of the entire process is to find a difference between two quantities, each of which is symbolized by a string of digits that conform to the conventions of place value notation. This set of notational conventions is permitted by a basic mathematical principle, additive composition of number. This principle expresses the fact that all numbers are composed of other numbers, and that each number can be decomposed into smaller numbers. Consider the number 9. It is composed of 8 and 1, 2 and 7, 10 and −1, 3 and 3 and 3, and so on. Nine is also an element, a part, of many other numbers: Combined with another 9 it forms 18, combined with 7 it forms 16, combined with negative 4 it forms 5, and so on. Place value notation uses the composition principle to permit us to write an infinite set of natural numbers without needing an infinite number of distinguishable symbols. It does this by assigning a value to each position in an ordered string so that an individual digit's values are determined by its position. This means that 324, for example, must be interpreted as a composition of 300 (itself a composition of 100 plus 100 plus 100) plus 20 (10 plus 10) plus 4 (1 plus 1 plus 1 plus 1).

Additive composition also justifies another permission that is central to the subtraction algorithm, the permission to calculate by partition. In doing a calculation, it is permissible to divide the quantities being operated on into any convenient parts, operate on the parts, and cumulate partial results. This is what allows subtraction to proceed column-by-column, rather than, say, by counting down by ones from the top to the bottom number. Calculation by partitioning is, however, subject to several constraints. In the case of subtraction, these constraints specify that (a) each part of the bottom number must be subtracted from a part of the top number, (b) each part of the bottom number may be subtracted only once (thus, each bottom part may be "touched" only once), (c) all of the bottom parts can be removed sequentially from the same top part (thus, some top parts may be touched several times and others may not be touched at all), and (d) in summing the partial results, any top part that has not been touched must be treated as if it were the result of a subtraction.[6]

In the course of calculating by partioning, it may be convenient to recompose the parts. In the case of subtraction, such recomposing is done to avoid accumulating negative partial results. Thus, when the top number in a column is smaller than the bottom number in that column, one adds to the top number to make it larger. This is called *borrowing,* or in more modern school parlance, *regrouping.* Regrouping is permitted by the additive composition principle, but it is subject to an essential constraint: Addition in one column must be compensated by subtraction in another column so that the total quantity in the top number

---

[6]This is what children are taught in school under the name of "bringing down" the top number in a column when the bottom of the column is empty; it is equivalent to subtracting 0 from each top part that has not otherwise been touched.

is conserved. The constraint of conservation via compensation is necessary because the original goal of the algorithm is to find a difference. If either of the numbers were allowed to change in the course of calculation, the difference between the numbers would also change.

Misunderstanding: Inadequate Constraints on Rule Construction.   This kind of analysis of algorithms as interacting permissions and constraints, each of which derives from basic features of the number system, allows us to give a new and more specific meaning to the idea of understanding rules and procedures. One understands a rule or procedure when one knows all of the constraints and permissions that govern it. Greeno, Riley, and Gelman (1984) have shown that this kind of analysis allows strong inferences about children's understanding of counting, even when the children are unable to verbalize explicitly their knowledge of constraints and permissions. Particularly strong inferences about understanding can be made when children construct variants of a standard procedure. In such cases, we can analyze the newly constructed procedures to see which constraints have been violated and which have been respected. If a constraint is violated, we can infer that the child either does not know the principle justifying the constraint or has failed to recognize its appropriateness to the procedure under construction.

With this in mind, we can now reconsider our three examples of errorful constructions. In each case, some constraints of the correct rule system are maintained while others are violated. In the case of buggy subtraction algorithms, most constraints imposed by the standard notational system for multidigit arithmetic are respected. These are the constraints I described earlier—under the rubric "critics"—of filling every column with one and only one digit, touching each column once, showing decrements and increments side-by-side and the like. At the same time, the constraints that derive from the principles just discussed—that is, those that derive from the need to treat the written numbers as representations of composed quantities, and of maintaining these quantities when exchanges are made among the parts—are contravened.

In our algebra malrules, implicit constraints in the rules taught in school are ignored in the process of driving a rule that will allow one to solve a type of problem (deciding whether expressions are equivalent or not) that has not been encountered previously. The result is a set of actions that one is too free to apply. It seems likely that greater attention to the referential meaning of algebra expressions would add constraints that would effectively block or modify many of the malrule constructions.

The story for decimal malrules is more complex, but also involves the kind of constraint trading that occurs in subtraction and algebra. Malrule 1 children appear to be violating many of the constraints of interpretation that derive from place value conventions, respecting only the constraint that "something" changes at the decimal point (so it cannot be totally ignored). In the malrule 2 invention, constraints of interpretation imposed by column values are applied, but constraints imposed by digit values are violated. In addition, constraints are applied that are derived from the principle that fractional pieces are larger when there are fewer pieces, and these interact with the column value constraints.

SYNTAX WITHOUT SEMANTICS: A PROBLEM
IN MATHEMATICS LEARNING

There is reason to believe that many children who construct buggy algorithms and symbolically based malrules know more about the underlying principles than they in fact apply. There are several sources of evidence for this claim. Elsewhere (Resnick, 1983), I have traced evidence for the elaboration of a part/whole schema over the early years of school arithmetic learning. This part/whole schema—which is related to the additive composition of number principle—probably begins in a nonquantitative form in children's experiences with uncompleted puzzles, and with cakes and other nondiscrete quantities that must be shared. Vergnaud (1982) has outlined a universe of basic *additive structures* that provides the reference domain for a wide variety of mathematical procedures and expressions involving addition and subtraction. Vergnaud's basic structures are isomorphic with the schemata that Riley, Greeno, and Heller (1983; see also Morales, Shute, & Pellegrino, 1985) have shown to underlie children's ability to solve basic addition and subtraction story problems. The now widely documented invented arithmetic procedures of children and certain unschooled or minimally schooled adults (e.g., Ginsburg, 1977; Russell & Ginsburg, 1984; Saxe & Posner, 1983; Scribner, 1984) are mostly based on these same additive structures and this gives us further reason to believe that the additive structures are acquired by virtually all humans.

Direct evidence that school children often know more about the principles underlying procedures than they apply when performing those procedures comes from some of our research on children's learning of place value. Resnick and Omanson (1987) have shown that children often demonstrate understanding of the principles of subtraction described earlier in this chapter when they work with concrete representations of number (such as Dienes blocks or color-coded chips), but do not interpret the scratch marks of written borrowing in terms of quantity exchange. Moreover, when children who had been diagnosed as having buggy subtraction algorithms were taught the principles of subtraction, their buggy performances did not necessarily disappear. The teaching in these experiments was done in individual tutorials, in a form that insured that knowledge of the principles was in fact linked by the children to justification of the steps in the subtraction algorithm. Detailed interviews established with considerable certainty that a number of children fully understood the principles and their application to written subtraction. Nevertheless, as soon as they returned to a situation of routine calculation performance, half of the children who had learned the principles reverted to using buggy algorithms. That is, they did subtraction in a way that violated principles they clearly knew.

This tendency to separate quantitative and symbolic representations seems to be a major stumbling block in mathematics learning, as it probably also is in learning other domains in which formal representational systems play an important role. Like natural languages, mathematical formalisms have syntax: Any expression in a mathematical notation obeys rules of what constitutes a well-formed expression, and transformations of expressions obey fixed rules for what will produce other allowable expressions within the system. Also like natural languages, mathematical expressions have semantics: The expressions describe quantities, relationships among quantities, and other mathematical *entities* (cf. Greeno, 1983a).

However, in the formal language of mathematics, unlike the natural language of human speech and writing, syntax and semantics can become detached from one another. When one is working with the language of mathematics, one does not automatically think about the quantities and relationships that are referenced. What is more, school instruction probably tends to aggravate this tendency for the formal language of mathematics to function independently of its referents. The focus in elementary school is on correct ways to perform procedures, a focus largely detached from reflection on the quantities and relationships to which symbolic expressions refer. This probably encourages children to attend to formal notations and rules for manipulating them without relating these rules to the semantics—that is, to the external referents—of the notations. Mathematics educators, long aware of this difficulty, have often proposed that it be counteracted by programs of instruction that focus on the underlying structures and principles of mathematics and show children how procedures are derived from these principles (cf. Resnick & Ford, 1981). Nevertheless, the problem persists, and findings such as those of our study on subtraction suggest that it is deeply rooted and not likely to respond to superficial changes in instructional practice.

The Nature of Mathematical Talent.   Some of our work suggests that one of the characteristics of very strong mathematics students is that they are much less likely to allow the mathematical symbols to become detached from their referents. A small number of mathematically precocious children that we have been following seem to reason ''ahead'' of their school instruction (i.e., to infer new mathematical relationships before these are introduced in school) and, subsequently, to attempt to relate the formal expressions and procedures introduced in school to their already developed conceptual knowledge. In future work, we plan to explore the hypothesis that this tendency to reason intuitively about formal systems, to link formal to more intuitively held knowledge, is what distinguishes excellent mathematics students from others. According to this hypothesis, ordinary students are more likely to treat school mathematics as an invitation to master puzzle-like rule systems. Students who are good at such rule learning—those who quickly discriminate among conditions of application, who have and use effective strategies for rehearsal and practice—will perform quite well in school mathematics. But they probably will never love the subject, nor be very creative at it, and they probably will stop studying mathematics as soon as the demands of school or profession allow. Those who are poor at rule learning and fail to link mathematical symbols to their referents are, very likely, those who populate our remedial and ''math anxiety'' classes.

If this hypothesis about the essential differences between good and poor mathematics learners turns out to be correct, it may be possible to help the weaker learners become stronger by giving them explicit help in drawing the connections between the formal rules they are taught and their more intuitive and informal knowledge of certain mathematical principles. Although there is regularly some effort to teach the principles and justifications underlying school arithmetic procedures, this effort is not usually very sustained. More important, it does not aim to explicitly link school math with children's intuitive knowledge about mathematics. In part, this is because we do not know very much about the form of children's knowledge, the terms in which they can express it, or the most congenial ways for children of making the links to symbolic formalisms. Here, I believe, mathematically advanced children can be important informants. These children are, in effect, ''articulate novices,'' able to express children's intuitive formulations of mathematical principles in ways that may well give us the terms in which to discuss these principles more effectively with other children who do not so easily talk about their intuitive understanding or link it to their school learning. For this reason, intensive study of the knowledge and reasoning of mathematically able children seems likely not only to shed light on the nature of mathematical talent in children, but also to provide knowledge that may help to improve our understanding and eventually our instruction of the less gifted.

LEARNING, DEVELOPMENT, AND SCHOOLING: WHAT RELATIONSHIP?

The main theme of this chapter has been the centrality of knowledge construction in school learning, and the various forms that such constructions can take. In pursuing this theme, certain common distinctions—between learning and development, between constructed knowledge and instructed knowledge, between knowledge acquisition that is intentional and responsive to external demands (such as demands in school) and knowledge acquisition that occurs unintentionally in the course of other activities—have failed to appear. In fact, this is not accidental: Acknowledging the pervasiveness of knowledge construction in human mental functioning leads one away from these distinctions and toward a more unified view of cognitive processing. Nevertheless, before concluding the chapter, it seems appropriate to consider these distinctions explicitly.

Consider first the relationship between constructed and instructed knowledge. If knowledge construction is pervasive, even in school, then what is the role of specific instruction? Does it make sense to speak of instructed knowledge as distinct from constructed knowledge? In one sense the answer is simple: The role of instruction is to provide material on which learners' constructive processes can operate. Instructed knowledge—knowledge as presented in school or *pedagogical knowledge* to use Glaser's (1984) apt term—is not expected to survive, but only to nourish and shape the knowledge construction process that is at the heart of learning. This function of instruction is manifestly evident in the examples developed in this chapter. All of the constructions examined are based upon material presented and even drilled in school. There is little likelihood that, in the absence of schooling, the particular knowledge constructions considered here would have taken place.

To say this, however, is only to set the stage for a much more complex answer to the question of how instructed and constructed knowledge are related, an answer that will have to be developed in the form of a well-elaborated constructivist psychology of instruction. We need now to develop a psychology of instruction that places the learner's active mental construction at the heart of the instructional exchange. This theory must be capable of guiding the design of interventions that aim to place learners in situations where the constructions that they will inevitably make will be powerful and correct ones, constrained by the principles that govern a domain. A constructivist instructional theory need not avoid prescriptions for intervention. The "hands off—let the children do it" attitude that has sometimes been suggested as a response to children's constructive capacities will not adequately guide and constrain knowledge construction. On the other hand, instruction should not be guided by an assumption that correct knowledge will be absorbed directly from demonstration and drills. What is needed now is a theory that helps us to understand how specific kinds of explanations and demonstrations are used in the knowledge construction process, what forms of practice will encourage the invention of correct and powerful procedures, and what kinds of feedback will optimally guide knowledge construction. Thus, a constructivist theory of instruction must address all of the traditional instructional questions.

I have claimed that instruction functions largely to set the immediate context within which knowledge construction takes place. It is notable that this kind of statement could be made not only about explicit school instruction, but also about any other sources of environmental and cultural influence on learning. That is, the environment and the culture provide the "material" upon which constructive mental processes will work, establishing both opportunities for and constraints upon knowledge construction. This constraining and enabling role of the environment produces similarities in the mental constructions of people in the same culture, and differences in mental constructions between cultures. The fact that school instruction and the culture and environment at large are conceived to participate in the knowledge construction process in similar ways suggests that there may be less difference than we have often thought between formal and informal learning, between intentional knowledge acquisition in school and unintentional knowledge acquisition elsewhere. For example, Sylvia Scribner's (1984) research on workers in a dairy plant gives evidence of invented mathematical procedures that must derive from processes very much like those discussed here—processes in which the workers' knowledge of constraints and permissions inherent in the number system allows them to construct procedures that save significant mental or physical labor in their daily tasks. The constructions that Scribner describes are successful and mathematically correct ones, as are the various procedures that have been reported for children, and for adults in various unschooled cultures. This is not surprising, for these are procedures that have been shaped and tested by use; they are the result of relatively long periods of living and working in a particular space of opportunity and demand. Thus, Scribner and others did not observe malrules and other incorrect conceptions that arise in the course of learning and that persist only if there is insufficient environmental pressure for building correct procedures and conceptions over time.

This brings me to the question of learning and development. There is an implicit correspondence between the intentional/unintentional and learning/development distinctions. When we think about deliberate acquisition of new skills or understanding, we tend to use the word *learning*. On the other hand, we usually speak of *development* when new competence results from activities that are not specifically intended to promote acquisition. Development is thought to be a natural process, learning a somewhat more artificial one. This distinction, in turn, maps onto the functionalist/structuralist contrast with which this chapter opened. In the past, psychologists who have studied intentional acquisition of competence (whether in school or in the laboratory) have tended to assume that the process is a direct one in which externally presented knowledge is exercised, absorbed, and reproduced. By contrast, many of those (and especially Piagetians) who have studied unintentional acquisition of competence (in play, outside school, often over long periods of time) have assumed that knowledge is constructed.

The arguments developed here suggest that it is false to assume that there are two different kinds of acquisition, one for formal and another for informal situations. Instead, I have tried to show that constructive processes are involved in school learning as well as in informal situations, but that the quality of the constructions depends on the kinds of representations used in reasoning. This being the case, focusing on distinctions between learning and development seems to me an unlikely way to make progress in understanding the nature of knowledge acquisition. We need instead to focus our attention and efforts to uncover the processes by which knowledge construction proceeds and the ways in which various kinds of environmental stimuli shape and constrain those processes. These are questions that our present scientific resources now permit us to address in a fresh and more fruitful way.

ACKNOWLEDGMENTS

The research reported herein was supported by the Office of Educational Research and Improvement as a project of the Center for the Study of Learning and in part by the Office of Naval Research (Grant No. N00014-84-K-0223).

REFERENCES

Anderson, J. R. (Ed.). (1981). *Cognitive skills and their acquisition.* Hillsdale, NJ: Lawrence Erlbaum Associates.

Brown, J. S., & Burton, R. R. (1978). Diagnostic models for procedural bugs in basic mathematical skills. *Cognitive Science, 2*(2), 155–192.

Brown, J. S., & VanLehn, K. (1982). Toward a generative theory of "bugs." In T. P. Carpenter, J. M. Moser, & T. A. Romberg (Eds.), *Addition and subtraction: A cognitive perspective* (pp. 117–135). Hillsdale, NJ: Lawrence Erlbaum Associates.

Burton, R. R. (1982). Diagnosing bugs in a simple procedural skill. In D. Sleeman & J. S. Brown (Eds.), *Intelligent tutoring systems* (pp. 157–183). New York: Academic Press.

Carry, L. R., Lewis, C., & Bernard, J. E. (1980). *Psychology of equation solving: An information-processing study.* Austin, TX: University of Texas.

Ginsburg, H. P. (1977). *Children's arithmetic: The learning process.* New York: Van Nostrand Reinhold.

Glaser, R. (1984). Education and thinking: The role of knowledge. *American Psychologist, 39*(1), 93–104.

Greeno, J. G. (1983a). Conceptual entities. In D. Gentner & A. L. Stevens (Eds.), *Mental models* (pp. 227–252). Hillsdale, NJ: Lawrence Erlbaum Associates.

Greeno, J. G. (1983b, August). *Investigations of a cognitive skill.* Paper presented at the Annual Meeting of the American Psychological Association, Anaheim, CA.

Greeno, J. G., Riley, M. S., & Gelman, R. (1984). Conceptual competence and children's counting. *Cognitive Psychology, 16*(1), 94–143.

Groen, G. J., & Resnick, L. B. (1977). Can preschool children invent addition algorithms? *Journal of Educational Psychology, 69*(6), 645–652. [University of Pittsburgh, LRDC Reprint Series 1978/5.]

Karmiloff-Smith, A., & Inhelder, B. (1974). If you want to get ahead, get a theory. *Cognition, 3,* 195–212.

Katona, G. (1967). *Organizing and memorizing: Studies in the psychology of learning and teaching.* New York: Hafner. (Original work published 1940)

Matz, M. (1982). Towards a process model for high school algebra errors. In D. Sleeman & J. S. Brown (Eds.), *Intelligent tutoring systems* (pp. 25–50). New York: Academic Press.

Morales, R. V., Shute, V. J., & Pellegrino, J. W. (in press). Developmental differences in understanding and solving simple word problems. *Cognition and Instruction, 2,* 41–57.

Neches, R. (1981). *Models of heuristic procedure modification.* Unpublished doctoral dissertation, Carnegie-Mellon University, Pittsburgh, PA.

Newell, A., & Simon, H. A. (1972). *Human problem solving.* Englewood Cliffs, NJ: Prentice-Hall.

Piaget, J. (1973). *To understand is to invent: The future of education.* New York: Grossman. (Original work published 1948)

Resnick, L. B. (1982). Syntax and semantics in learning to subtract. In T. P. Carpenter, J. M. Moser, & T. A. Romberg (Eds.), *Addition and subtraction: A cognitive perspective* (pp. 136–155). Hillsdale, NJ: Lawrence Erlbaum Associates.

Resnick, L. B. (1983). A developmental theory of number understanding. In H. P. Ginsburg (Ed.), *The development of mathematical thinking* (pp. 109–151). New York: Academic Press. [LRDC Reprint Series 1984/38.]

Resnick, L. B., & Ford, W. W. (1981). Teaching the structures of mathematics. In L. B. Resnick & W. W. Ford (Eds.), *The psychology of mathematics for instruction* (pp. 101–127). Hillsdale, NJ: Lawrence Erlbaum Associates.

Resnick, L. B., & Neches, R. (1984). Factors affecting individual differences in learning ability. In R. J. Sternberg (Ed.), *Advances in the psychology of human intelligence* (Vol. 2, pp. 275–323). Hillsdale, NJ: Lawrence Erlbaum Associates [LRDC Reprint Series 1984/41.]

Resnick, L. B., Nesher, P., Leonard, F., Sackur-Grisvard, C., Omanson, S., Peled, I., & Magone, M. (in preparation). *Constructing a concept of decimal numbers.*

Resnick, L. B., & Omanson, S. F. (1987). Learning to understand arithmetic. In R. Glaser (Ed.), *Advances in instructional psychology* (Vol. 3, pp. 41–95). Hillsdale, NJ: Lawrence Erlbaum Associates.

Riley, M. S., Greeno, J. G., & Heller, J. I. (1983). Development of children's problem-solving ability in arithmetic. In H. P. Ginsburg (Ed.), *The development of mathematical thinking* (pp. 153–196). New York: Academic Press.

Russell, R. R., & Ginsburg, H. P. (1984). Cognitive analysis of children's mathematics difficulties. *Cognition and Instruction, 1*(2), 217–244.

Sackur-Grisvard, C., & Leonard, F. (1985). Intermediate cognitive organization in the process of learning a mathematical concept: The order of positive decimal numbers. *Cognition and Instruction, 2,* 157–174.

Saxe, G. B., & Posner, J. K. (1983). The development of numerical cognition: Cross-cultural perspectives. In H. P. Ginsberg (Ed.), *The development of mathematical thinking* (pp. 291–317). New York: Academic Press.

Scribner, S. (1984). Studying working intelligence. In B. Rogoff & J. Lave (Eds.), *Everyday cognition: Its development in social context* (pp. 9–40). Cambridge, MA: Harvard University Press.

Simon, H. A. (1976). Identifying basic abilities underlying intelligent performance of complex tasks. In L. B. Resnick (Ed.), *The nature of intelligence* (pp. 65–98). Hillsdale, NJ: Lawrence Erlbaum Associates.

Sleeman, D. (1982). Assessing aspects of competence in basic algebra. In D. Sleeman & J. S. Brown (Eds.), *Intelligent tutoring systems* (pp. 185–199). New York: Academic Press.

Vergnaud, G. (1982). A classification of cognitive tasks and operations of thought involved in addition and subtraction problems. In T. P. Carpenter, J. M. Moser, & T. A. Romberg (Eds.), *Addition and subtraction: A cognitive perspective* (pp. 39–59). Hillsdale, NJ: Lawrence Erlbaum Associates.

Wertheimer, M. (1959). *Productive thinking.* New York: Harper & Row. (Original work published 1945)

3 Necessity: The Developmental Component in School Mathematics

Frank B. Murray
University of Delaware

Like their performance on virtually every other intellectual task, children's performance on arithmetic problems improves steadily throughout the elementary school grades (Fey & Sonnabend, 1982; Romberg & Carpenter, 1986). They become more accurate and faster in their performance on ordinary addition and subtraction problems and in their performance on unusual problems that require borrowing and carrying across several digits. Although children, on the whole, are consistently successful on the National Assessment of Educational Progress (NAEP) Tests of whole number computation and some measurement tasks, they are noticeably unsuccessful on tasks that involve fractions, percentages, and basic mathematical problem solving (NAEP, 1979). Still, despite a marked unevenness in children's performance across various mathematical domains and between one cohort of pupils and another, children—especially throughout the early grades—show a steady improvement in basic computational skill.

Can it be said, however, that anything is developing as children's performance improves—as they become more accurate and faster at subtracting 15 from 91, for example? What could be developmentally interesting about these changes in children's performance? At one level these changes meet the minimum criterion for a developmental change, namely they are changes that take place over relatively long periods of time—over months and years. Were they changes that took place over much shorter periods—minutes, hours, or days—we would be more likely to think of them as changes in behavior that were due to nondevelopmental mechanisms, like learning or motivation.

51

THE CONSISTENCY BETWEEN CHILDREN'S
ARITHMETICAL PERFORMANCE AND OPERATIVITY

The arithmetical errors children make, the bugs, repairs, and malrules that are cited by Resnick (this volume) and others (e.g., Brown & VanLehn, 1982) are completely consistent with the typical pre-operational responses that are so familiar to researchers working in the Genevan tradition. The competence, for example, to simultaneously treat two or more aspects of the same thing is a hard-won developmental achievement that takes on the order of 7 years to accomplish and even then it is expressed in only a few conceptual domains. Thus, we expect place value notation to be difficult for the pre-operational pupil and even, in certain contexts, for the concrete operational child. The numeral 9 is not always a 9; sometimes it is 900 or 9/10ths and so forth—and sometimes, as students of measurement find out, it is a nominal entity that cannot even be said to come after 8 and before 10.

To some extent the issue in the child's arithmetical performance, particularly in the case of some striking deficiencies and inconsistencies, is an issue of the child's metacognition of a notational system and the various algorithms, as arbitrary and serviceable as they are. The issue in the child's performance on school arithmetic tasks is often more a question of his or her cognition of numerals in place of numbers—or as Resnick (this volume) and others claim, the separation of syntactics from semantics, or as others claim (Hiebert, 1986), the separation of performance from understanding.

Far from a challenge to the Genevan view, the very existence of malrules and bugs is entirely consistent with the Genevan view of intellectual development. What, after all is the origin of these bugs and malrules, let alone the mathematical principles that supplant them? Children cannot be said to have learned them, because like the young child's persistent syntactical errors, there would be no opportunity for these errors to have been learned or imitated. No adult does mathematics this way and no teacher teaches malrules and bugs to children. These malrules are invented, and like all cognitive constructions or inventions, they are attempts by the child to understand, to produce greater coherence, and to resolve or reduce contradiction. The fact that these inventions often yield failure and incorrect answers does not mean that they fail to confer a degree of understanding or coherence. In fact, it can be argued that even adult errors in logical reasoning are not truly errors in logic because what adults have done is to convert the logical problem into another problem about which they reason perfectly (Henle, 1962).

From still another Genevan perspective it is reasonable to view these malrules, bugs, and repairs—all of which make a certain sense of one level—as a part of the so-called "justification-at-any-price" phenomenon. This phenomenon, introduced by Piaget as a defining attribute of pre-operational thought, but unexplained by him, is found when the child is over his or her head and, so to speak, pushed to the wall. It is found in the fantastic lies children offer when they are pressed for explanations of events they do not fully understand. However, the lies and justifications children offer as explanations are not random. Upon close examination, these preposterous explanations often have a certain sense and coherence. For example, a nonconserver in an early investigation (Murray, 1965) told the researcher that the reason one stick in a Muller–Lyer configuration looked longer, or became longer, than another stick of initially equal length was that his mother had put the stick in the oven. What could the child possibly mean by such an explanation as neither his mother nor an oven were present? Surely the child's explanation was not a random utterance and consequently it must indicate something about the child's primitive view of the way things in the universe change—get bigger in this case. Perhaps the child in this example had observed that things, like cakes, get bigger after being in the oven and when presented with a similar mysterious increase (a stick's length from the Muller–Lyer distortion), the child concluded that a similar force was at work. His preposterous explanation is then an appeal to his primitive physics of "magical"—or action at a distance—causes. These justification-at-any-price explanations are potentially a rich source of clues to the young child's physics and so on.

Presumably mature physics or mathematics develops out of immature physics or mathematics, although the two may have no functional relationship to each other. On the other hand, it may very well turn out that bugs and malrules are necessary elements in the developmental pathway of mathematical understanding in much the same way that preoperational thought—with all its "failures"—is a necessary construction in the development of operativity (Sinclair & Sinclair, 1986). Thus, from several perspectives the child's invention of bugs, malrules, and repairs and the other changes in arithmetical performance and understanding are consistent with the general claims made in Piagetian theory about the child's grasp of any intellectual skill.

DEVELOPMENT AND ARITHMETIC

The developmentally interesting questions about arithmetical understanding and performance are, as they always are for each cognitive domain, what structure is developing and toward what developmental end is it going; that is, what is the developmental end point of mathematical understanding in the domain? The developmental mechanism, however it is specified, is that which provides coherence to all the algorithms, procedures, and notational systems; it is the glue, so to speak, that holds the notational system to the quantities and allows the notations and procedures to form a system. From the Genevan perspective, it is a system of algorithms that has the well-known operational features of reversibility, compensation, and so on. Thus, addition and subtraction are integrated into a system in which it is really not possible to think of one apart from the other because the existence of one requires and implies the existence of the other. Similarly, the notational system, owing to the general power of the semiotic function, becomes a symbolic system capable of an efficient attachment and re-attachment to various entities.

What develops, in other words, is the notion of mathematical necessity. It is not just that 15 from 91 is 76, true as that is, but that it has to be 76, that it cannot be anything else however notated. Moreover, if it were anything else, an entire mental system of other known things would have to be changed. The development of necessity requires the invention of a system in which otherwise separate events are connected together on some common dimension. Thus, the algorithms of addition and subtraction are shown to be reversible aspects of the same operation or structure. Similarly, the malrule of decimal contradictions in the decimal notation in which the numbers to the right of the decimal point decrease as the connotations of their labels increase (tenths, hundredths, thousandths) is shown to be an instance of reversibility in the place value notation. The dimension or structure that links the algorithms is what is invented or constructed by the child and confers necessity, not just regularity and truth, on the learned relationships between any set of elements.

From where does this necessity come—how does it become attached to what we otherwise know to be true, what we learn is true? These are the overriding developmental questions. How is this necessity constructed, and how is it occasionally suspended so that other possible systems of wider range consistency and necessity can be constructed to serve in its place? Cognitive development, from this perspective, is the extension of necessity to other domains of things we know are true. Not to press the point too far, we could say that learning mechanisms yield truth and cognitive developmental mechanisms yield necessity. The algorithms, notations, basic concepts that are learned somewhat rotely and arbitrarily in the typical instructional sequence at some point develop into a coherent system, in fact an operational system in the Genevan sense. This at least would be the developmental interpretation of the changes that take place in children's arithmetical performance. What evidence is consistent with this view?

The development of core structures that tie the algorithms together into an operational system, marked by reversibility, is consistent with Resnick's (this volume) observation that the cognitive processes used in mathematical problem solving are the same for both correct and incorrect outcomes, the difference being that each flows from a different representation of the problem. The source of these differing representations, like the source of the horizontal decline, is still quite unknown. Similarly, there is Resnick's claim that there are certain mathematical principles of quantity, such that if the child had these in mind, the bugs, repairs, and malrules would not occur or would not have been invented by the child in the first place. These principles surely will be found to have a close resemblance to the Genevan operativity structures.

NECESSITY AND OPERATIONAL THOUGHT

The classic operativity tasks despite their exhalted and reified status, are merely diagnostic tasks, tasks that can be used to assess the child's appreciation of logical necessity. The tasks are not about what the child knows in the sense of how well-informed the child may be. In fact, to the extent that school learning—information in the curriculum—contributes to the child's performance on the operativity tasks, the tasks will yield a false positive diagnosis because although the child may arrive at the correct answer he or she may do it in a way that precludes his or her deducing it and seeing the necessity of it. It is one thing to know that 3 and 5 are 8 or that a flattened clay ball weighs the same as when it was shaped like a ball and even that it can be rolled back into a ball, but it is quite another matter entirely to know that it must be 8 or that it must weigh the same. Being correct, but not understanding the necessity of the correct answer, is not conservation; it is what the Genevans have called *pseudo-conservation*.

It can be noted, in passing, that the diagnosis of logical necessity with the conservation task can also yield a false negative diagnosis when, for example, the pupil, although admittedly wrong and misinformed, thinks that the flattened ball not only is heavier but that it must be heavier, always would be heavier, and could not conceivably be lighter. This would be pseudo-nonconservation and would indicate the presence of the operational structures the Genevans believe support the feelings of logical necessity. Thus, correct performance on the task may not indicate necessity and incorrect performance may indicate it, which is why the Genevans have always embedded the diagnosis of cognitive level in a clinical setting that was designed to minimize the false positive and negative errors.

No doubt, it has puzzled, perhaps even irritated, many American developmental and educational psychologists that the Genevans rarely acknowledge the vast American literature on conservation and other related topics. On the whole, the non-Genevan literature on conservation has almost nothing to do with the questions the Genevans attempted to answer in their considerations of conservation. The proper questions are how the child moves from a grasp of empirical necessity to logical necessity, from induction to deduction, from empirical revertibility[1] to mental reversibility, and from covariation to compensation. Conservation, as Pinard (1981) points out, is not a concept to be acquired or a principle or a specific cognitive operation; it is, rather, a simple consequence of reversibility and is a fundamental component of every concept the child learns.

---

[1]The term *revertibility* is a translation of the word "renversabilité," attributed to Rita Vuyk (*Overview and Critique of Piaget's Genetic Epistemology, 1965–1980*, New York: Academic Press, 1981). It has also been translated elsewhere as *empirical reversibility* (see J. Piaget, *The Equilibration of Cognitive Structures*, translated by Terrance Brown and Kishore Julian Thampy, Chicago: The University of Chicago Press, 1985) which may make the meaning more transparent.

How the child comes to discriminate the large set of statements that are true or false from the smaller set that are necessarily true or false is a significant issue for any theory of the development of the intellect because having a concept of necessity is a criterial attribute of a rational mind.

The Genevans have attempted to diagnose the presence of the child's concept of necessity with many tasks, but most notably with the conservation task. This task has the structure of a transitive inference or deduction once the child makes the assumption that the transformed object is equivalent to the untransformed object. How the child comes to make that assumption has been an important research question with many theorists searching only for the efficient causes of the assumption. The others continue to point out that the specification of only the efficient cause provides an incomplete account of conservation. The added specification of the structure of the conservation response and the necessity it diagnostically represents must be given along with the specification of the place and purpose of the concept of necessity in the formation of the mature mind. The initial debates, naturally focused upon criteria that would implicate the restricted versus the full range of Aristotelian causes (viz., material, efficient, formal, and final causes).

It is important to realize that the tests of genuine conservation that the Genevans use only make sense insofar as they are attempts to certify that the child's conservation response was a deduction, that is a necessary conclusion. A determination of the child's feeling of the necessity of his or her response could be made, but almost never is. For example, the child could be asked whether the outcome could ever have been different, or would it always or just sometimes be what the child said it was. Typically, the feeling of necessity is assessed indirectly by one or more of the following five criteria that only make sense if they are indicators of necessity. Otherwise they are unreasonable criteria—criteria we would not employ for the acquisition of any other kind of information. The five criteria are:

1. Durability. Conservation assessment is repeated at later time intervals up to 1 or 2 months on the assumption that the notion of necessity is never given up once it is acquired.

2. Resistance to countersuggestion. In this case, counterevidence, pressure, argument is offered by the experimenter in an attempt to change the child's conservation response on the assumption that necessary conclusions are not modifiable. Easily changed responses are said to indicate pseudo-conservation, that is a judgment based upon something other than necessity.

3. Specific transfer. Conservation is assessed with different materials and perhaps with different transformations on the assumption that the logical form of the task should transcend particular task features.

4. Nonspecific transfer. Conservation is assessed in different domains or

with different operativity tasks (e.g., seriation, transitivity, class inclusion) because these all manifest necessity.

5. Trainability. This criterion is in some sense the converse of the countersuggestion criterion because it is applied to the nonconservation response on the
assumption that a quick and abrupt change in response after feedback, hints,
cues, and so on indicates that the original nonconservation was not valid (or was
pseudo-nonconservation) because development takes a relatively long time.

It should be noted that the classical Genevan explanations for conservation,
namely identity, negation, and reciprocity, are valid justifications only in cases
where conservation and necessity are presupposed (Murray, 1982). In sum, the
criteria the Genevans imposed on conservation assessment, namely reversibility
reasons, durability, specific and nonspecific transfer, and resistance to extinc-
tion, only make sense when the conservation is seen as a way to diagnose the
presence of logical necessity in the child's reasoning. Otherwise, they are inadequate and even give irrelevant and useless information about the task. That the
pancake can be rolled back into a ball really tells us nothing about whether
weight or anything else, except shape, changed.

The other standard operativity tasks follow the same pattern. Class inclusion
is about the necessity of the whole's being greater than the part; seriation is about
each stick's necessarily unique position in the array; horizontality about the
necessary relationships that obtain from the grid of absolute space; and classification about the necessarily unique placement of class members in a classification
scheme.

Unfortunately, the conservation problem, like the other operativity tasks, is
not solely a logical reasoning task even though success on it is taken by Piaget as
the best indicator of the presence of the logical groupings of operational thought.
The conservation problem, despite the Genevan intention, tells us as much about
the child's understanding of certain natural regularities as it does of his understanding of logical necessity. The problem, as Piaget and others have noted, is
contaminated by a mixture of logical and physical principles. The information
that the clay ball and a clay pancake are equal in weight and the information that
weight is transitive both have nonlogical sources. How the child comes to know
these things and how he or she uses what he or she knows is one question that
separates the various theories of conservation and is a question that remains
unanswered.

Indeed, in the Genevan account cognitive advancement for the child and adult
comes when the person invents or constructs for each mental event an opposite or
negation where none had existed previously. The invention of the negation,
inverse, reverse requires the construction of a link or a dimension on which the
two events (the positive and the negative) become indissociable so that the
thought of one now necessarily entails the thought of the other, not as a separate
entity, but as a mutual member of the same structure. For example, the child's

initial notion of addition, as we have noted, may be entirely independent of his or her initial notion of subtraction, but at some later point, each is seen as linked in a single structure in which each necessarily entails the other, is the reverse of the other so that one cannot be thought of apart from the implication or possibility of the other. Equilibration is seen as the mechanism by which these reversible links are constructed.

The conservation and other operativity problems can be seen as the development of necessity but all the old issues remain. Does, for example, our notion of necessity undergo qualitative changes over the life span or is it essentially the same notion throughout but applied at different rates to different cognitive domains? Does knowing that ''sisters have to be girls'' or that ''parents have to be older than their children'' require the same structural competence as knowing that ''4 from 9 has to be 5 and could not be another number'' or that ''A must equal C if both A and C equal B?'' Whether or not it requires the same structural competence, we do know that there is a wide age range over which children come to appreciate the necessity of various events—a range that spans the preoperational and formal operational periods (Pieraut-LeBonniec, 1980).

How, in fact, does the feeling of necessity get attached to what we otherwise know to be true? The problem of necessity is fundamental to a whole set of curricular and pedagogical decisions. Of all the things that are true, how do we know which, if any, must be true? Although Piaget's theory, and the data that support it, make it clear that there are sizable aptitude treatment interactions—that is, the instructional effort is unquestionably constrained by the pupil's cognitive level—how is it possible that the pupil comes to believe that some events are necessarily true? Whatever the answer, conservation and the other operativity tasks are about this question.

EMPIRICAL CONNECTIONS BETWEEN OPERATIVITY AND NECESSITY

Formal Operations.   The link between formal operational thought and the notion of necessity—especially as it is manifested in deductive reasoning—is virtually guaranteed by the definition of formal operational thought as the adolescent's competence to make deductions from possible as well as actual events and circumstances. Thus, the adolescent is able to say, ''if this were the case, which it is not, but if it were, then such and so would follow necessarily.''

Fetzer and Murray (1971) investigated the link between syllogistic reasoning and operational thought. It has been known for some time that syllogisms based upon familiar content are easier to process than those that employ symbols or unfamiliar content (Wilkins, 1928), and that the subject's attitude toward the content (Janis & Frick, 1943) or the emotional aspects of it (Lefford, 1946) are determiners of the subject's appreciation of the necessity or the validity and invalidity of an argument. Even though nonstructural performance factors, such as these, influence reasoning, it is reasonable, nevertheless, to suppose the existence and development of an underlying logical competence as a significant part of the explanation of reasoning on logical and mathematical tasks, let alone reasoning in other domains. Because a syllogism may be logically valid and yet composed of empirically false statements, or conversely logically invalid and composed of empirically true statements, it is a useful device for examining the child's sensitivity to necessity, particularly in cases where necessary and contingent cues agree or conflict. Fetzer and Murray (1971) investigated children's performance on valid and invalid categorical and linear syllogisms, whose premises and conclusion were all either empirically true, false, or neutral, and also their performance on some concrete and formal operativity tasks.

In all, 206 children (Grades 3–9) received 4 conservation tasks, 6 linear syllogisms, 23 categorical syllogisms and 2 formal operational tasks (beam-balance proportionality and incidence and reflection). The 12 categorical syllogisms had premises and conclusions that were either empirically true (ET), empirically false (EF), or empirically neutral (EN). The conclusions either followed logically from the premises, i.e., logically valid (LV), or they did not follow, i.e., logically invalid (LI). An example of an empirically true and logically invalid syllogism (ETLI) was "All collies have long hair; Lassie has long hair; therefore, Lassie is a collie." The empirically false and logically valid syllogism (EFLV) was, for example, "All candy is blue; all horses are candy; therefore, all horses are blue," and an example of an empirically neutral and valid syllogism was "All Sally's friends are blondes; the Smith's are Sally's friends; therefore, the Smith's are blondes."

Six linear syllogisms, two instances of three types (ET, EN, EF) were also presented as two statements followed by a choice of two conclusions. Examples of each type were: ET—A skyscraper is higher than a garage and a garage is higher than a doghouse, with a conclusion of (a) A skyscraper is higher than a doghouse, or (b) A doghouse is higher than a skyscraper; EN—John is taller than Dick, and Dick is taller than Tom, with a conclusion of (a) John is taller than Dick, or (b) Tom is taller than John; EF—A canoe is bigger than a tugboat and a tugboat is bigger than a battleship with a conclusion of (a) A canoe is bigger than a battleship, or (b) A battleship is bigger than a canoe.

Only 10% of the children were correct on the formal operational tasks, a typical finding for a sample of this size and age range. A Guttman scale with a reproducibility factor of 92.3 indicated the tasks from least to most difficult were ET, ETLV, EFLI; conservation of weight, ENLV, EN, ENLI, ENLI; EFLV, EF, conservation of volume, ETLI. The clusters of tasks separated by semicolons in the preceding sentence were significantly different from each other in difficulty. Syllogisms in which there was a "conflict" between truth and necessity were (viz., ETLI, EFLV, EF) significantly more difficult than the syllogisms in which there was no conflict between truth and necessity (viz., EFLV, EFLI,

ET) and we well, significantly more difficult than the neutral syllogisms (ENLV, ENLI, and EN). Overall, the proportions of the subjects who were correct on the "conflict" syllogisms were low (ETLI, .09; EFLV, .22; EF, .23) compared to the "no conflict" syllogisms (ETLV, .97; EFLI, .87; ET, .95) and neutral syllogisms (ENLV, .84; ENLI, .34; EN, .65). The very low performance on the ETLI (.09) may indicate that it is harder to overcome true content and judge it to be invalid, than to override false content (EFLV .22) and accept it as necessary. However, of those who were correct on the empirically neutral and valid (ENLV) task, 27% were also correct on the "conflict" EFLV tasks, and of those who were correct on the empirically neutral and invalid (ENLI) task, 23% were correct on the "conflict" ETLI task, which indicates that the effect of the conflict between contingent and necessary truth is minimal for those who have the logical competence (as measured by the neutral problems).

Evidence for the link between necessity (as measured by performance on "conflict" syllogisms) and formal operational thought comes from two sources—(a) the relatively superior performance of children who by an age criterion of 12–15 years should be in the formal operational stage, and (b) children's performance on the formal operativity tasks themselves. Older children (ages 12–15) simply gave significantly more correct and fewer incorrect responses than younger children (ages 8–11) in the "conflict" syllogisms, that is, those syllogisms in which the child's appreciation of necessity overrode what was merely true about the statements. However, by any reasonable criterion of operational thought (for example, at least 50% correct) the children and adolescents failed to demonstrate formal operativity on the formal operational tasks and on the volume conservation task. It was only quite late that a criterion of 50% correct was met on the "conflict" syllogisms (EF, 15 years; ETLI, 44% at 15 years; EFLV, 14 years). Nevertheless, there were significant associations between conflict syllogisms and the formal operativity measures (viz., volume conservation, equal angles, and equilibrium) but not between the syllogisms and conservation on weight.

The high proportion of success on the three "no-conflict" syllogisms (ET, ETLV, EFLI), especially by youngest subjects, indicates that the empirical content, not an appreciation of the necessity of the outcome, was probably the determiner of the child's success. The next four tasks in difficulty, conservation of weight and the three neutral syllogisms, suggest that concrete operational thought, as measured both by weight conservation and the age of the subjects, supported the syllogistic inference in these instances.

The next four items in difficulty, the "conflict" syllogisms and volume conservation, presumably require formal operational thought. This notion is supported by the age of successful subjects on these tasks and the significant association of the "conflict" syllogisms and the formal operativity tasks. However, it is by no means clear whether the ability to solve the conflict syllogism should be attributed to a change in underlying logical competence over and above that needed to solve the easier neutral syllogisms, or to change in some performance variable, or to some function that seasons or strengthens logical competence so that it may prevail in the conflict condition. This latter alternative is consistent with Feather's (1964) finding that high scorers on neutral reasoning tasks do better on reasoning tasks on controversial content where, presumably, the subjects must disregard their prejudices.

The child's difficulty in rejecting a conclusion as not necessary as opposed to accepting one as necessary was a clear finding in these data and may be related to the "consideration of absent possibilities" characteristic of formal operational thought. The detection of the "not necessary" may implicitly require an awareness of the possibility of another conclusion (viz., the necessary one) whereas the detection of necessity may not require an awareness that other possibilities are not necessary but simply the recognition that the given conclusion is necessary.

Although it is probably the case that young subjects' (up to 14 years) judgments were largely determined by the empirical content of the statements, it is probably not the case that they were simply evaluating the truth of the conclusions alone and not attending to the premises because significant differences were found at all ages between valid and invalid neutral syllogisms. If one were looking only at the neutral conclusions, there should be no more reason to accept or reject one neutral conclusion than another. However, a set to accept all but patently false conclusion statements could account for the younger subjects' performance on the syllogism task and would indicate, as Henle (1962) suggests that subjects simply did not accept the task as a logical one. Similarly, the younger subjects in the linear syllogisms could have been accepting any but a patently false alternative. Consequently, although the young child may appear to reason logically on these tasks, he or she may be relying exclusively on extralogical cues and have no real appreciation of the logical structure of the problem.

When more direct attempts are made to assess necessity, the results confirm its link to formal operativity in several domains. For example, Murray and Armstrong (1978) examined 188 subjects' (Grades 2, 3, 5, 7, 9, 11, and college) responses to a set of arithmetical problems—some with necessary outcomes and some with indeterminate outcomes. In this study, subjects responded to six tasks—to one simple probability reasoning task and five conservation tasks. One of these was a traditional conservation of number task, whereas the other four were number conservation of equivalence tasks that differed in the types of transformation performed on the arrangement of beads in jars (jar 1, red beads; jar 2, blue beads; jar 3, green beads). For example, in one problem, after six red beads were taken from jar 1 and placed in jar 2, subjects were directed to imagine that two red beads and four blue beads were returned to jar 1. (Answer: number of red beads in jar 1 is always equal to the number of blue beads in jar 2.) In another problem, after six red beads were taken from jar 1 and mixed with the blue beads in jar 2, subjects were directed to imagine that the experimenter without looking took six beads from jar 2 and put them in jar 1. (Answer: number of red beads in jar 1 is always equal to the number of blue beads in jar 2.)

To determine subjects' judgments of the effects of the transformation and also to determine whether subjects appreciated whether the result of the transformation was necessary or merely probable, they were asked two questions: *Question 1,* whether there were the same number of red beads in the red bead jar as blue beads in the blue bead jar or a different number, or whether they didn't know one way or the other; and *Question 2,* if, after the transformation was performed many times the number of red beads in the red bead jar would *always, sometimes,* or *never* equal the number of blue beads in the blue bead jar (etc.).

A factor analysis (Gorsuch, 1974) of all subjects' responses to the six tasks revealed the same two main factors whether responses to Question 1 or Question 2 were analyzed. All the problems loading on the first factor had necessary outcomes and, accordingly, the factor was labeled *Necessity.* The second factor appears to be a *Probability* factor in the sense that the subjects took the tasks to have probable or indeterminate outcomes.

It was only by the seventh grade that the subjects consistently exceeded a 50% correct criterion on both questions and by the ninth grade there was clear and consistent discrimination, even if sometimes incorrect, between what was necessarily true and what was not.

Concrete Operations.   Cauley, Murray, and Smith (1983) gave 38 kindergarten and first grade pupils four operativity tasks—conservation of mass, seriation, transitivity, and class inclusion. They were asked about their appreciation of the necessity of their judgments in three ways—(a) whether the outcome they stated for each task would always be what they said it was or just sometimes, (b) whether it had to be, and (c) whether it could ever be some plausible alternative that was advanced by the experimenter. Almost all children were correct on each task (.82–.92). About 68% of these responded that the outcome would always be the same, had to be what it was, and could not be different or something else.

Similarly, Murray and Armstrong (1976, 1978) found that nearly all conservers of number, length, amount, and weight held their judgment by necessity insofar as each felt that no matter how many times the conservation transformation were performed the result would always be the same, namely, what they just said it was. In a second study (unpublished), 17 of 20 conservers of number, amount, and weight clearly deduced their judgments from premises implicit in the conservation paradigm (Murray, 1981); that is, they were aware of the implicit steps in the paradigm, thought the outcome would always be what it was and could never be different from what it was.

Pre-operational Links.   Substantial numbers of pre-operational children, by the usual measures, appear to hold their incorrect judgments about operativity tasks by necessity. As well, they appreciate the necessary and non-necessary aspects of several other kinds of events. For example, when 6-year-olds are given a 6-item test about the necessity or non-necessity of everyday notions and events, we have found in several samples that about 70% of them know that sisters must always be girls, that fathers have to be older than their children, that crayons do not have to be blue, and so on, that two cookies plus one cookie are always three cookies, that any jelly bean taken out of a jar of red jelly beans has to be red and could never be green, and so on.

Similarly, we have found in several samples that about half of the nonconservers appear to have deduced their erroneous conclusions (Murray & Armstrong, 1976). In one unpublished sample, 16 of 34 of 6-year-old nonconservers of number, amount, and weight gave evidence of necessity that was indistinguishable from that given by the conservers previously cited; they knew all the implicit premises embedded in the conservation paradigm and simply thought that the extended row of objects, for example, would always have more objects than the unextended row and that it could never be less, and so on. By any reasonable test, it appears that some "nonconservers" can support their conclusions with reasons that appear to have all the features of genuine necessity and operativity (see Murray, 1981, 1982 for elaborations of this argument).

Murray and Smith (1985) examined whether this kind of nonconserver necessity was genuine—whether it was logical or merely empirical in nature. They raised the question of whether the nonconservers who show this kind of "necessity" would be the ones who would make cognitive gains after they have been contradicted in a peer social interaction conservation training manipulation modeled after Ames and Murray (1982). Three outcomes, each of which provides interesting evidence on the nature of this preoperational "necessity," were considered:

1. Some nonconservers who assert "necessity" may be children without operativity who are merely misinformed and who think that the conservation transformation really affects amount, length, and so on. In the peer situation, they would be expected to maintain their original positions or at most, switch to another nonconservation position, in which the transformation still affects amount, and the like, but in a different way. Thus, their "necessity" assertion reflects only their firm belief or certainty that flattening, for example, always affects the weight of an object in some way.

2. Some nonconservers who show this pre-operational "necessity" may also be children without operativity who are merely adamant about their positions, who are socially dominant and who are prepared to argue their position, whatever it is. They would be expected to resist the peer's contradiction, and not adopt the peer's position after the social interaction. The necessity measures in this case would only measure the child's certainty and not the child's true appreciation of logical necessity.

3. Some nonconservers' "necessity" may signify the operation of a logically

deductive system but one that reaches an incorrect conclusion based on incorrect premises. If operativity is present, then these nonconservers may be more likely than the others to acquire the conservation response, when contradicted by a peer asserting the opposite position, because the operativity allows the conservation conclusion, rather than the opposing nonconservation conclusion, to be reached.

In this study, 18 of 26 children (17 girls and 9 boys, age 5.4 years) answered correctly at least three of the four questions about the necessity of their nonconservation judgments, while the remaining eight children, those with less than three correct answers, were said not to have an appreciation of necessity. There were insignificant age differences between the necessity ($N = 18$) group and the non-necessity group ($N = 8$) of nonconservers. Children were asked (a) to give judgments and reasons (the usual conservation criteria), (b) to rate how sure they were about their answers (not sure, pretty sure, very sure), and (c) to respond to a series of four questions to assess the necessity of their responses [viz., whether their answers (a) would always or just sometimes be what they had just said, (b) had to be what they had just said, (c) could ever be one alternative (e.g., "more"), and (d) could ever be the other alternative (e.g., "same")].

In the training session, each child was paired with a nonconserver who held the opposite nonconserving point of view about the result of the transformation (Ames & Murray, 1982). The two children were instructed to discuss the three possible answers (same, more, less) until they agreed on one response. Immediately after they gave their answer and again 4 weeks later, each child was tested individually on the pretest tasks.

Nonconservers without necessity made no significant gains on the two posttests, both of which included the training task and transfer tasks. Only nonconservers with necessity made significant gains on these two posttests. The gains, although significant, were small, viz., about 2 points out of 6, but in line with the results of other peer interaction studies in which neither participant in the interaction dyad solved the problem correctly on the pretest (e.g., Ames & Murray, 1982; Doise, Mugny, & Perret-Clermont, 1975, 1976).

If the "necessity" asserted by these nonconservers were simply an indication of a certainty, we might expect these nonconservers to be socially dominant in the pair, offer more reasons, and remain stoutly loyal to their position even after the interaction, but this was not the case.

If this "necessity" asserted by nonconservers was an empirical necessity, based on empirical regularities and beliefs about how the world operates, we might expect children to either maintain their original judgments, or at most, to switch to the opposite nonconservation position because they think that conservation transformation is relevant. However, as we have seen, nonconservers with necessity were more likely than the others to show cognitive growth and shift to conservation. On the other hand, the nonconservers without necessity were more likely to switch back and forth between the different nonconservation positions.

Although the restricted variability in the children's responses to questions of how sure they were of their answers limits the interpretation of any relationship between certainty and necessity, it was the case that the results of the certainty measures were not significantly related to necessity measures.

Several reasons for the cognitive gains made by the necessity group can be offered speculatively. Piaget and his colleagues, in their recent work *Le Possible and Le Necessaire* (1983), suggest that children construct the two realms, what is possible and what is necessary, side by side in their construction of reality. Initially, for the young child, what happens represents all of what is possible and is necessary simply because it happens. Later, the child begins to see the real as only a subset of the possible (e.g., the pancake could be more, or less, or the same). Similarly, the necessary comes to be seen later as only a subset of what happens; the construction of this latter subset arises out of the implications within the system (e.g., because more is not less, and less is not more, then the pancake cannot be *both* more and less). For Piaget, in addition to pseudo-necessities that are merely empirical generalities (e.g., that flattening has certain effects), pre-necessities that are local and incomplete are also possible in preoperational thought, as it undergoes the process of constructing necessities. However, these are not considered by Piaget to be truly logically necessary, because the coordination of implications in the fully reversible system is not present.

In the Murray and Smith (1985) study, one might characterize the children in the non-necessity group as those who, by the very nature of their responses to the necessity questions, considered most of the alternatives to be possible, but none of them really necessary. Thus, for this group, what is possible cannot be differentiated from what could be real, because the search for reasons has not proceeded far enough to generate reasons why some possibilities might be more expected than others and some other possibilities excluded. For the nonconservers with necessity, again by the nature of their responses to the necessity questions, there were already reasons why some of the possibilities could not be real or true.

These early, pre-operational "pre-necessities" may signal the availability of a deductive principle before the concrete operational system is complete in any particular domain. Whether or not the premises are true, and whether or not the premises are complete, what is required for a valid deductive argument is that, if the premises were true, then the conclusion could not be false. By this criterion, nonconservers' arguments—although based on untrue and incomplete premises—are nevertheless valid deductive arguments. If flattening really does change the amount of clay, then it cannot be false that the pancake is truly more or less. In fact, Piaget (1983) notes, in his discussion of "necessitation" in later stages, that:

Whether these deductions become true or false, what is of interest is that the consequences drawn from them by the subject are deductively necessary, but of a necessity at the same time more conditional and more inferential than in (stage) IIA . . . . (p. 30)

For whatever reasons, nonconservers with necessity seem more capable of growth than nonconservers without necessity in the peer-interaction situation. By Piaget's definition, this necessity cannot be the complete logical necessity associated with operativity, because it lacks the complete system of compensatory implications. However, it does appear to be a logical and not merely empirical necessity. As such, it may represent an important component, along with the construction of physical knowledge about relevant and irrelevant transformations, and the full coordinated system of implications, in the child's acquisition of operativity in any domain.

ARITHMETIC AND NECESSITY

Although all the kindergarten and first grade children in the Cauley, Murray, and Smith (1983) study knew that $2 + 1 = 3$, only 60% knew that it would always be 3 and that it could not be any other number. In another sample of 4- to 5-year-olds ($N = 22$) we found that although nearly all could accurately add single digits below 5 and be confident that they had the correct answer, about 70% of them believed that the correct answer could be a different number as well—that is, although they were sure the answer was 3, for example, and they would always add the numbers that way, they also agreed that the answer could be 2 or 1. When pressed for an explanation, they resorted to justification-at-any-price responses (my mother told me; 1 and 2 could be 12; can be a lot of numbers, because numbers don't stop; because; it is the answer now; it could be a 7 if you wanted; I saw it on TV; in another school it could be a 4). Yet in 1 or 2 years, the children would be firm in their insistence that only one number could be the right answer. How do they come to know that only one number could be correct? At what point is this conviction buttressed with a system of necessary structures that simply precludes the idea that the sum could be another number.

Cauley (1985) has been able to show, for example, that only about one third of second and third graders who are flawless in their proficiency on multi-digit subtraction problems recognized that the value of the whole top number is conserved during the borrowing manipulations. Cauley distinguished logical knowledge of subtraction—that which confers necessity—from procedural knowledge (the subtraction algorithms) and conceptual knowledge (e.g., knowing the meaning and goals of subtraction in the way most adults' knowledge of the square root differs from their knowledge of how procedurally to extract it). On the whole, the connections between these three aspects of the pupils knowledge were disjointed and relatively independent with only about 15% of the sample giving evidence that they had integrated the knowledge into a system that provided a level of understanding that matched the pupils' computational proficiency. Only 40% of the proficient students knew that the minuend was the same amount after borrowing as before. Very few in fact knew the value of what was borrowed—whether it was 100, 10, and so on.

The relationship between our ability both to perform a task and to understand the task and why our action was appropriate appears to be complicated. On the one hand, there may be no functional relationship at all between action and understanding, especially in the basic behavioral areas that are critical for the continuation of the species. The development of our species, let alone the individual's development, surely requires that certain actions and procedures be carried out nonreflectively and without any appreciation of the meaning or explanation of the action. For example, our ability to speak a language, particularly a native tongue, is quite independent of any formal knowledge on our part of the syntactic rules that in fact describe our speaking.

On the other hand, there are the well-worn examples from the experimental psychology literature on the transfer of training of the close interaction between successful practices and theoretical knowledge of them—with each, on occasion, facilitating the development or exhibition of the other. The symbiotic relationship between practice and theory or understanding is undeniable from either the historical perspective of the development of the academic disciplines or from the perspective of the individual who is able to solve a novel problem, never encountered before, based upon his or her notions of how other things work.

The fact that the relationship between practice and understanding is complicated and seems to encompass instances that run from the closest symbiosis to functional independence only means that school's work is more difficult than is ordinarily thought. It is simply not obvious what the schools should strive for in this area. Is the fact that children can flawlessly compute arithmetical functions with virtually no idea of the logic of the algorithms they employ a non-problem or is it a problem that deserves the attention of educational researchers and policy makers? The relationship between conceptual and procedural knowledge is obviously the key to further advances in our understanding of how children and adults do mathematics and how they think about and understand what they do.

Following the principle of genetic epistemology that intellectual progress on a difficult matter that presents itself as an "either/or" dichotomy of polar opposites can be made if a way can be found to link the two putative opposites (computational skill and understanding, for example) on a common dimension, it is a good beginning to realize that the object of the search is the "relationship" or the dimensions upon which the opposites are merely the poles. It is a good sign of progress when the dimension can be named and conceptualized so that the nature of the relationship can be examined and tested. Several candidates can be put forward, and each can be viewed as an attempt to clarify the meaning of necessity. The dimension can be seen as an Ausubelian scale of meaning, ranging from rotely acquired and unconnected items to items that have ever increasing connections to other mental events. Necessity is then a function of number of and complexity of the unalterable connections to other ideas. Or the scale may merely be one of the increasing automaticity of repeatable and reliable procedures in which necessity is a synonym for unchallenged regularity and predictability of the procedure or idea.

Or, in conclusion, the scale may be more profitably seen as a developmental scale in which the initial mathematical actions are themselves the objects of other actions or "operations" in the Genevan sense (Sinclair & Sinclair, 1986), and these give rise to a system of counting actions that no longer yields contradictory outcomes. The necessary is then the outcome of such a system.

ACKNOWLEDGMENTS

The author is indebted to several colleagues whose efforts and opinions have influenced this work—namely, Sharon Armstrong, Kathy Cauley, Carol Harding, Maria Rayias, and Debbie Smith.

REFERENCES

Ames, G., & Murray, F. (1982). When two wrongs make a right: Promoting cognitive change by social conflict. *Developmental Psychology, 18*(6), 892–895.

Brown, J. S., & VanLehn, K. (1982). Towards a generative theory of "bugs." In T. Carpenter, J. Moser, & T. Romberg (Eds.), *Addition and subtraction: A cognitive approach.* (pp. 117–135). Hillsdale, NJ: Lawrence Erlbaum Associates.

Cauley, K. (1985, April). *The construction of logical knowledge: A study of borrowing in subtraction.* Paper presented at the American Educational Research Association, Chicago.

Cauley, K., Murray, F., & Smith, D. (1983, March). *Necessity in children's reasoning: Criteria for conservation and operativity.* Paper presented at the Eastern Educational Research Association, Baltimore, MD.

Doise, W., Mugny, G., & Perret-Clermont, A-N. (1975). Social interaction and the development of cognitive operations. *European Journal of Social Psychology, 5*(3), 367–383.

Doise, W., Mugny, G., & Perret-Clermont, A-N. (1976). Social interaction and cognitive development: Further evidence. *European Journal of Social Psychology, 6*(2), 245–247.

Feather, N. T. (1964). Acceptance and rejection of arguments in relation to attitude strength, critical ability, and intolerance of inconsistency. *Journal of Abnormal Social Psychology, 69,* 127–136.

Fetzer, M., & Murray, F. (1971, April). *The effect of empirical falsity on the development of syllogistic reasoning.* Paper presented at the American Educational Research Association meetings, New York.

Fey, J., & Sonnabend, T. (1982). Trends in school mathematics performance. In G. Austin & H. Garber (Eds.), *The rise and fall of national test scores* (pp. 143–161). New York: Academic Press.

Gorsuch, R. L. (1974). *Factor analysis.* Philadelphia: Saunders.

Henle, M. (1962). On the relation between logic and thinking. *Psychological Review, 69,* 366–378.

Hiebert, J. (1986). *Conceptual and procedural knowledge: The case of mathematics.* Hillsdale, NJ: Lawrence Erlbaum Associates.

Janis, I. L., & Frick, F. (1943). The relationship between attitudes toward conclusions and errors in judging logical validity of syllogisms. *Journal of Experimental Psychology, 43,* 73–77.

Lefford, A. (1946). The influence of emotional subject matter on logical reasoning. *Journal of Genetic Psychology, 34,* 127–151.

Murray, F. (1965). Conservation of illusion-distorted lengths and areas by primary school children. *Journal of Educational Psychology, 56,* 62–65.

Murray, F. (1981). The conservation paradigm: Conservation of conservation research. In I. Sigel, D. Brodzinsky, & R. Golinkoff (Eds.), *New directions and applications of Piaget's theory* (pp. 143–175). Hillsdale, NJ: Lawrence Erlbaum Associates.

Murray, F. (1982). The pedagogical adequacy of children's conservation explanations. *Journal of Educational Psychology, 74,* 656–659.

Murray, F., & Armstrong, S. (1976). Necessity in conservation and nonconservation. *Developmental Psychology, 12,* 483–484.

Murray, F., & Armstrong, S. (1978). Adult nonconservation of numerical equivalence. *Merrill-Palmer Quarterly, 24,* 255–263.

Murray, F., & Smith, D. (1985). Pre-operative necessity in the acquisition of operativity. *Cahiers de Psychologie Cognitive, 5,* 314–315.

National Assessment of Educational Progress (NAEP). (1979). *Changes in Mathematical Achievement, 1973–1978.* Denver: Education Commission of the United States.

Piaget, J. (1983). *Le Possible et le Necessaire.* (Vol. 2.) *L'evolution du Necessaire Chez l'enfant.* Paris: Presses Universitaires de France. (Portions translated by D. Smith).

Pieraut-LeBonniec, G. (1980). *The development of model reasoning: Genesis of necessity and possibility notions.* New York: Academic Press.

Pinard, A. (1981). *The conservation of conservation.* Chicago: University of Chicago Press.

Romberg, T., & Carpenter, T. (1986). Research on teaching and learning: Two disciplines of scientific inquiry. In M. Wittrock (Ed.), *Handbook of research on teaching* (3rd ed., pp. 850–873). New York: Macmillan.

Sinclair, H., & Sinclair, A. (1986). Children's mastery of written numerals and the construction of basic number concepts. In J. Hiebert (Ed.), *Conceptual and procedural knowledge: The case of mathematics* (pp. 59–73). Hillsdale, NJ: Lawrence Erlbaum Associates.

Wilkins, M. C. (1928). The effect of changed material on ability to do formal syllogistic reasoning. *Archives of Psychology, 102,* (whole issue).

4 The Role of Learning in Children's Strategy Choices

Robert S. Siegler
Christopher Shipley
Carnegie-Mellon University

What is the relation of learning to development? The issue can be approached either definitionally or empirically. Definitional approaches separate the two constructs on a priori grounds, such as the time scale of the cognitive change, the population undergoing the change, the change's magnitude, and its relation to physical maturation. Cognitive changes occurring over short time periods are usually viewed as learning, whereas those occuring over longer periods are typically viewed as development. Cognitive changes of adults are almost always viewed as learning, whereas those of children may be viewed as either learning or development. Cognitive changes of limited scope are most often regarded as learning, whereas large scale changes are often said to involve development. Cognitive changes with no known maturational basis are usually attributed to learning, whereas those with a strongly suspected or established maturational base are more frequently said to reflect development.

These definitional distinctions are useful in explicating some of the considerations that lead us to apply one label or the other to particular intellectual changes. However, they are only tangentially related to an issue that is near the heart of the learning/development distinction: the similarity or difference of the cognitive mechanisms that produce the changes that we call learning and development. Regardless of whether two changes occur over short periods or long, in children or adults, on a large or small scale, and with a maturational or no maturational involvement, the cognitive mechanisms involved in them could be similar or different.

An example may help illustrate this point. Consider rule induction as a cognitive mechanism. Both children and adults induce both trivial and profound rules. Some rules, such as the rule that larger things are usually heavier, are induced very quickly; others, such as the rule that torques equal mass times distance, take much longer to induce. We can at least imagine rule inductions that depend on attainment of a certain level of maturation (e.g., a sufficiently large STM capacity), and others for which early maturational levels are sufficient. In sum, the a priori considerations do not tightly constrain what cognitive operations may be active in a given intellectual change.

How can the similarity or difference of such cognitive mechanisms be established? Ideally, we would be in a position to compare the cognitive mechanisms involved in tasks classified as *learning* with those involved in tasks classified as *development*. Unfortunately, current understanding of such cognitive mechanisms, even as they contribute to particular changes, is relatively primitive. Sophisticated analyses of cognitive processes involved in performance on particular tasks are fairly numerous, but understanding of change processes is less advanced (Sternberg, 1984).

For these reasons the goal of this chapter is to analyze in detail the processes involved in one type of cognitive change. Once investigators have performed a number of such analyses in situations said to involve learning and situations said to involve development, it will be possible to compare the proposed mechanisms and establish dimensions of similarity and difference. This will provide an empirical basis for deciding whether learning and development involve fundamentally different cognitive mechanisms, and if so, what the differences are.

The cognitive change on which we focus in the present chapter involves children's choices of strategies. Early in their experience with many tasks, such as adding, subtracting, and multiplying numbers and reading and spelling words, children use a variety of overt (visible and audible) strategies. In adding numbers for example, children often count on their fingers. As they gain greater experience with the problems, children progressively abandon the overt strategies, instead relying on internalized solution procedures. The questions of central interest are what mechanisms lead children of a given age to choose overt strategies on some problems and not others, and what mechanisms lead to changes in the relative frequency of different strategies at different ages?

Our discussion of strategy choices, and the cognitive changes that they undergo, is organized into six sections. First the issue of strategy choice is discussed at a general level. Then consideration turns to data on young children's strategy choices on elementary addition problems and to a model of the mechanisms that we believe underlie strategy choices in this, and other, domains. The model is formalized as a set of mathematical equations. Next is an analysis of how strategy choices develop. The analysis is expressed as a running computer simulation that both performs and develops. Following this, we briefly summarize new findings on strategy choices in subtraction, multiplication, and spelling. The findings suggest clear parallels between strategy choices in addition and in the other domains. Next, we relate the current research on strategy choices to previous research on the rules children use to solve balance scale problems. Finally, we discuss several conclusions that arise from the present research.

THE ISSUE OF STRATEGY CHOICE

Cognitive and developmental psychologists often have phrased their models in terms that suggested that all people, or at least all people of a given age, performed a given task in a given way. These models defy the every day observation that people often perform a given task in different ways on different occasions. For example, a child one day might write down a word's spelling as retrieved from memory, but the next day look up the same word in a dictionary. We suspect that the universalistic phrasings stem more from the difficulty of formulating and providing evidence for alternatives than from deep conviction that all people use the same approach. The effect, however, has been to divert attention away from an important phenomenon: How do people decide what to do from among the various things that they might do?

Good reasons exist for people to know and to use multiple strategies for achieving a goal. Strategies differ in their accuracy, in the amounts of time they require, in their memory demands, and in the range of problems to which they apply. Strategy choices involve tradeoffs among these properties so that people can cope with cognitive and situational constraints. The broader the range of strategies that people know, the more they can shape their approaches to meet these changing circumstances. As becomes evident in this chapter, even young children can choose strategies in adaptive ways. But how do they do so?

The main possibility that has been explored to date involves metacognitive knowledge. In this view, children use knowledge of their own cognitive capacities, the demands of the material, and available strategies to explicitly choose which strategy to use. For example, when confronting a complex problem, they might think, "This is a tough problem, too tough to solve unless I do X, I'd better do X."

It almost certainly is the case that people sometimes proceed in this manner. As a general explanation of strategy choices, however, the approach seems less promising than it once appeared. On an empirical level, research has revealed only modest correlations between explicit knowledge about cognitive capabilities and strategy use (Brown, Bransford, Ferrara, & Campione, 1983; Cavanaugh & Perlmutter, 1982; Flavell & Wellman, 1977; Sternberg & Powell, 1983). On a theoretical level, there is considerable lack of clarity about how metacognitive knowledge would lead to strategy choices. Do people make explicit judgments about their intellectual capacities, available strategies, and task demands every time they face a task they could perform in two or more ways? If not, how do they decide on which tasks to do so? Do they consider every strategy that they could conceivably use on a task or only a subset of them? If only a subset, how do they decide which ones? How is cognitive capacity estimated, especially cognitive capacity for novel material? In light of these empirical and conceptual uncertainties, it seems worthwhile to at least entertain the possibility that people can arrive at adaptive strategies without explicitly assessing their intellectual abilities, available strategies, and task requirements. That is, the inherent workings of the memory system may account for some range of strategy choices. The distribution of associations model describes how this might occur.

THE DISTRIBUTION OF ASSOCIATIONS MODEL

The distribution of associations model was motivated by several findings about 4- and 5-year-olds' addition of numbers. These findings were first obtained by Siegler and Robinson (1982) and later replicated by Siegler and Shrager (1984). In both experiments, preschoolers were presented all 25 addition problems involving augends (1 to 5) and addends (1 to 5). They were asked, "If you had n oranges and I gave you m more, how many would you have then?" Their performance was videotaped, to allow detailed analyses of the strategies they used to solve the problems.

The preschoolers were found to use four strategies. Sometimes they put up their fingers and counted them (the *counting fingers strategy*). Sometimes they put up their fingers but answered without any apparent counting (the *fingers strategy*). Sometimes they counted aloud without any obvious external referent (the *counting strategy*). Finally, sometimes they answered without any overt behavior intervening between presentation of the problem and statement of the answer. For reasons that later should become apparent, this was labeled the *retrieval strategy*. Solution times differed systematically on the four strategies. Retrieval was the fastest, fingers the next fastest, and counting and counting fingers the slowest.

The most interesting findings, however, concerned relations between how difficult a problem was (with difficulty measured either by percentage of errors or length of solution time) and percentage of use of overt strategies. Simply put, the harder the problem, the more often children used overt strategies. For example, Siegler and Robinson (1982) reported a correlation of $r = .91$ between percentage of errors on each of 25 problems and percentage of overt strategy use on that problem. Those data, along with the data of a replication and two extensions to new sets of problems, are shown in Fig. 4.1.

The distribution of associations model was designed to account for which strategies children used, the relative solution times of the strategies, and the close relations among errors, solution times, and overt strategy use on each problem. The label *distribution of associations model* was chosen because within the model, errors, solution times, and overt strategy use all are functions of a single variable: the distribution of associations between problems and potential answers. The model includes a representation and a process. The representation consists of associations of varying strengths between each problem and possible answers to the problem. The numerical values in the Figure 4.2A matrix are the estimated strengths of these associations.[1] For example, an associative strength of .05 links the problem 1 + 1 and the answer "1," and an associative strength of .86 links 1 + 1 and "2."

The process that operates on this representation can be divided into three phases: retrieval, elaboration of the representation, and counting. As shown in Fig. 4.2B, the child (who we here imagine as a boy) first retrieves an answer. If he is sufficiently confident of it, or is unwilling to search further, he states it. Otherwise, the child generates a more elaborate representation of the problem, perhaps by putting up his fingers, and tries again to retrieve an answer. If he is sufficiently confident of the answer he states it. Otherwise, he counts the objects in the representation and states the last number as the answer.

Now we can examine the process in greater detail. The first phase (Steps 1–8) involves an effort at retrieval. The child sets two parameters: a confidence criterion and a search length. The confidence criterion defines a value that must be exceeded by the associative strength of a retrieved answer for the child to state that answer. The search length indicates the maximum number of retrieval efforts the child will make before moving on to the second phase of the process. The values of these parameters are selected randomly on each trial, with the confidence criterion varying from .01 to .99 and the search length from 1 to 3.

Once the parameters are set, the child retrieves an answer. The probability of any given answer being retrieved on a particular retrieval effort is proportional to the associative strength of that answer for that problem. Thus, the probability of retrieving "2" as the answer to "1 + 1" would be .86 (Fig. 4.2A). If the associative strength of the retrieved answer exceeds the confidence criterion, the child states that answer. Otherwise, the child examines whether the number of searches that have been conducted is within the permissible search length. If so, the child again retrieves an answer, compares it to the confidence criterion, and advances it as the solution if its associative strength exceeds the criterion. Retrieval efforts continue as long as the associative strength of each retrieved answer is below the confidence criterion and the number of searches does not exceed the search length.

If the point is reached at which the number of searches that the child has undertaken equals the search length for that trial, the child may optionally use an

---

[1]These estimated strengths are based on performance in a separate experiment. In this experiment, 4- and 5-year-olds were presented the Siegler and Robinson procedure except that they were explicitly asked to "just say what you think the right answer is without putting up your fingers or counting." The purpose of these instructions was to obtain the purest possible estimate of the strengths of associations between problems and answers.

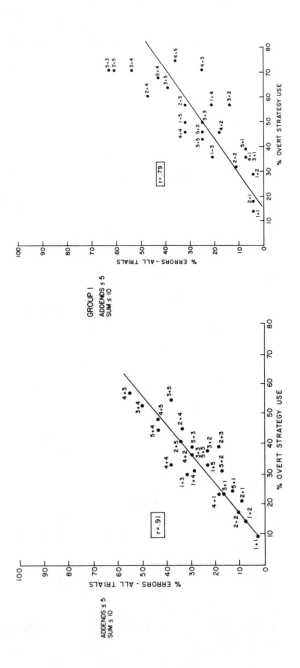

GROUP 1

ADDENDS ≤ 5
SUM ≤ 10

ADDENDS ≤ 5
SUM ≤ 10

76

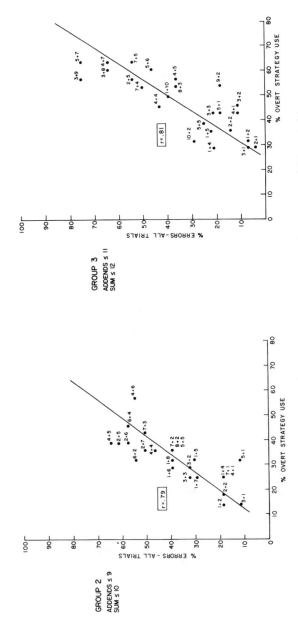

FIGURE 4.1. Relations between overt strategy use and errors on addition problems.

A. <u>REPRESENTATION</u> (ASSOCIATIVE STRENGTHS)[a]

Problem	Answer												OTHER
	0	1	2	3	4	5	6	7	8	9	10	11	
1 + 1		.03	.90	.01	.01		.01					.01	.02
1 + 2			.07	.77	.03		.02		.01	.04	.01	.01	.03
1 + 3		.01		.08	.74	.04	.01	.04	.01				.06
1 + 4			.01		.07	.66	.10	.07				.01	.08
1 + 5					.08	.12	.61	.09	.02	.02	.01		.04
2 + 1		.04	.04	.82	.03		.01		.01				.03
2 + 2	.01		.03	.03	.86	.03		.03					
2 + 3			.02	.06	.26	.42	.11	.07	.03	.01			.02
2 + 4		.01		.04	.01	.34	.39	.10	.06		.02		.02
2 + 5		.01		.03	.01	.12	.33	.29	.04		.03	.01	.11
3 + 1		.01	.01	.06	.77	.02	.03	.03	.04				.02
3 + 2	.01		.06	.07	.07	.64	.09	.01	.01				.04
3 + 3	.02			.04	.13	.09	.61	.01	.02	.01	.01		.04
3 + 4				.03	.09	.18	.18	.37	.02	.02	.02		.10
3 + 5				.04		.08	.19	.17	.27	.06	.07	.01	.12
4 + 1			.02	.02	.06	.72	.04	.03	.04	.01			.04
4 + 2			.04	.09		.14	.48	.11	.06		.02		.06
4 + 3				.03	.11	.07	.18	.36	.16	.01	.02		.07
4 + 4	.02		.01	.01	.01	.20	.06	.04	.50	.01	.04		.09
4 + 5			.01		.02	.06	.17	.09	.11	.29	.09	.02	.14
5 + 1			.02		.03	.04	.79	.03	.02		.02	.01	.02
5 + 2			.03	.13	.01	.11	.19	.46	.03	.01	.02		
5 + 3			.02	.07	.08	.11	.09	.13	.34	.04	.04		.07
5 + 4					.07	.13	.14	.07	.11	.29	.07	.01	.11
5 + 5	.02					.04	.18	.08	.03	.02	.51	.03	.08

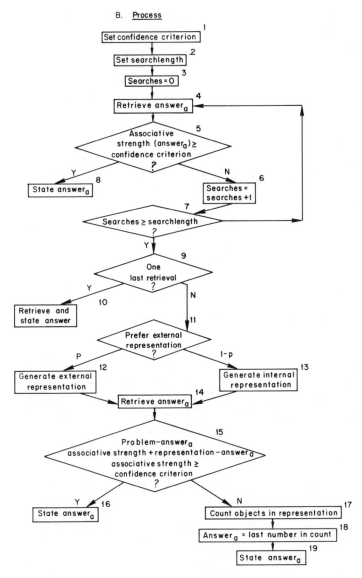

B. Process

1. Set confidence criterion
2. Set searchlength
3. Searches = 0
4. Retrieve answer$_a$
5. Associative strength (answer$_a$) $\geq$ confidence criterion ?
6. Searches = searches +1
7. Searches $\geq$ searchlength ?
8. State answer$_a$
9. One last retrieval ?
10. Retrieve and state answer
11. Prefer external representation ?
12. Generate external representation
13. Generate internal representation
14. Retrieve answer$_a$
15. Problem–answer$_a$ associative strength + representation – answer$_a$ associative strength $\geq$ confidence criterion ?
16. State answer$_a$
17. Count objects in representation
18. Answer$_a$ = last number in count
19. State answer$_a$

FIGURE 4.2 Representation and process for distribution of associations model of 4- and 5-year-old's addition.

[a]Numerical values in matrix based on performance in overt-strategies-prohibited experiment (see Footnote 1).

alternative form of retrieval. This form could be labeled the *sophisticated guess-ing* approach. It involves simply retrieving one last answer and stating whichever answer is retrieved. Intuitively, this can be likened to trying to spell "schuss," not having great confidence that any retrieved spelling is correct, and writing out one of the spellings rather than looking up the word in a dictionary.[2]

If children do not state a retrieved answer, they proceed to elaborate the representation of the problem. They can generate either an elaborated external representation, for example one in which they put up their fingers, or an elabo-rated internal representation, for example one in which they form a mental image of objects corresponding to augend and addend. Putting up fingers or forming an image adds visual associations between the elaborated representation and various answers to the already existing association between the problem and various answers. If the elaborated representation involves the child's fingers, it adds kinesthetic associations as well. We refer to these visual and kinesthetic associa-tions as *elaborated representation–answer associations* as opposed to the *prob-lem–answer associations* discussed previously.

Having formed the elaborated representation, the child again retrieves an answer.[3] If that answer's associative strength exceeds the confidence criterion, the child states it as the answer. If it does not, the child proceeds to the third phase, an algorithmic process in which he or she counts the objects in the elaborated representation and advances the number assigned to the last object as the sum.

It may be useful to examine how a child using the model would solve a particular problem. Suppose a girl was presented the problem "3 + 5." Initially, she randomly selects a confidence criterion and a search length. For purpose of illustration, we assume that her confidence criterion is .50 and that her search length is 2. Next, she retrieves an answer. As shown in Fig. 4.2A, the proba-bility of retrieving 3 is .04, the probability of retrieving 5 is .08, the probability

---

[2]This aspect of retrieval is an addition to the Siegler and Shrager (1984) model. Several consid-erations argued for introducing it. It allowed formulation of a mathematical equation for solution times that was closer to our theoretical ideas than was the one in the earlier paper. The equation appears on p. 89, in the context of the overall mathematical model. The change also made the performance of the model more like that of the children by increasing the frequency of use of the retrieval strategy and decreasing the accuracy of performance on retrieval trials. In the present version of the mathematical model, children use this approach on a randomly chosen 10% of trials on which they failed to retrieve an answer with sufficient associative strength to state the answer. The value 10% is only one of a large range of values that could be used; the particular number is arbitrary.

[3]The probability of a given answer being retrieved at this point is determined by adding the problem–answer and the representation–answer associative strengths and dividing by 1 plus the representation–answer associative strength. In the computer simulation (to be described on pp. 94–100), it was arbitrarily decided that each external representation added a constant .05 to the answer corresponding to the number of objects in the representation. Thus, if the problem 1 + 4 was represented with 5 fingers, and the initial associative strength of 1 + 4 = 5 was .61, the new associative strength would be .66/1.05 = .63.

of retrieving 6 is .19, and so on. Suppose that the child retrieves 6. This answer's associative strength, .19, does not exceed the current confidence criterion, .50. Therefore, the girl does not state it as the answer. She next checks whether the number of searches has reached the search length. Since it has not, she again retrieves an answer. This time she might retrieve 8. The associative strength of 8, .27, does not exceed the confidence criterion, .50.

Because the number of searches, 2, has reached the allowed search length, the child may state whatever answer she next retrieves from the distribution of associations. If she did this, she would have a probability of .04 of retrieving and stating 3 as the answer, a probability of .08 of retrieving and stating 5, a probability of .19 of retrieving and stating 6, and so on.

If the girl does not take this route, she next elaborates the problem representation, either by forming a mental image or by putting up fingers. Suppose that she puts up three fingers on one hand and four on the other. Next, she again retrieves an answer. As indicated in Footnote 3, combining the problem–answer and the representation–answer associative strengths increases her probability of retrieving 8 from .27 to .30. Suppose that she retrieves 8. Its associative strength still does not exceed the .50 confidence criterion. Therefore, the girl does not state it. She instead proceeds to the third phase of the process. Here, she counts her fingers and states the last number as the answer to the problem. If she counts correctly, she will say "8."

This model accounts for the strategies that children use, for the temporal characteristics of the strategies, and for the close relations among the percentage of overt strategy use, the percentage of errors, and the mean solution times on each problem. First consider how it accounts for the existence of the four strategies. The retrieval strategy appears if children retrieve an answer whose problem-answer associative strength exceeds their confidence criterion (Steps 1–5, sometimes Steps 6 and 7, Step 8). It also appears if children use the "sophisticated guessing" form of retrieval in which they first fail to retrieve an answer with associative strength exceeding the confidence criterion and then retrieve one last answer and state it (Steps 1–7 and 9–10). The fingers strategy emerges when children fail to retrieve an answer whose problem–answer associative strengths exceeds their confidence criterion, put up their fingers, and then retrieve an answer where the sum of the problem-answer and the elaborated representation-answer associative strengths exceeds their confidence criterion (Steps 1–7, 9, 11–12, 14–16). The counting fingers strategy appears if children fail to retrieve an answer whose problem–answer associative strength exceeds their confidence criterion, put up their fingers, fail to retrieve an answer where the sum of the elaborated representation–answer and problem–answer associative strengths exceeds the confidence criterion, and finally count their fingers (Steps 1–7, 9, 11–12, 14–15, 17–19). The counting strategy is observed if children fail to retrieve an answer whose exceeds their confidence criterion, form an elaborated internal representation, fail to retrieve an answer where the sum of the elaborated representation–answer and problem–answer associative strengths exceeds the confidence criterion, and finally count the objects in the internal representation (Steps 1–7, 9, 11, 13–15, 17–19).

The relative solution times of the strategies arise because the faster strategies are component parts of the slower ones. To use the fingers strategy, children must execute all of the steps in the retrieval strategy and five additional ones (four additional ones if they use the form of retrieval where they retrieve one last answer and state it). To execute the counting fingers strategy, children must proceed through all of the steps in the fingers strategy and two additional ones. To execute the counting strategy, children must execute all of the steps in the retrieval strategy plus six others. If we can equate the time needed to form elaborated internal and elaborated external representations, children using the counting strategy must execute all of the steps in the fingers strategy plus two others. Thus, the retrieval strategy should be faster than any of the other strategies, the fingers strategy should be faster than the counting fingers strategy, and, if the time needed to form an external representation does not exceed the time needed to form an internal one, the fingers strategy also should be faster than the counting strategy.

Perhaps the most important feature of the model is that it generates close associations among percentage of errors, mean solution time, and percentage of overt strategy use on each problem. The associations arise because all three dependent variables are functions of the same independent variable: the distribution of associations, such as that for 2 + 1 in Fig. 4.3, with those of a flat distribution, such as that for 3 + 5. (A peaked distribution is one in which most associative strength is concentrated in a single answer; a flat distribution is one in which several answers have relatively similar associative strengths. The data in Fig. 4.3 are direct graphical translations of the tabular data in the Fig. 4.2A matrix).

A low percentage of use of overt strategies, a low percentage of errors, and a short mean solution time all accompany the peak distribution. Relative to the flat distribution, the peaked distribution results in (a) less frequent use of overt strategies (because the more unequal the associative strengths of different answers within a distribution, the more likely that the answer that is retrieved will have sufficiently high associative strength to exceed the confidence criterion), (b) fewer errors (because of the higher probability of retrieving and stating the answer that forms the peak of the distribution, which generally will be the correct answer, and (c) shorter solution times (because the probability of retrieving on an early search an answer whose associative strength exceeds any given confidence criterion is greater the more peaked the distribution of associations).

At least two nonintuitive predictions follow from this model. One is that the correlation between percentage of errors on each problem and the percentage of overt strategy use on that problem is primarily a correlation between the *percentage of errors on retrieval trials on each problem* and the percentage of overt

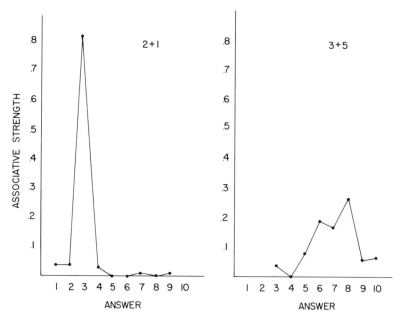

FIGURE 4.3. A peaked (left) and a flat (right) distribution of associations.

strategy use on the problem. The other is that the correlation between solution times on each problem and percentage of overt strategy use on that problem is primarily a correlation between the *mean solution time on retrieval trials on each problem* and the percentage of overt strategy use on the problem. The reasoning underlying these predictions is that percentage of overt strategy use on a problem, percentage of errors on retrieval trials on that problem, and mean solution time on retrieval trials on the problem all depend entirely on the distribution of associations. In contrast, percentage of errors and mean solution times on non-retrieval trials on the problem depend on other factors.

This logic may become clearer when we examine the model's account of the way in which errors and solution times are produced by each of the four strategies. First consider errors. On retrieval trials, the percentage of errors on each problem only depends on the distribution of associations. Errors can be made in two ways. In one, an incorrect answer retrieved from the distribution exceeds the confidence criterion. The flatter the distribution, the greater the proportion of retrieval trials on which an incorrect answer will be retrieved and the greater the likelihood that such an answer, once retrieved, will be stated. In the other, children fail to retrieve an answer whose associative strength exceeds the confidence criterion, and then states whichever answer they next retrieve from the distribution. Again, the flatter the distribution, the more likely they are to retrieve and state an incorrect answer. Thus, the peakedness of the distribution of associations, which earlier was shown to determine percentage of overt strategy use on each problem, also determines the percentage of errors on retrieval trials.

In contrast, the percentage of errors on counting and counting fingers trials is unaffected by the distribution of associations. The counting and counting fingers strategies arise when children fail to retrieve a statable answer. Instead, they answer by counting the objects in their elaborated representations. Errors are made when they misrepresent the number of objects in the problem or when they miscount them. The greater the sum, the more objects that can be misrepresented or miscounted, and therefore the greater the likelihood of errors. Thus, co-linearity with the sum should account for whatever correlation emerges between the percentage of errors on counting and counting fingers trials on each problem and the percentage of overt strategy use on the problem.

Correlations involving the percentage of errors on fingers strategy trials should occupy a middle ground. Recall that the fingers strategy is produced when children first fail to retrieve an answer whose associative strength exceeds their confidence criterion, then elaborate the representation by putting up their fingers, and then retrieve an answer where the sum of the problem–answer and the elaborated representation–answer associative strengths exceeds the confidence criterion. Under such circumstances, the percentage of errors is a function of both the distribution of associations between problems and answers and the distribution of associations between elaborated representations and answers. A relatively peaked distribution of associations increases the probability that the problem–answer and elaborated representation–answer associations together will lead to retrieval of an answer whose associative strength exceeds the confidence criterion. However, the sum also may influence this likelihood. Presumably, children more often correctly represent the addends on problems with small sums, which will lead to the elaborated representation–answer association more often being added to the correct rather than to an incorrect answer on these problems. Thus, the percentage of errors on fingers strategy trials on each problem should correlate somewhat with percentage of overt strategy use on that problem, but not as highly as percentage of errors on retrieval trials on the problem.

The logic of these predictions can be summarized as follows:

A. If percentage of overt strategy use on each problem is a function only of the distribution of associations; and

B. If percentage of errors on retrieval trials on each problem also is a function only of the distribution of associations; and

C. If percentage of errors on fingers trials is in part a function of the distribution of associations; and

D. If percentage of errors on counting and counting fingers trials is not at all a function of the distribution of associations, instead being a function of the sum;

Then

1. Percentage of errors on retrieval trials should correlate highly with percentage of overt strategy use.
2. Percentage of errors on counting and counting fingers trials should correlate less highly with percentage of overt strategy use, especially when the contribution of the sum is partialed out.
3. Percentage of errors on fingers trials should show an intermediate degree of correlation with percentage of overt strategy use.

Similar logic can be applied to analyzing the correlation between solution times and overt strategy use. Solution times on retrieval trials should derive exclusively from the peakedness of the distribution of associations. Again, this holds true for both types of retrieval. First, consider retrievals that occur when the associative strength of a retrieved answer exceeds the confidence criterion. The more peaked the distribution, the fewer retrieval efforts children should require to retrieve an answer whose associative strength exceeds their confidence criterion.

Now consider the sophisticated guessing retrievals that occur after children have failed to retrieve an answer whose associative strength exceeded the confidence criterion. Such retrieval trials are by definition more time consuming than the other forms of retrieval, because they only occur after the maximum search length has been reached. Frequency of use of this most time-consuming form of retrieval is directly proportional to the likelihood that children failed to retrieve an answer whose associative strength exceeded the confidence criterion. Again, solution times depend on the peakedness of the distribution of associations, which determines the likelihood of retrieving an answer that exceeds the confidence criterion.

On counting and counting fingers trials, the influences on solution times are different. Amount of time needed to generate an elaborated representation and to count the objects in it are the key factors. These depend on the number of objects that need to be represented and counted, in short, on the sum. The model made no direct prediction concerning solution times on fingers trials on each problem. Thus, the prediction of the model was that the correlation between percentage of overt strategy use and mean solution times on retrieval trials on each problem would be higher than the correlations between percentage of overt strategy use and mean solution times on counting and counting fingers trials. The pattern would be most evident with the contribution of the sum partialed out from both correlations.

Empirical Tests of the Model

Siegler and Shrager (1984) reported several tests of the distribution of associations model to children's addition performance. First the fit of the model to the Siegler and Robinson (1982) data was examined. The focus was on whether the source of the correlations among percentage of errors, mean solution times, and percentage of overt strategy use on each problem was percentage of errors and mean solution times on retrieval trials on each problem. Then an effort was made to replicate the initial empirical findings, to establish their generality across new sets of addition problems, and to test the model's ability to account for them.

Siegler and Shrager's replication and extension experiment involved three groups of problems. Children in Group 1 of this experiment (the replication condition) were presented the same 25 problems as the children studied by Siegler and Robinson. These were all of the problems on which both addends were less than or equal to 5 and on which the sum was less than or equal to 10. Children in Group 2 were presented 25 problems on which the sum again was less than or equal to 10 but on which either addend could be as great as 9. Children in Group 3 were presented a third set of 25 problems. In this set, the sum could be as high as 12 and the addends as large as 11. As in Siegler and Robinson, the children were 4- and 5-year-olds and the problems were presented in the form "If you had n oranges and I gave you m more, how many would you have then?".

In all three replication and extension conditions, the same strategies were used as in Siegler and Robinson (1982): retrieval, fingers, counting, and counting fingers. The relative solution times of the strategies also were the same: retrieval was always significantly faster than fingers, which in turn was always significantly faster than counting and counting fingers.

Most important, the relations among overt strategy use, errors, and solution times were strong in all three replication and extension groups, and the source of the correlations in them and in the Siegler and Robinson data was errors and solution times on retrieval trials. First consider the correlations data across all trials. The correlations were of similar magnitudes to the ones observed in the initial Siegler and Robinson experiment. On the error data, the correlations ranged from $r = .79$ to $r = .88$ for the three groups. On the solution time data, the correlations ranged from $r = .81$ to $r = .92$ for the three groups. These correlations were higher for all three groups on both measures than the correlations produced by either Groen and Parkman's (1972) min model or Ashcraft's (1982) sum squared model.

The comparisons of the correlations involving performance on retrieval trials and performance on counting and counting fingers trials provided a more stringent test of the model. The analyses of the error data are shown in Table 4.1. On all eight of the sets of raw and partial correlations, the correlation between overt strategy use and errors on retrieval trials was greater than the corresponding correlation between overt strategy use and errors on counting and counting fingers trials. On six of the eight comparisons, the difference between the correlations' magnitudes was significant. On all four of the raw correlations, the relation between errors and overt strategy use was actually stronger when only errors on retrieval trials were considered than when errors on all trials were. Also as predicted, the correlations between errors on fingers trials and percentage of overt strategy use were intermediate in magnitude. They were smaller than the correlations involving errors on retrieval trials, but larger than the correlations involving errors on counting and counting fingers trials.

TABLE 4.1
Source of Correlations Between Overt Strategy Use and Errors in Addition[a]

A. Raw Correlations

	Retrieval trials	Fingers trials	Counting and counting fingers trials
Siegler & Robinson (1982)	.92	.68	.36
Siegler & Shrager (1984)			
Group 1	.83		.51
Group 2	.80	.68[b]	.47
Group 3	.88	.	.37

B. Partial Correlations (Correlations with the Sum Partialed Out)

	Retrieval trials	Fingers trials	Counting and counting fingers trials
Siegler & Robinson (1982)	.87	.56	−.23
Siegler & Shrager (1984)			
Group 1	.67		.42
Group 2	.56	.66[b]	.23
Group 3	.70		.26

[a]Numbers in table indicate correlations of percentage of overt strategy use on each problem with the variable specified in the table. For example, the top left value of .92 indicates a raw correlation of $r = .92$ between percentage of errors on retrieval trials on each problem and percentage of overt strategy use on that problem for Group 1.

[b]Because the fingers strategy was used relatively infrequently in Siegler and Shrager (1984), performance when using it was summed across the three conditions in the experiment.

TABLE 4.2
Source of Correlations Between Overt Strategy Use and Solution
Times

A. *Raw Correlations*

	Retrieval trials	*Counting and counting fingers trials*
Siegler & Robinson (1982)	.76	.83
Siegler & Shrager (1984)		
Group 1	.79	.42
Group 2	.75	.54
Group 3	.84	.79

B. *Partial Correlations (Correlations with the Sum Partialed Out)*

	Retrieval trials	*Counting and counting fingers trials*
Siegler & Robinson (1982)	.68	.71
Siegler & Shrager (1984)		
Group 1	.75	.10
Group 2	.50	.00
Group 3	.74	.38

As shown in Table 4.2, the solution time data were similarly consistent with the model's predictions. On six of the eight comparisons, the correlation between overt strategy use and solution times on retrieval trials exceeded the corresponding correlation involving solution times on counting and counting fingers trials. On four of the eight comparisons, the difference between correlations was significant. Even after the influence of the sum was partialed out, the correlations remained strong.

In summary, the model successfully predicted a large number of characteristics of the data of the replication and extension experiments and of the original Siegler and Robinson data. It accounted for the four strategies that children used, the relative solution times of the strategies, the relations among percentage of errors, mean solution times, and percentage of overt strategy use on each problem, and the source of the relation between errors, solution time, and strategy use being errors and solution times on retrieval trials. The last prediction was solely attributable to the model, because prior to formulating it, we had no expectation whatsoever that the source of the correlation would be performance on retrieval trials.

The model also possessed several other properties that seemed desirable. It allowed children to strike a balance between speed and accuracy demands. When possible, they would use the relatively rapid retrieval approach. However, when retrieval yielded no answer that was sufficiently strongly associated with the problem, they would fall back on successively more time-consuming overt approaches. The model also had the advantage of treating all problems in the same way. Unlike prior models of addition (Ashcraft, 1982; Groen & Parkman, 1972), it did not assume that ties have a special status or that the mental distance between sums increases exponentially with their sizes. Finally, as is discussed in more detail later in the chapter, the model suggested how development might occur. As children's distributions of associations become increasingly peaked, they rely increasingly on retrieval, advance the correct answer more often, and answer more quickly. In short, their performance becomes increasingly adult-like.

A Mathematical Expression of the Model

We wanted to provide a rigorous test of the sufficiency of the model to produce strong relations among overt strategy use, frequency of errors on retrieval trials, and length of mean solution times on each problem. Therefore, we translated the model's predictions into algebraic equations, inserted a large range of parameter values into the model, and compared the model's behavior to that which children had displayed.

The following equations were used to describe for each problem the probability of retrieving an answer that exceeded the confidence criterion on any given search of memory, the probability of overt strategy use, the probability of an error on a retrieval trial, and the expected solution time on a retrieval trial.

Probability of Retrieving Answer that Exceeds Confidence Criterion =

$$R = \frac{\displaystyle\sum_{a=1}^{A} (AS_a)\,(p(AS_a > CC))}{\left(\displaystyle\sum_{a=1}^{A} AS_a\right)}$$

Probability of Overt Strategy Use on a Problem =

$$(1 - R)^N - .1(1 - R)^N)$$

Probability of Errors on Searches on Retrieval Trials on Each Problem =

$$1 - \frac{(AS_{ca})\,(p(AS_{ca} > CC)) + (.1(1 - R)\,AS_{ca})}{R + .1(1 - R)}$$

Expected Number of Searches on Retrieval Trials on Each Problem =

$$\sum_{n=1}^{N} R((1-R)^{n-1})(\sum_{n=1}^{N} nR((1-R)^{n-1})) + .1(N+1)(1 - (\sum_{n=1}^{N} R((1-R)^{n-1})))$$

$$\sum_{n=1}^{N} R((1-R)^{n-1}) + .1(1 - (\sum_{n=1}^{N} R((1-R)^{n-1})))$$

R = probability of retrieving answer on each search whose associative strength exceeds the confidence criterion, A = number of answers associated with problems, AS_a = associative strength of answer$_a$, AS_{ca} = associative strength of correct answer, CC = confidence criterion, N = number of searches in searchlength

The correspondence between each equation and the process it models is quite straightforward. The probability on each problem of retrieving an answer that exceeds the confidence criterion on a given search is the sum of the associative strengths of answers to that problem that exceeded the criterion divided by the sum of the associative strengths of all answers to the problem. This term, labeled R, is used extensively in the three equations predicting the behavioral variables. Indeed, it embodies our ideas of why the correlations among them occur.

The other three equations share a similar form with each other. The first term in the numerator in each equation is the product of two terms: the probability that an answer whose associative strength exceeds the confidence criterion will be located within N searches and the impact that such an event would have on the particular dependent variable. The second term in the numerator in each equation indicates that on one-tenth of the trials on which a statable answer has not been retrieved after N searches, the child will state whichever answer he or she next retrieved from the distribution of associations. The two terms in the denominators of the error rate and solution time equations are the probability of retrieval via the first and second route respectively.

With this introduction, we can consider the equations that predict percentage of overt strategy use, percentage of errors, and mean solution time on each problem. The probability of overt strategy use equals nine-tenths the probability that on none of the searches will an answer be retrieved that exceeds the confidence criterion. The probability of a correct answer on a retrieval trial is the sum of the probabilities of retrieving and stating the correct answer by the two possible routes divided by the sum of the probabilities of retrieving and stating any answer by these routes. The equation predicting solution time on retrieval trials is the most complex of the three. The initial term in the numerator is the product of two terms: the probability of retrieving on the *Nth* search an answer whose associative strength exceeds the confidence criterion and the number of searches to that point. The second term in the numerator weights the *N + 1* searches necessary to retrieve an answer via the sophisticated guessing route by the probability of the route being used. The denominator indicates the probabilities of using retrieval via either route.

We examined the operation of this mathematical model under the 72 possible combinations of confidence criterion (.05, .10, .15, .20, .30, .40, .50, .60, .70, .80, .90, 1.00) and search length (1 to 6). For each confidence criterion/search length pair, we applied the four equations to each of the 25 problems that children had been presented. Then we combined the results for each problem to obtain expected percentages of errors on retrieval trials, mean solution times on retrieval trials, and percentages of overt strategy use.

The model was tested in two ways, corresponding to measures of internal and external validity. First we wanted to establish the sufficiency of the equations to generate the high correlations among the three variables that we had observed. To do this, we entered into the equations the Fig. 4.2A associative strengths and used the output of the equations to estimate percentages of errors, mean solution times, and percentage of overt strategy use on each problem. Then we correlated the results for the three dependent varaibles. If the equations operated as anticipated, the correlations would be high.

The equations passed this test. The correlations among the output of the equations for errors, solution times, and overt strategy use ranged from $r = .97$ to $r = .99$. Thus, in the mathematical model as well as in the verbal statement of the theory, the three dependent variables were highly correlated.

The next test was to determine whether the mathematical model could predict children's errors, solution times, and overt strategy use. For each variable, the output of the mathematical equations for the 25 problems was correlated with the performance of children in the Siegler and Robinson experiment. Recall from Footnote 1 that the mathematical model was operating on a different data set collected under different conditions than those in the Siegler and Robinson experiment. Thus, this was a test of external validity.

The correlations again were high. The percentage of overt strategy use on each problem produced by the mathematical equations correlated with the children's percentage of overt strategy use $r = .92$. The model's percentage of errors on retrieval trials correlated with the children's percentage of errors on retrieval trials $r = .88$. The model's and the children's mean solution times on retrieval trials correlated $r = .87$. The results demonstrated that the mathematical equations operated as anticipated, that the equations accurately predicted the children's behavior, and that estimates of associative strengths obtained in one experiment could predict errors, solution times, and overt strategy use in another.

THE DEVELOPMENT OF STRATEGY CHOICES
ON ADDITION PROBLEMS

This account raises the question of how distributions of associations develop. How do some problems come to have peaked distributions and others flat ones? Siegler and Shrager hypothesized that children associate whatever answer they state with the problem on which they state it. Therefore, the issue reduced to why children state certain answers to certain problems. We hypothesized that three factors were influential: pre-existing associations from the counting string, frequency of exposure to each problem, and the sum of the addends.

Three Influences on Development

Counting String Associations.   As Gelman and Gallistel (1978) demonstrated, most 4- and 5-year-olds know the counting numbers from 1 to 10. This knowledge appears to both help and hurt their addition performance. Counting helps by providing backup strategies to use when children do not retrieve a statable answer. It can also hurt, however, by suggesting incorrect answers. This is illustrated by children's performance on the six ascending series problems (items on which the second addend is the larger one, such as 2 + 3) where the correct answer is not the number one greater than the second addend. On all six of these problems, in two separate experiments, the most frequent error made by 4- and 5-year-olds on retrieval trials was to say that the answer was the number one greater than the second addend (Fig. 4.4). That is, they answered that 3 + 3 = 4 and 3 + 5 = 6. The result suggested that such problems triggered associations with children's knowledge of the counting string. The children momentarily forgot that they were adding and reverted to the better known procedure for

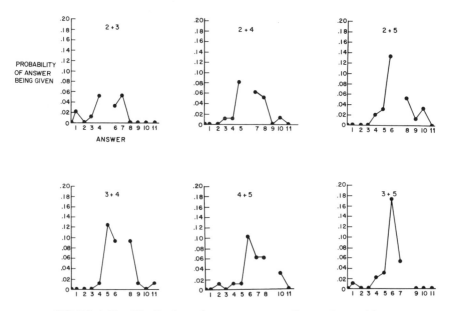

FIGURE 4.4A. Distribution of errors on ascending series problems (data from retrieval trials in Siegler & Robinson, 1982, and Group I of Siegler & Shrager, 1984, overt-strategies-allowed experiment).

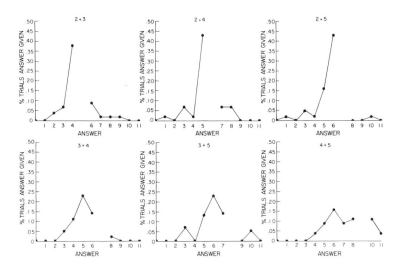

FIGURE 4.4B. Distribution of errors on ascending series problems (data from overt-strategies-prohibited experiment, Siegler & Shrager, 1984).

counting. Ironically, these counting associations may help children on "1+" problems, such as 1 + 3 and 1 + 4, where the counting association is the correct answer.

The Sum of the Addends. A second factor that we hypothesized influenced the development of distributions of associations was the sum of the addends. Presumably, the more objects children need to represent, and the more objects they then need to count, the more likely they are to err. In line with this view, Gelman and Gallistel (1978) reported that 3- and 4-year-olds erred more often as the sets they counted grew larger.

Exposure to Problems. We hypothesized that a third influence on the development of the distribution of associations was amount of exposure to each problem. Parents, teachers, and other children may present some problems more often than others. To test this possibility, Siegler and Shrager invited parents of 2- to 4-year-olds to teach their children to solve addition problems, as they might at home. The goal was to see how often parents presented each problem.

The results indicated that parents presented the easier problems more often. Overall, the frequency of problem presentation correlated $r = .69$ with the percentage of errors in Siegler and Robinson. In addition, the results helped explain several otherwise anomalous results. Numerous investigations have found that ties are easier than their minimum numbers would suggest (Groen &

Parkman, 1972; Siegler & Robinson, 1982; Svenson, 1975). Parents presented ties much more often than other problems with large minimum numbers. Further, addition researchers consistently have found that "+1" problems such as "3 + 1" and "4 + 1" are easier than the corresponding "1+" problems, such as "1 + 3" and "1 + 4" (Groen & Parkman, 1972; Siegler & Robinson, 1982; Svenson, 1975). Parents were found to present "+1" problems five times as often as the corresponding "1+" problems.

To test the adequacy of this three-factor account of development, we quantified each of the hypothesized predictor variables and examined how well they together accounted for the Fig. 4.2A distribution of associations. The acquisition model was expressed as a regression equation with three independent variables. One predictor was associations from the counting string. All ties and ascending series problems on which counting string associations yielded a correct answer (e.g., 1 + 3) were assigned a value of 2, all ties and ascending series problems on which such associations yielded an incorrect answer (e.g., 2 + 3) were assigned a value of 0, and all descending series problems (e.g., 3 + 2) were assigned a neutral value of 1. A second predictor was the likelihood that children would err in counting the objects in their elaborated representations. This variable was defined operationally as the sum of the numbers in the problem, because the more objects children had to represent, and the more objects they had to count, the more likely they would be to err. The third predictor was the frequency of exposure to each problem. The data on frequency of parental presentation of each problem was the operational measure of exposure to that problem.

The regression analysis supported the previous analysis of development in several ways. The three predictor variables accounted for 85% of the variance in the percentage of errors on the 25 problems in Fig. 4.2A. Each of the predictors added significant amounts of variance to that explained by the other two. The sum variable was the first to enter the equation, accounting for 68% of the variance, the counting associations variable was the next to enter, adding 10%, and the parental input variable also added significant variance, 7%. These results were consistent with the view that preexisting associations from the counting string, likelihood of mistakes in counting objects in elaborated representations, and frequency of exposure to different problems contribute to the development of associations between problems and answers.

A Computer Simulation of the Development of the Distribution of Associations

A number of critics of information-processing approaches, among them Neisser (1976) and Beilin (1983), have argued that computer simulations have not, and probably cannot, account for development. They noted that most existing simulations of development generate performance but do not undergo transitions from one state to the next. Transition mechanisms are postulated at a verbal level, but not incorporated into the simulations themselves. In this section, we discuss a computer simulation of addition that incorporates learning and performance mechanisms into a single model. The model progresses from producing relatively poor performance at the outset to eventually producing the sophisticated performance typical of 4- and 5-year-olds.

An Outline of the Simulation.   The simulation can be described in terms of its representation and process at the outset and in terms of seven features of its operation. At the outset, the representation includes only two types of knowledge. The first is the understanding that numbers as a general class are appropriate answers to addition problems. We depicted this information as a set of minimal associations (associative strength = .01) between each problem under consideration and each possible answer (each whole number between 1 and 11). Second, when an ascending or tie problem is presented, the association between that problem and the answer one higher than the second number is momentarily strengthened, much as in semantic priming.

Now consider the initial state of the process. Biology has given it the ability to retrieve information from memory. Direct instruction and modeling have taught it to put up fingers (or their equivalent) and count them. Thus, the process at the beginning of the stimulation resembles that shown in Fig. 4.2B.

This initial representation and process are insufficient to produce performance as advanced as that of 4- and 5-year-olds. For example, when we presented to the simulation in its initial state a set of 10,000 problems, 400 each of the 25 problems with addends no greater than 5, it stated a retrieved answer on only 7% of trials. Percentage of errors and percentage of overt strategy use on each problem correlated $r = .01$.

On the other hand, the initial representation and process do provide a base from which learning can occur. Seven aspects of the acquisition process seem critical.

1. The simulation is presented the 25 problems in accord with their relative frequency in the parental input study just described.[4]

2. Before each problem, the simulation generates a confidence criterion and a search length. Both are selected by a random process, with the confidence criterion varying from .05 to .99 and the search length from 1 to 3.

3. The probability of retrieving an answer is proportional to its associative

---

[4]In the relatively small sample of parental input data that we had available at the time that this chapter was written, parents had never presented some problems. This seemed unlikely to reflect the real-world input. Therefore, we added a constant to each percentage in the input data. This ensured that all problems would be encountered on at least 2% of trials, while also ensuring that the simulation most frequently encountered the problems that parents presented most often.

strength compared to the associative strengths of all answers to the problem. A retrieved answer is stated if its associative strength exceeds the current confidence criterion. Retrieval attempts continue until either the associative strength of a retrieved answer exceeds the confidence criterion or the number of searches matches the allowed search length.

4. On one-tenth of trials on which no answer has yet been advanced, one last answer is retrieved and stated. The probability that a given answer will be stated is proportional to its associative strength relative to all answers' associative strengths, as in the usual retrieval process.

5. If no answer has been stated and the end of the retrieval phase has been reached, the program generates an elaborated representation of the number of objects in the augend and addend. In accord with the empirical data on use of the three overt strategies, an external representation is generated on 75% of trials that reach this point and an internal representation on 25%. If an external representation is generated, the model temporarily (for the duration of the trial) adds .05 to the associative strength of the answer corresponding to the number of objects represented. In either case, the simulation then retrieves an answer (with the usual relative probabilities), and states it if its associative strength exceeds the confidence criterion.

6. If no answer has been stated, the model counts the objects in a elaborated representation. On each count, there is a fixed probability of skipping over the object being counted and a fixed probability of counting it twice.

7. Every time the system advances an answer, the association between that answer and the problem increases. The increment is twice as great for correct answers, that presumably are reinforced, as for incorrect answers, that presumably are not.

The Simulation's Behavior.   The simulation runs in two phases: a learning phase and a test phase. The learning phase is designed to resemble children's experience with addition prior to the time at which they enter the experiment. The test phase is intended to resemble behavior in the experimental setting, given children's prior experience.

The learning phase includes 2,000 trials, an average of 80 for each of the 25 problems. During this period, children develop more or less peaked distributions of associations on each problem. In accord with the previously discussed regression equations, three variables shape the learning process: associations from the counting string, frequency of presentation of each problem, and the sum of the numbers. To highlight the contribution of each of these variables, we compare a pair of problems that differ on that variable but whose status is the same on the other two variables.

First consider 1 + 4 and 2 + 3, problems that have identical sums and frequencies of presentation, but one with a helpful and one with an interfering association from counting. As shown in Fig. 4.5A, the item that has the helpful association, 1 + 4, rapidly builds a peak at the answer 5. The association between the item with the interfering association, 2 + 3, and the answer 5 starts from a lower point and grows more slowly. At the end of the learning phase, after 2,000 trials, the answer 5 has 77% of the total associative strength for 1 + 4 versus 46% for 2 + 3. The peak for 1 + 4 also is higher in absolute terms: .67 versus .37. The greater percentage of total associative strength at 5 for 1 + 4 means that the simulation will retrieve 5 more often on this problem. The higher absolute peak for 1 + 4 means that when the simulation retrieves 5, it will state it more often.

Figure 4.5B illustrates the developmental course for two problems that have identical sums and that lack specific counting string associations, but that differ in frequency of presentation. The problem 4 + 1 is presented on 5.4% of trials, whereas the problem 3 + 2 is presented on 3.7%. The presentation rate has a marked effect on how high the peak rises as well as some effect on how peaked the distribution is. After 2,000 trials, the absolute associative strength of the peak for 4 + 1 was .80, whereas for 3 + 2 the associative strength was .51. The percentage of associative strength for the problem that were located in that problem's peak were 76% and 69% respectively. These differences indicate that 4 + 1 would be retrieved somewhat more often than 3 + 2, and would be stated on a considerably higher percentage of those trials on which it was retrieved.

Finally, as shown in Fig. 4.5C, the sum exerted an effect even when the frequency of presentation and the type of counting string association was constant. The problems 3 + 4 and 4 + 5 are identical in frequency of presentation and in having an interfering counting association. However, they differ in their sums. The peak of the item with the lower sum rises somewhat more rapidly and at the end of 2,000 learning trials is higher (.39 vs .32) than that for the item with the higher sum. The distribution also is somewhat more peaked, with the peak of 3 + 4 having 50% of the total associative strength and the peak of 4 + 5 having 43%. Thus, all three variables influence the percentage of trials on which the correct answer is retrieved and the probability that it will be stated once it is retrieved.

After the simulation completes the learning phase, it proceeds to the test phase. Where the learning phase was intended to model children's experience prior to the experiment, the test phase was intended to parallel their experience in the experiment. The test phase differed from the learning phase in only two respects. First, to parallel the empirical experiments that we conducted, all problems were presented equally often in the test phase. Second, because each child who participated in the empirical experiments received only two exposures to each problem, thereby providing very little opportunity to learn, we turned off the learning mechanism that added associative strength to each answer that was stated. The goal was to model a large number of children, each having a brief experimental session, rather than a single child having a very long session.

A. Problems Differing in Type of Counting Association

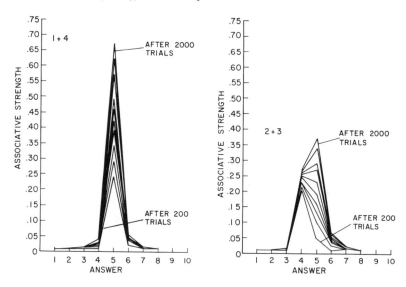

B. Problems Differing in Frequency of Presentation

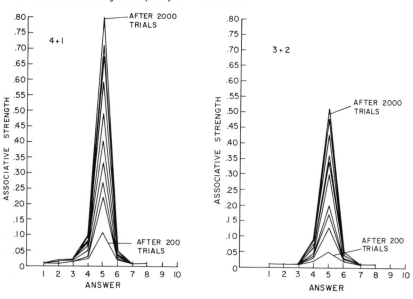

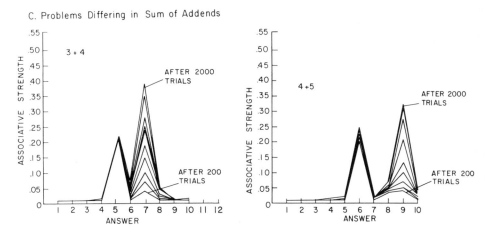

C. Problems Differing in Sum of Addends

FIGURE 4.5. Computer simulation's learning of associations: (A) Effects of counting-string associations, (B) frequency of presentation, and (C) sum. Curves represent associative strengths after each 200 trials; the lowest curve represents strengths after 200 trials, the next lowest after 400 trials, and so on.

The computer program's behavior in the test phase closely resembled that of children in Siegler and Robinson (1982) and Siegler and Shrager (1984). It generated the strategies that the children used. The relative solution times of the strategies were identical to those of the children. The simulation's error patterns also were like the children's; the simulation's most frequent error on all six ascending problems was the answer one greater than the second addend.

Most important, the simulation's performance resembled that of the children in which problems elicited the greatest percentage of errors, which took the longest to answer, and which elicited the highest percentage of overt strategies. As shown in Table 4.3, all of the correlations of greatest interest between the simulation's behavior and that of the children exceeded $r = .80$. Moreover, the

TABLE 4.3
Computer Simulation's Performance

Intramodal Correlations	Correlations Between Children's and Model's Behavior[a]
$r_{\text{% errors and % overt strategy use}} = .97$	$r_{\text{% errors produced by model and children}} = .88$
$r_{\text{% errors and } \bar{x} \text{ solution times}} = .97$	$r_{\text{% overt strategy use produced by model and children}} = .92$
$r_{\text{% overt strategy use and } \bar{x} \text{ solution times}} = .99$	$r_{\bar{x} \text{ solution times produced by model and children}} = .87$

[a]Children's data are combined results of retrieval trials in Siegler and Robinson and in replication condition of Siegler and Shrager.

intra-simulation correlations among percentage of errors on retrieval trials, percentage of overt strategy use, and mean solution times on retrieval trials on each problem all exceeded $r = .90$.

In sum, a computer simulation that takes into account relative frequency of problem presentation, associations from the counting string, and the likelihood of errors in executing overt strategies can produce performance much like that of 4- and 5-year-olds. The simulation both learns and performs. At the outset, its performance is not very accurate, and is unlike that of 4- and 5-year-olds in many ways. After having an opportunity to learn, its performance is much more child-like. The simulation demonstrates that children could acquire their distributions of associations through the three hypothesized mechanisms, and that if they did, their performance would be much like that which we observed.

STRATEGY CHOICES IN SUBTRACTION, MULTIPLICATION, AND SPELLING

Is the strategy choice procedure depicted in the distribution of associations model unique to the addition task, or is it one of a family of related strategy choice procedures? An initial question was whether related strategy choice models in other areas could even be hypothesized. It proved possible to hypothesize the same basic type of model in several areas, among them subtraction, multiplication, and spelling. In all of these tasks, the representations could be of identical form: a distribution of associations between each problem and various answers. The processes also showed some generality, at the level of including the same three phases: retrieval, elaboration of the representation, and an algorithmic backup strategy.

Because the tasks were different, the models necessarily differed in some ways as well. The aspects of the models that proved to be unique to the particular task involved the types of elaborations that are performed and the nature of the algorithmic back-up processes. We hypothesized that subtraction would be the most similar to addition, differing only in which fingers are put up and which are put down at different times. Our hypotheses about multiplication differed in that the elaboration of the representation would involve writing down one of the multiplicands the number of times indicated by the other, and the algorithm would involve adding up the multiplicands that have been written. In spelling, the elaborative process could involves assigning letters to the sounds within the word or writing out alternative possible spellings, and the algorithm could involve looking up the word in the dictionary.

To test the generality of the model, we presented subtraction, multiplication, and spelling problems to children in the process of learning these problems. To study subtraction, we presented 34 kindergarteners and first graders with the 25 problems that were the exact inverses of the 25 addition problems used in the original Siegler and Robinson (1982) study. For every problem "a + b = c" in that experiment, here there was a problem of the form "c − b = a." For example, for the addition problem "3 + 5 = 8," the corresponding subtraction problem was "8 − 5 = 3." To study multiplication, we presented 56 third graders with the 100 multiplication problems formed by the possible combinations of multiplicand (0 to 9) × multiplier (0 to 9). To study spelling, we presented 28 second graders with sets of 20 words, half from their second-grade spelling book and half from a third-grade book. The main goals were to establish which strategies the children would use, whether the relation among errors, solution times, and overt strategy use would be present, and if the relation was present, whether its source was in errors and solution times on retrieval trials.

The experiments indicated that on each task, children use several strategies. In subtraction, children used the same four strategies that we observed in addition: counting fingers, counting, fingers, and retrieval. In multiplication, they used five strategies. One was retrieval. Two others involved elaboration of the representation: repeating the problem orally, and writing down the problem on the answer sheet. The remaining two were algorithmic approaches that involved both elaboration of the representation and computing of the number of objects in the elaborated representation. One of these, repeated addition, was previously described. The other was literal representation and counting. A child using this strategy to solve "4 × 3" might draw four bundles, each having three lines in it, and then count the lines. In spelling, we detected four strategies: retrieval, writing of alternative spellings and selection of one as correct, overt sounding out of words, and looking up words in the dictionary. (For additional information about the fine structure of these strategies, their frequency of use, and their accuracy and temporal characteristics, see Siegler, 1986.)

On all three tasks, strong relations between frequency of overt strategy use, frequency of errors, and length of solution times also were present. The correlations between percentage of overt strategy use and percentage of errors on the three tasks ranged from $r = .82$ to $r = .87$. The correlations between percentage of overt strategy use and mean solution times ranged from $r = .86$ to $r = .91$ on them. These correlations were of similar magnitude to those observed in the addition experiments.

For us, the most convincing evidence of the model's applicability to tasks other than addition was the finding that the overall correlations among overt strategy use, errors, and solution times derive primarily from errors and solution times on retrieval trials. (These findings are only for subtraction and multiplication; the corresponding analyses for spelling have not yet been done.) The correlations involving subtraction errors are shown in Fig. 4.6. On both subtraction and multiplication, the correlation between overt strategy use and errors on retrieval trials was significantly greater than the correlation between overt strategy use and errors on overt strategy trials. The correlations between overt strategy use and solution times on retrieval trials on the two tasks also were greater

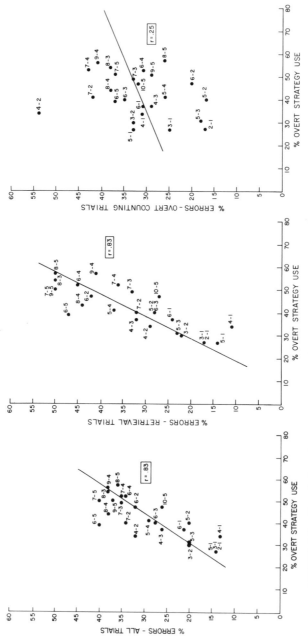

FIGURE 4.6. Correlations between errors and overt strategy use in subtraction (Siegler & Shrager, 1984).

than the correlation between overt strategy use and solution times on overt strategy trials (although the difference failed to reach significance on the subtraction problems.) In general, however, the data were consistent with the pattern predicted by the distribution of associations model (again, see Siegler, 1986, for a more detailed presentation of these data).

The findings on subtraction, multiplication, and spelling suggest that the applicability of the distribution of associations model is not limited to addition of numbers as a task nor to preschoolers as a population. Rather, the types of strategies predicted by the model and the particular relations among errors, solution times, and overt strategy use that it leads us to expect fit children's behavior in several areas and over a range of ages. In the next section, we consider how the model might be extended to a Piagetian task that previously has been analyzed from a quite different perspective.

STRATEGY CHOICES ON THE BALANCE SCALE TASK

In earlier articles, Siegler (1981, 1983) concluded that much of children's knowledge can profitably be characterized as rules for solving problems. The present account of addition, subtraction, multiplication, and spelling has a different flavor. The emphasis on the role of associations is unlike the earlier analyses of balance scales, conservation, projection of shadows, and other problems and concepts. This difference raises the question of how the two types of analyses might be related.

One important difference between the two sets of tasks involves the amounts of experience that children have with items on the two sets of tasks. Children have large amounts of experience with particular arithmetic and spelling problems. This gives them an opportunity to build associations between individual items and particular answers. In contrast, prior to the experimental session, children ordinarily have never encountered balance scale, conservation, or projection of shadows problems of the types presented in typical experiments. Therefore, they have no associations between individual items and answers to those items.

This analysis suggests that if children had substantial amounts of experience with particular balance scale, conservation, or projection of shadows problems, associative knowledge would influence their performance much as it does in the arithmetic and spelling tasks. To test this view, Roman Taraban and I provided 24 fifth to eighth graders with substantial experience with a few balance scale problems. Then we tested the children on these and other balance scale problems to examine how they chose strategies to solve the problems.

The balance scale apparatus was the same one used in Siegler (1976). On each side of the fulcrum were four pegs on which metal weights could be placed. The arm of the balance could tip left or right or remain level, depending on how the weights were arranged. However, a lever was set to hold the arm motionless. The task was to predict which (if either) side would go down if the lever were released.

The experimental design involved a pretest, training, and a posttest. The pretest was similar to that described by Siegler (1976). It was used to identify children who used Rule III on the balance scale task. That is, it was used to identify children who could solve all balance scale problems other than ones where there was more weight on one side and the weight on the other side was farther from the fulcrum. These were called conflict problems, since the two cues to which side would go down suggested conflicting predictions. Considering weight alone suggested that one side would go down, and considering distance from the fulcrum alone suggested that the other would. Children who used Rule III would respond correctly to all non-conflict problems, but would answer the majority of conflict problems incorrectly.

The training session involved repeated presentation of 6 conflict problems. These 6 problems were drawn from a set of 12, so that one half of the children received training with one group of 6 problems and one half with the other group. Training continued until children could draw the configuration of weights on pegs for each of the 6 problems without looking at them, and could consistently recall which side would go down.

The posttest included 18 problems of three types. Six were non-conflict problems that Rule III would solve correctly. Six were the conflict problems with which the children had had substantial experience. Six were the conflict problems that the child had not previously encountered. The dependent measure of greatest interest was children's solution times on the three types of problems.

At least two hypotheses concerning the relative duration of these solution times seemed plausible. Siegler and Atlas (cited in Siegler & Klahr, 1982) found that children who could accurately solve both conflict and non-conflict problems responded more quickly to the non-conflict problems. This suggested the prediction that even if children learned to accurately answer the six conflict problems with which they had extensive experience, they would answer them more slowly than the non-conflict problems. The experience seemed likely to lead to faster responding on familiar than on unfamiliar conflict problems. Thus, the children would answer the non-conflict problems most rapidly, the trained conflict problems next most rapidly, and the untrained conflict problems the least rapidly.

The distribution of associations model made a different prediction. This prediction was based on the greater experience with particular balance scale problems of children in the present study compared to children in the Siegler and Atlas study. Because the children in the Siegler and Atlas study had not had substantial experience with any balance scale problems, they needed to use a rule to answer all of them. Within this rule, non-conflict problems could be answered more rapidly than conflict problems. However, the children in the present study, who had had substantial experience with some conflict problems, could answer

these problems through retrieving associations between the balance scale config-
urations and particular answers. Only if they could not retrieve an answer with
sufficient confidence to state it would they fall back on the rule that led to non-
conflict problems being answered more rapidly than conflict problems. Therefore, the distribution of associations model predicted that children who had
substantial experience with some conflict problems would answer those conflict
problems the most rapidly, non-conflict problems the next most rapidly, and
untrained conflict problems the least rapidly.

This prediction of the distribution of associations model proved accurate.
Children answered the trained conflict problems significantly faster than the non-
conflict problems, and answered both types of problems significantly faster than
the untrained conflict problems. Children answered correctly on more than 95%
of both trained conflict problems (where they could retrieve the correct answer)
and the non-conflict problems (where their rule would lead to correct answers).
They answered correctly on less than half of the untrained conflict problems,
where neither their rule nor associations would indicate the correct answer.

An interesting implication of these results concerns the relations between
associative and rule-based responding. Developmental psychologists often think
of rule use as somehow more advanced than reliance on associations. In the case
of the balance scale, however, children progressed from sole reliance on a rule to
reliance on a mix of associative and rule-based knowledge. They relied on
associations when they had extensive associative knowledge and on their rule
when they did not.

This approach has the same advantages as the general strategy choice procedure described earlier. It leads to fast and accurate responding when that is a
possibility, and to slower (and more accurate responding than is otherwise possible) when the associations are weak or nonexistent. The pattern also resembles
that found in studies of expert performance. In chess, for example, experts have
been found to rely both on pattern recognition skills and on general strategies.
Novices, on the other hand, rely more heavily on the general strategies (Chase &
Simon, 1973). The main point is that as people gain exposure to particular
problems, whether they involve arithmetic, spelling, balance scales, or chess,
they rely increasingly heavily on retrieval and pattern recognition, and less
heavily on general rules and backup strategies.

CONCLUSIONS

Within the present analysis, changes in children's strategy choices in arithmetic
and spelling emerge as a consequence of learning. Changing associations between particular problems and particular answers are seen as producing the
observed changes in strategy use. Knowledge of related operations, the types of
difficulty encountered in executing backup strategies, and amount of exposure to

particular problems all seemed to influence the development of the distribution of associations, and thus the strategy choices that children made. These same factors are influential in a simulation model of the acquisition of subtraction strategy choices that we are currently formulating.

One conclusion that we draw from the present work is that simple learning processes can allow children to acquire intelligent problem-solving procedures. The children's behavior, and that of the model, was intelligent in at least two senses: accuracy and efficiency. When it was possible to use the rapid and nearly effortless retrieval procedure and to still produce accurate performance, the children and the model did so. When this was impossible, and use of retrieval would have led to inaccurate performance, children made greater use of the backup strategies. To have always used retrieval would have produced inaccurate performance; to have always used the backup strategies would have produced unnecessarily long solution times. The strategy choice procedure that children seemed to use produced behavior that was both accurate and fast.

A second, related conclusion concerns the types of tasks that may be useful for cognitive developmentalists to study. Piaget believed that performance on unfamiliar tasks provided the clearest index of children's basic reasoning. Much has been learned from studying these tasks, but they are not the only ones that may help reveal the nature of cognitive development. Children devote a large percentage of their thoughts to grappling with familiar tasks such as arithmetic and spelling. These cognitive activities not only are interesting areas of study in and of themselves, they also may influence the way in which children try to solve less familiar problems. Omitting them from study produces an imbalanced picture of children's thought processes. Seen from another perspective, the distinction between cognitive development and the development of skills in classrooms seems increasingly artificial; we may learn a great deal about cognitive change processes by including the acquisition of academic skills within the purview of cognitive development.

A final conclusion involves the need for detailed analyses of cognitive changes that we label as *learning* and those that we label as *development*. As mentioned at the outset of this chapter, we typically attribute particular cognitive changes to learning or to development on various a priori grounds: time scale of the change, population involved, magnitude of the change, and whether maturation is strongly suspected to be involved. Whether these distinctions reflect substantive differences in the cognitive processes involved in intellectual changes is unknown, however. Our understanding of the relation between learning and development as general processes is limited by our understanding of particular learnings and particular developments. Progress in understanding the general issue may follow progress in understanding particular instances.

REFERENCES

Ashcraft, M. H. (1982). The development of mental arithmetic: A chronometric approach. *Developmental Review, 2,* 213–236.

Beilin, H. (1983). The new functionalism and Piaget's program. In E. K. Scholnick (Ed.), *New trends in conceptual representation: Challenges to Piaget's theory?* (pp. 3–40). Hillsdale, NJ: Lawrence Erlbaum Associates.

Brown, A. L., Bransford, J. D., Ferrara, R. A., & Campione, J. C. (1983). Learning, remembering, and understanding. In P. H. Mussen (Ed.), *Handbook of child psychology: Cognitive development volume* J. H. Flavell & E. M. Markman (Eds.), (pp. 77–166). New York: Wiley.

Cavanaugh, J.C., & Perlmutter, M. (1982). Metamemory: A critical examination. *Child Development, 53,* 11–28.

Chase, W. G., & Simon, H. A. (1973). The mind's eye in chess. In W. G. Chase (Ed.), *Visual information processing* (pp. 215–281). New York: Academic Press.

Flavell, J. H., & Wellman H. M. (1977). Metamemory. In R. V. Kail, Jr. & J. W. Hagen (Eds.), *Perspectives on the development of memory and cognition* (pp. 3–33). Hillsdale, NJ: Lawrence Erlbaum Associates.

Gelman, R., & Gallistel, C. R. (1978). *The child's understanding of number.* Cambridge, MA: Harvard University Press.

Groen, G. J., & Parkman, J. M. (1972). A chronometric analysis of simple addition. *Psychological Review, 79,* 329–343.

Neisser, U. (1976). General, academic, and artificial intelligence. In L. B. Resnick (Ed.), *The nature of intelligence* (pp. 135–144). Hillsdale, NJ: Lawrence Erlbaum Associates.

Siegler, R. S. (1976). Three aspects of cognitive development. *Cognitive Psychology, 8,* 481–520.

Siegler, R. S. (1981). Developmental sequences within and between concepts. *Monographs of the Society for Research in Child Development, 46*(2), Whole No. 189.

Siegler, R. S. (1983). Five generalizations about cognitive development. *American Psychologist, 38,* 263–277.

Siegler, R. S. (1986). Unities across domains in children's strategy choices. In M. Perlmutter (Ed.), *Perspectives on intellectual development: The Minnesota Symposia on child psychology* (Vol. 19, pp. 1–48). Hillsdale, NJ: Lawrence Erlbaum Associates.

Siegler, R. S., & Klahr, D. (1982). When do children learn: The relationship between existing knowledge and the ability to acquire new knowledge. In R. Glaser (Ed.), *Advances in instructional psychology* (pp. 121–211). Hillsdale, NJ: Lawrence Erlbaum Associates.

Siegler, R. S., & Robinson, M. (1982). The development of numerical understandings. In H. Reese & L. P. Lipsitt (Eds.), *Advances in child development and behavior* (pp. 242–312). New York: Academic Press.

Siegler, R. S., & Shrager, J. (1984). A model of strategy choice. In C. Sophian (Ed.), *Origins of cognitive skills* (pp. 229–293). Hillsdale, NJ: Lawrence Erlbaum Associates.

Sternberg, R. J. (1984). Mechanisms of cognitive development: A componential approach. In R. J. Sternberg (Ed.), *Mechanisms of cognitive development* (pp. 163–186). New York: Freeman.

Sternberg, R. J., & Powell, J. S. (1983). The development of intelligence. In P. H. Mussen (Ed.), *Handbook of child psychology: Cognitive Development* J. H. Flavell & E. M. Markman (Eds.) (pp. 341–419). New York: Wiley.

Svenson, O. (1975). Analysis of time required by children for simple additions. *Acta Psychologica, 39,* 289–302.

5 Information Processing and Piagetian Theory: Conflict or Congruence?

Lynn S. Liben
The Pennsylvania State University

The empirical study of cognition in children has often been approached from an information-processing framework. Much of this work stems from questions and paradigms developed in research on adult cognition. In the area of memory, for example, the model proposed by Atkinson and Shiffrin (1968) to conceptualize adult memory was imported into experimental child psychology to organize the study of children's sensory registers, their short-term storage capacity, and the use of control processes such as rehearsal and clustering strategies (e.g., see Kail & Hagen, 1977; Ornstein, 1978).

For psychologists committed to studying phenomena that may be uniquely developmental, however, the more interesting application of information processing has been in areas related directly to tasks derived from Piagetian theory, as, for example, in computer simulations of children's solution to seriation and class inclusion tasks (e.g., Baylor & Gascon, 1974; Gascon, 1969; Klahr & Wallace, 1976), or in task analyses of balance bar, shadow projection, probability, and conservation tasks (Siegler, 1981).

Information-processing interpretations of children's performance on Piagetian tasks are not the first attempts to use alternative theoretical approaches to reinterpret phenomena first observed by Piaget. Early attempts, made from the perspective of traditional learning theory (e.g., Gagné, 1968), were quickly dismissed as antithetical to the constructive nature of Piagetian theory. The more recent information-processing analyses are more difficult to categorize with respect to whether or not their core features are congruent with a Piagetian approach. If the two approaches *are* fundamentally congruent, then the easily replicable procedures, mathematically precise data, and well-delineated flow charts of information processing might well argue for displacing the difficult to

109

concretize and reproduce interviews of the clinical method, the largely categorical data, and the abstract formal logic of Piagetian theory.

Spokespersons of information processing appear to view their approach to cognitive development as having already displaced earlier approaches, including, presumably, Piaget's. In the opening paragraph of his recent Mussen *Handbook* chapter on "Information Processing Approaches to Cognitive Development," Siegler (1983) writes:

> In the 1970 edition of this *Handbook,* information processing was the primary topic in none of the 29 chapters. The subject index included only two references to it. Thirteen years later, the information processing approach is arguably *the* leading strategy for the study of cognitive development. I would be surprised if the subject index of the current *Handbook* included fewer than 100 references to it. (p. 129)

Siegler must, then, have been surprised to discover that, apart from the 8 column inches of the index that refer the reader directly back to Siegler's own chapter, there are only 13 references to "Information Processing" in all four volumes of the *Handbook* combined. This stands in sharp contrast to the more than 30 column inches of references to Piagetian theory that contain some 150 entries, again even after eliminating references to pages in the *three* chapters devoted specifically to Piagetian work.

Thus, the contention that Piagetian theory has been displaced by information processing finds no support from a gross content analysis of the classic handbook of the field. This observation does not, however, preclude the possibility that such displacement will eventually take place, nor does it address the more telling conceptual issue of whether or not the two approaches are fundamentally comparable. This latter issue is considered in the present chapter by analyzing Siegler's recent work. Although evaluating an entire approach through the examination of a single research program is necessarily restrictive, the particular focus is easily defended: Siegler is undoubtedly the leading spokesperson for the information-processing approach to cognitive development, as evidenced by the invitation to author the *Handbook* chapter just mentioned, as well as by his long-standing, elegant, and heavily cited program of research. A fuller discussion of whether the analysis of Siegler's work also extends to other information-processing developmentalists is found in the Epilogue.

Before turning to an analysis of Siegler's recent work, it is useful to put it in the context of his larger program of research. Siegler's early work (e.g., 1976, 1981) was directed primarily toward establishing the efficacy of the rule assessment technique and to applying it to a number of different kinds of problems. In the rule assessment technique, alternative rules that children might use to solve a particular kind of problem are generated by rational task analyses, existing theories, and previous empirical work. Problems are then devised that will elicit different patterns of responses, depending on which rule the child is following.

Finally, in cases in which there are theoretical predictions concerning either the sequencing or simultaneity of rule use, individual children's responses are examined for systematic patterns of rule use across different problem types.

As a consequence of applying these rule assessment techniques to a number of Piagetian tasks (balance beam; shadow projection; probability; and conservation of liquid quantity, solid quantity, and number), Siegler (1981) concluded that children do use different rules at different points of their development, and that for each particular type of problem, there are orderly changes in which rules are used (the *within-concept* data). Although the progressions observed differ in detail from those offered by Piaget, Siegler's general position that children's approaches to particular problems differ with development is consistent with the stage-related descriptions found in Piagetian theory.

In contrast, however, Siegler argues that his data on children's rule use across problem types (the *between-concept* data), do not support the Piagetian contention that there is general consistency in the way that different tasks are approached. As a consequence, Siegler rejects the Piagetian stance that children's behavior across a wide array of tasks may be understood by reference to logical structures such as the groupings of concrete operations.

Although Siegler's early work was thus focused primarily on these state descriptions (rules), and on arguing that Piaget's characterization of overarching structures was unsatisfactory, it did not offer a substitute conceptualization for integrating performance across tasks, nor did it explicate the mechanisms by which children progressed from elementary to more advanced rule systems. It is in this context that the current work by Siegler (1986; Siegler & Shipley, this volume) is an important advance because it directly focuses on both these issues, that is, on integration and progression. Partly because these are core issues of *any* developmental theory, their explication is particularly relevant for evaluating the conceptual question raised earlier of whether or not information processing is fundamentally compatible with traditional Piagetian theory. Thus, the present chapter begins with a discussion of the integrative conceptualization presented by Siegler (1986), followed by an examination of the developmental mechanisms proposed by Siegler and Shipley (this volume), and concludes with a discussion of how these issues are related to the overarching theme of the volume, that is, the relationship between development and learning.

UNITIES IN COGNITIVE FUNCTIONING

As just noted, Siegler (1981) concluded that his empirical data, and those of many other researchers, were not consistent with the Piagetian position that children's thinking could be understood as realizations of logical structures such as the group, grouping, and lattice. Probably the most common response to these seemingly contradictory data has been to abandon the attempt to provide a uniformly applicable logical model of children's reasoning such as that formulated by Piaget, and substitute instead a series of detailed, stage-like descriptions focused on ever and ever smaller content domains, such as the skill sequences formulated by Fischer (1980). These kinds of local solutions to the descriptive goal of developmental psychology, however, lose in theoretical power what they gain in predictive accuracy. Hilgard (1956) described this problem with respect to the functionalism of the 1950s by arguing that the disadvantage of stating issues in a readily testable fashion was that the resulting collection of individual laws lacked hierarchical integration. To be an "economical scientific system," data must be "logically structured as well as empirically sound" (Hilgard, 1956, p. 364). Citing Hilgard's comments, Beilin (1983) has suggested that this observation is equally applicable to current functional approaches, among which he places information-processing approaches such as Siegler's:

> The decompositional approach to functional analysis is a powerful research tactic for what it displays of the nature of functional entities but, without corresponding constructive methods that build or search for the interrelations among functions (i.e., that search for functional correspondences and structural isomorphisms), the new functionalism will proliferate strategies and functions for each task studied until the enterprise sinks from its own weight, as Hilgard saw with an earlier functionalism. (p. 33)

Indeed, it is undoubtedly the dissatisfaction with having a potentially infinite set of models for each domain or skill that has led Siegler (1986) to identify what he has called "unities in thinking." Specifically, he proposed:

> to explore the proposition that unities in thinking that are not evident at the behavioral level can become evident through analyses of underlying mechanisms. This Piagetian-sounding proposition will be explored in some distinctly non-Piagetian-sounding domains—addition, subtraction, multiplication, and spelling—as well as on the more Piagetian-sounding balance scale task. The basic hypothesis is that in all of these domains, children employ the same general procedure for choosing which strategy to use to solve particular problems. (p. 1)

The purpose of this section of the chapter is to consider these unities, with a particular focus on how they contrast to the "structures d'ensemble" of Piagetian theory with respect to first, their scientific derivation and function, and second, the content domains in which they are studied.

Derivation and Function of Unities

All but the most reductionistic of psychologists (positivists) recognize that it is an impossible task to describe behavior successfully by a catalogue of objective observations alone. First, observations themselves are theory-laden (Hanson, 1958; Kuhn, 1962; Lauden, 1977; Lewis, 1983; Overton, 1984). Second, unstructured observations would be quantitatively so vast that they would be cognitively unmanageable. Thus, a major goal of any developmental theory is to provide some coherent system for organizing past observations, for interpreting incoming data, and for generating predictions that should be explored in future empirical work.

Siegler (1986) suggests that the search for "unities" can be conducted at different levels of aggregation, including the levels of traits, behaviors, and internal mechanisms. By unities in traits he refers to similar approaches to cognitive tasks such as concrete or abstract thinking, animistic or scientific, precausal or causal. By unities in behaviors, Siegler refers to similarity in passing or failing all problems (presumably of a particular type, although this is not specified in his description of this level). By unities at the level of internal mechanisms, he refers to similarities in reasoning that occur "because all of the behavior derives from similar structures or from similar representations and processes" (p. 1).

Siegler asserts that it is at the first two levels that the search for unities is conducted in Piagetian theory, and concludes further that "Efforts to identify unities in reasoning at the level of trait descriptions and at the level of behavior have yielded somewhat disappointing results" (p. 1). Siegler thus urges that the search for unities be conducted at the third level instead, suggesting that his own program of research falls under this rubric.

One might, however, take issue with Siegler's characterization. First, of the three approaches he outlines, the third seems far more compatible with the structural approach of Piagetian theory than do the first two. Second, Siegler's characterization ignores the radically different nature of the derivation, evaluation, and purpose of unities in the two theoretical traditions. Siegler's approach, and information-processing approaches more generally, fit within the conventionalist research program (see Overton, 1984, 1985) in which empirical data are primary. Nonobservable propositions (unities) are then derived from these empirical data so that general propositions serve *"only as convenient and conventional ways of ordering and organizing hard data,* i.e., observations. They do not influence the data base itself. Rather, they operate like pigeonholes to classify, arrange, and organize hard data into coherent units" (Overton, 1984, p. 196). As the empirical data change, the propositions change as well. Thus, in this approach, the "genuine progress of science . . . takes place . . . on the ground level of proven facts [i.e., hard data] and changes on the theoretical level are merely instrumental" (Lakatos, 1978, p. 106).

Siegler and Shipley's model (i.e., computer program) of children's addition strategies provides an excellent illustration of a data-driven approach:

> The computer program's behavior in the test phase closely resembled that of children in Siegler and Robinson (1982) and Siegler and Shrager (1984). It generated the strategies that the children used. The relative solution times of the strat-

egies were identical to those of the children. The simulation's error patterns were also like the children's; the simulation's most frequent error on all six ascending problems was the answer one greater than the second addend (Siegler & Shipley, this volume, p. 99).

Piaget's approach, in contrast, fits within a rationalist (Kantian) epistemological tradition in which legitimate scientific knowledge is derived *not only* from observation, but from mental activity (reason) as well (Overton, 1984). After identifying the function of a psychological structure (itself an interpretive task), the investigator next attempts to discover, through rational analysis, the organization (formal explanation; structure) of that function (Beilin, 1983, 1985a, 1985b; Overton, 1984; Piaget, 1985). Is is important to emphasize that the structural analyses are *rationally,* not empirically derived, and as such, are *not* subject to the same kind of empirical falsification that is appropriate for propositions formulated within conventionalist approaches such as Siegler's (see Overton, 1984). They are, however, subject to revision, as evidenced in Piaget's continual search for ever more powerful structural models (Beilin, 1985b; Montangero, 1985; Piaget, 1985).

Although the formal explanation is thus a rational construction and hence "made up" by the investigator, this does not negate the role of empirical observations. As just explained, the formal explanations are motivated by observations in the first place, and continue to be "kept in check by the fact that later empirical tests will be made to determine whether the rules are in fact a good representation of the organization of behavior" (Overton, 1984, p. 209). In addition, even if true experiments (i.e., manipulation of independent variables) are not used to *derive* the organization, they may be used to examine whether or not the organization will be manifest in behavior under particular circumstances (Overton & Newman, 1982). Thus, empirical data are essential to Piagetian theory, importantly differentiating it from the realm of arm-chair philosophical analysis that Piaget so vehemently and creatively rejected.

Although empirical data are essential to the Piagetian approach, they are not used to derive unities (structures) directly. Indeed, it is this separation between empirical data and general propositions (structure) of Piagetian theory that defends it against Brainerd's (1978) criticism that the relationship between theory and data is a circular one. Interestingly, as noted earlier by Overton (1985), the criticism of circularity is more legitimately applied to information-processing approaches in which the competence model is empirically derived directly from observed performance, as illustrated in the preceding quotation from Siegler and Shipley (this volume, see p. 99). That is, given that the particular computer program was written expressly to simulate children's observed behaviors, it is not remarkable that there is a good match between them.

In summary, Piagetian theory and information processing differ radically with respect to the method used to derive unities and the heuristic purpose that these unities serve. In light of these radical differences, Siegler's assertion—that past empirical data do not support the unities formulated in Piagetian theory, and that alternative approaches must therefore be substituted—must be recognized as an assertion formulated within one, but not the only, scientifically legitimate framework.

Domains of Unities

The argument presented above is that unities are derived differently, and serve different functions in information processing and in Piagetian theory. Another dimension on which the two approaches may be compared concerns the substantive areas in which these unities are studied.

Siegler's own characterization of the major difference between the contents studied in his recent research and Piaget's is with respect to whether the tasks used are familiar or unfamiliar. Siegler and Shipley (this volume) argue that whereas Piaget chose unfamiliar tasks to provide "the clearest index of children's basic reasoning," they focus on "familiar tasks such as arithmetic and spelling," arguing that "these cognitive activities not only are interesting areas of study in and of themselves, they also may influence the way in which children try to solve less familiar problems" (p. 106).

One difficulty with studying familiar domains is that one cannot be certain when one is observing a novel invention, and when one is observing a learned routine. For example, consider the child described by Siegler and Shipley (this volume, p. 101) who solved the problem "4 × 3" by drawing four bundles, each with three lines, and then counting the lines. Was he demonstrating an understanding of multiplication, or simply calling up an algorithm motivated by workbook upon workbook filled with problems depicted in precisely this manner?

A second and deeper issue concerns the breadth of contents covered. Although it would probably be difficult to reach consensus about how to characterize the breadth of particular content areas, there would probably be general agreement that spelling and the arithmetic skills studied by Siegler are less far-reaching than the categories of space, time, number, and causality addressed in the Piagetian work. If it is only a matter of time before the kinds of analyses already applied to the former group of contents can be applied to the latter, the difference would be trivial. However, that the difference between the two kinds of domains is probably more profound may be seen by examining Siegler and Shipley's attempt to expand their model to incorporate findings from the balance beam task. It is telling that children's rule structures identified in earlier research on the balance beam (Siegler, 1976) were *not* integrated into the flow charts used to model children's addition strategies. Instead, entirely new data were collected on the balance beam by Siegler and Taraban (reported in Siegler & Shipley, this volume) using a revised paradigm in which children were provided with experiences that experimentally built up a set of associations to the balance beam task. In essence, then, the balance beam task was transformed from a novel reasoning task to a familiar problem which could be solved (not necessarily accurately) by drawing upon past associations to similar problems. Once having transformed the task in this manner, it is not surprising that it could be modeled similarly to performance on "familiar" tasks such as addition and subtraction.

Parenthetically, it might be noted here that task transformations have plagued reinterpretations of original Piagetian work in other domains as well. By making seemingly superficial changes in the original Piagetian tasks to make the tasks more "comprehensible" to young children, the task demands are changed to an entirely different level. Examples of this problem may be found in the domain of class inclusion (e.g., see Dean, Chabaud, & Bridges, 1981) and spatial representation (see Liben, in press).

In short, Siegler and Shipley (this volume) propose that they have demonstrated the applicability of a model that originated in the study of arithmetic skills to a qualitatively different domain, the balance beam problem. In the process of application, however, they have transformed the balance beam task from one that is unfamiliar and thus requires active problem solving, to one that is highly familiar and thus can draw upon a set of past associations. As a consequence, the range of domains addressed in Siegler and Shipley's work is neither as diverse as might appear on first glance, nor as broad as those addressed within Piagetian theory.

The argument made above is that the range of domains incorporated by the unities in Siegler's work and in Piagetian theory differs significantly. An examination of any single content domain also suggests fundamental differences between the two approaches. For example, both Siegler and Shipley (this volume) and Piaget (1965) are interested in children's approaches to number. But, whereas Piaget was asking fundamental questions about the nature of numbers and how children go about acquiring an understanding of that nature, Siegler and Shipley focus on children's skills at applying algorithms to solve problems that happen to involve numbers. (See Macnamara, 1984; and Murray, this volume for excellent discussions of the differences between the kinds of questions asked by Piaget and those addressed by researchers using computer modeling in the study of number.)

In summary, the subject matter on which the unities are built differs significantly between Piagetian theory and the work of Siegler and Shipley. Differences may be seen in the familiarity of tasks, the breadth of content domains, and the foci within particular content areas.

DEVELOPMENTAL MECHANISMS

The issues considered in the preceding section of this chapter are concerned primarily with how one chooses to characterize children's cognition at any given time, that is, with the descriptive task of cognitive developmental psychology. The other major, indeed, the more important goal of developmental work, is to characterize the mechanisms that are responsible for leading the child from less, to more mature levels of functioning. Piagetian theory has often been criticized for failing to explain precisely how the processes of assimilation and accommodation operate. Information-processing approaches have similarly been criticized for failing to account for development:

> Yet, the lack of success they experience in modeling developmental mechanisms should make one pause. For as long as they fail to model the properties of a constructive self-regulating system of schemes with abstract properties that progressively integrate the results of the child's experience into existing structures, they will continue to rediscover radical empiricism and nativism. (Beilin, 1983, p. 34)

Perhaps this constitutes the strongest similarity between Piagetian theory and information processing: both have been criticized for failing to attend to explanatory mechanisms!

Siegler and Shipley (this volume) directly acknowledge Beilin's criticism in introducing the section of their chapter in which they discuss "a computer simulation of addition that incorporates learning and performance mechanisms into a single model" (p. 95). As noted in the introduction to the current chapter, it is Siegler and Shipley's direct acknowledgment of this issue and their attempt to deal with it that make their chapter an especially valuable contribution. The mechanisms they present are thus considered below, again, with particular attention to how they compare to mechanisms proposed in Piagetian theory.

Specified Causal Mechanisms

The developmental analysis of Siegler and Shipley's formulation must begin with the distribution of associations because the child's behavior, or "strategy choice" is ultimately determined by this parameter: "within the model, errors, solution times, and overt strategy use are all functions of a single variable: the distribution of associations between problems and potential answers" (Siegler & Shipley, this volume, pp. 74–75). The impact of the distributions of associations may be seen most easily by comparing patterns of performance on problems for which the child has a flat distribution (i.e., one in which several answers have relatively similar association strengths) versus performance on problems for which the child has a peaked distribution (i.e., one in which most association strength is concentrated in a single answer). The specific differences in patterns of performance are explained in detail in Siegler and Shipley (see especially pp. 82–83), and are summarized by them as follows: "As children's distributions of associations become increasingly peaked, they rely increasingly on retrieval, advance the correct answer more often, and answer more quickly. In short, their performance becomes increasingly adultlike" (p. 89). Once having proposed that the differences in patterns of performance are attributable to differences in the degree to which distributions of associations are peaked, the significant question evolves into why problems *have* different distributions of associations. The developmental question, in turn, becomes why these distributions change over time: "How do some problems come to have peaked distributions and others flat ones? Siegler and Shrager hypothesized that children associate whatever answer they state with the problem on which they state it. Therefore, the issue reduce[s] to why children state certain answers to certain problems" (pp. 91–92). Siegler and Shipley hypothesize that three factors are influential: "preexisting associations from the counting string, frequency of exposure to each problem, and the sum of the addends" (p. 92).

First, consider pre-existing associations from the counting string. These associations are such that any given number has a strong association to the next whole number. As a consequence, when the counting string associations control the child's responses to addition problems, they will increase the likelihood of a correct response for "1+" problems (e.g., "1 + 3" "1 + 6") because the number following the second addend in the counting string, as well as the correct answer, are identical (i.e., 4 and 7 in the previous examples). Under the same circumstances, however, these associations will *decrease* the likelihood of a correct response on other ascending series problems (i.e., problems other than "+1" problems in which the second addend is greater than the first, such as "2 + 3"). Siegler and Shipley report that on the latter kind of ascending series problems:

> the most frequent error made by 4- and 5-year-olds on retrieval trials was to say that the answer was the number one greater than the second addend. . . . The result suggested that such problems triggered associations with children's knowledge of the counting string. The children momentarily forgot that they were adding and reverted to the better known procedure for counting. (pp. 92–93)

The child thus appears to be at the mercy of well-established routines that may be mindlessly triggered by hearing the name of a particular digit. Such an influence has a strongly mechanistic, associationistic, reflexive nature to it, and is apparently devoid of deeper levels of cognitive processing. It might be noted that the earlier discussion of "familiar" versus "unfamiliar" tasks is relevant here because it is precisely an attempt to avoid accessing automatic responses of this kind that presumably led Piaget to select tasks that had *not* been encountered before. Thus, it is not so much that an alternative view of the influence of the counting string would be offered by Piagetian theory, but rather that its impact would be reduced by selecting different kinds of tasks.

Differences in the two theoretical approaches may also be seen by considering a second factor identified by Siegler and Shipley—the sum of the addends. This factor concerns a characteristic of the problem per se apart from the child's experiences with them. Piaget, too, recognized that task difficulty could vary in relation to task characteristics. With respect to seriation, for example, Piaget (1952) noted that a child who could not order 10 sticks might succeed with 3 or 4. Similarly, children who cannot conserve number with 7 or 8 items might well be able to conserve number with small sets that can be encompassed within the limits of subitization. It is noteworthy that when considered from this perspective, the work of Gelman and Gallistel (1978) showing preschoolers' abilities to deal with very small numbers is consistent with, rather than contradictory to, Piaget's original work. Piaget's use of larger sets is attributable to his interest in testing the boundaries of children's understanding of the concepts in question, boundaries which can be tested only when the perceptual solution to a task is placed in conflict with the mature conceptual solution. Thus, both research traditions acknowledge that tasks that differ quantitatively may elicit different kinds of response strategies, although they choose to focus on somewhat different implications of these task differences.

The third factor identified by Siegler and Shipley—frequency of exposure to each problem—is probably the most interesting of the three to consider with respect to a comparison of the two theoretical approaches. Siegler and Shipley suggest that "parents, teachers, and other children may present some problems more often than others" (p. 93). They test this hypothesis empirically by bringing parents into the lab, and asking them to teach their own 2- to 4-year-old children "to solve addition problems, as they might at home." Consistent with their expectations, Siegler and Shipley found that the distributions of problems presented by parents were not random, but instead fit nicely with the data from children's patterns of performance on addition problems. That is, there was a significant correlation between the children's accuracy and parents' presentation patterns: problems that parents presented more often were the problems that children were more likely to solve correctly.

What makes Siegler and Shipley's presentation of this factor particularly interesting from the perspective of a comparison with a Piagetian approach, is the strikingly passive picture of the child it paints. There are at least two alternative interpretations of the differential exposure notion that would credit children themselves with some of the responsibility for differential exposure to different addition problems. One alternative would still invoke parental input, but in a manner that simultaneously acknowledges the child's input into the process. That is, one might suggest that parents' and teachers' problem selections are influenced by their sensitivity to the child's understanding of number (much as language input via "motherese" is conceptualized in language development literature). An even more self-directive view of differential frequencies of exposure would posit that children self-present problems differentially. This interpretation fits more comfortably within the Genevan tradition, in which children are viewed as active constructors of their own knowledge. Sinclair (this volume) provides excellent examples of self-presentation of numerical problems in describing a variety of behaviors of Katya, a 4-year-old girl. This description emphasizes the self-motivated, constructive, cognitive struggle in learning something about number and thus stands in sharp contrast to the associationistic picture painted by Siegler and Shipley in which the child is viewed primarily not a problem seeker, but rather the passive recipient of externally provided problems.

Unspecified Causal Mechanisms

Siegler and Shipley are highly specific about the three mechanisms just discussed. There remains, however, a substantial degree of mystery concerning the origins of the observed strategies and the organization of the flow chart that moves the child *through* these strategies. The closest that Siegler and Shipley come to specifying the establishment of these strategies and their hierarchical arrangement (see flow charts in Siegler & Shipley, this volume) is by analogy to the computer simulation. In the simulation, the initial state of the process includes these strategies and rules for their execution: "Biology has given it the ability to retrieve information from memory. Direct instruction and modeling have taught it to put up fingers (or their equivalent) and count them" (p. 95).

Interestingly, although there is room in the model for individual differences in the numbers assigned to various parameters (e.g., the probability of executing one last retrieval; the amount of exposure to problems in the domain, see Siegler, 1986), the *organization* of the flow chart appears to be identical across individuals. Only the preference for external versus internal representations appears to be open to individual variation. Thus, although the responses produced by the system will vary as a function of the particular confidence criteria and search lengths that are set by particular children in particular settings, the available strategies and their organization are comparable across settings and appear to be directly wired into the system from the start. As noted by Beilin (1985a), the nativist solution to the issue of origins is not an uncommon one among those identified with the information-processing position.

Although Siegler appears to attribute strategies, organization, and the changes in them to hardwiring, other information-processing theorists—most notably Klahr—have suggested mechanisms for change (in rules and flow chart organization) under the umbrella of "self-modifying systems." Although the focus of the present chapter on Siegler's work precludes a detailed discussion of Klahr's proposals, it is interesting to note that a recent analysis undertaken by Beilin (1985a) led to the conclusion that the self-modifying principles proposed by Klahr are fundamentally associationistic (see, especially, pp. 19–20). Thus, the self-regulating activities such as assimilation, accommodation, and reflective abstraction offered by Piaget, although somewhat ethereal (but decreasingly so, e.g., see Inhelder, Sinclair, & Bovet, 1974; Piaget, 1985), at least offer a true alternative of self-constructive activity to the choices of empiricism and nativism offered—albeit cloaked in contemporary language—in information-processing accounts of cognitive development.

In summary, just as the kinds of unities sought and the purposes they serve differ in Siegler and Shipley's approach from Piaget's, so too, their views of developmental mechanisms are radically different. Piaget's emphasis is on activity, organization, and self-regulated constructions controlled by the child to yield significant developmental change. In contrast, Siegler and Shipley focus almost exclusively on the consequences of externally-determined experiences that are largely beyond the child's own control, and appear to rest on a significant degree of hard-wiring.

DEVELOPMENT AND LEARNING

The concluding section of this chapter focuses directly on the theme of the volume: "Development and Learning: Conflict or Congruence?" Before one can ask whether development and learning are in conflict or congruence, however, it is necessary to define what is meant by each concept, recognizing, of course, that even basic terms used in these definitions may be understood differently depending upon one's research program (see Overton, 1985, pp. 213–216). Following a discussion of these definitional issues, the relationship between development and learning within each theoretical tradition is considered. Finally, issues in cross-theory relationhips are addressed.

Definitions of Development and Learning

Both Piaget and Siegler and Shipley have specifically defined the terms *development* and *learning*. Piaget (1964) defines *development* as "a process which concerns the totality of the structures of knowledge" with the "development of knowledge [as] a spontaneous process, tied to the process of embryogenesis" (p. 8). In contrast, he defines *learning* as:

> the opposite case. In general, learning is provoked by situations—provoked by a psychological experimenter; or by a teacher, with respect to some didactic point; or by an external situation. It is provoked, in general, as opposed to spontaneous. In addition, it is a limited process—limited to a single problem, or to a single structure. (p. 8)

More recently, Piaget (1970) has contrasted learning and development by suggesting that the term *learning:*

> is restricted to denote essentially exogenous acquisitions, where either the subject repeats responses, parallel to the repetition of external sequences (as in condition-

ing), or the subject discovers a repeatable response by using the regular sequences generated by some device, without having to structure or reorganize them himself through a constructive step-by-step activity (instrumental learning). (p. 713)

In contrast, *development* concerns:

> *invention* and not . . . mere copying. And neither stimulus–response generalization nor the introduction of transformational responses can explain novelty or invention. By contrast, the concepts of assimilation and accommodation and of operational structures (which are created, not merely discovered, as a result of the subject's activities), are oriented toward this inventive construction which characterizes all living thought. (p. 714)

In short, the core of the contrast between the two concepts is the constructive, broad, spontaneous, structural nature of change in development, compared to the exogenously given, narrow, provoked, nonstructural nature of learning.

Siegler and Shipley (this volume) distinguish learning and development with respect to four dimensions. Learning is said to refer to changes that (a) take place over short periods, (b) occur in adults, (c) apply to restricted domains, and (d) do not depend on a maturational base. Development, in contrast, is said to refer to (a) changes that take place over long periods, (b) occur in children, (c) apply to extensive domains, and (d) have (or are suspected to have) a maturational base.

Any one of these definitional criteria could itself be the subject of an entire paper. The distinction between changes in children versus adults, for example, would be vehemently rejected by life-span developmental psychologists who have argued convincingly that development continues beyond adolescence (e.g., Perry, 1970). Similarly, the question of whether or not there is a maturational base is problematic as soon as one begins considering the interactions between maturational and experiential factors such as those studied in the field of developmental psychobiology (e.g., see Gottlieb, 1983). Without evaluating each of these criteria in detail, however, it is still possible to characterize them as criteria that distinguish development from learning primarily with respect to different *domains* of application rather than different processes.

The Relationship Between Development and Learning

Given that the terms development and learning are used so differently in the two theories, it is necessary to consider first the relationship between development and learning *within* each theory separately.

Siegler and Shipley (this volume), once having defined the terms as explained here, directly address the relationship as follows:

> These definitional distinctions are useful in explicating some of the considerations that lead us to apply one label or the other to particular intellectual changes.

However, they are only tangentially related to an issue that is near the heart of the learning/development distinction: the similarity or difference of the cognitive mechanisms that produce the changes that we call learning and development. . . . How can the similarity or difference of such cognitive mechanisms be established? Ideally, we would be in a position to compare the cognitive mechanisms involved in tasks classified as *learning* with those involved in tasks classified as *development*. . . . Once investigators have performed a number of [analyses of processes] in situations said to involve learning and situations said to involve development, it is possible to compare the proposed mechanisms and establish dimensions of similarity and difference. (pp. 71–72)

There are several noteworthy features of this statement. First, it posits that the relationship between development and learning—like the generation of models in the first place—is ultimately an empirical question. Second, although Siegler and Shipley argue that the learning versus development issue can be resolved by a collection of analyses of "situations said to involve learning and situations said to involve development," they fail to categorize the cases *they* study as examples of either development or learning, referring to them by the neutral term "cognitive change" (p. 72)! Perhaps classifications of *situations* is not possible.

A far more fundamental issue is revealed by a close reading of the above passage, namely that both learning *and* development are conceptualized as *outcomes* rather than as causal *mechanisms*. That is, it is not that learning has led to certain changes, nor that development has led to certain changes, but rather that learning and or development have occurred as the result of "cognitive mechanisms." This means that it is the "cognitive mechanisms" that are at the heart of the theory. These mechanisms are those that were discussed in the preceding section of this chapter. It was concluded that these mechanisms are fundamentally externally driven associations, and as such, seem to fit under the rubric of what is generally referred to as "learning." From this theoretical perspective, then, learning is fundamental. It may sometimes yield "cognitive change" with a limited domain of application, in adults, without an identified or suspected maturational base (referred to by Siegler and Shipley as "learning"), and it may sometimes yield "cognitive change" which has a broad domain of application, in children, and with an identified or suspected maturational base (referred to as "development"). But in both situations, the primary impetus for change appears to be learning.

In contrast to Siegler and Shipley, Piaget clearly rejects the possibility that development may be viewed as a product of learning exogenously given information. Nevertheless, like Siegler and Shipley, Piaget may also be said to view development as an *outcome,* insofar as he specified four causes *of* development: maturation, experience with objects, social experience, and equilibration (Piaget, 1964, 1970). Thus, just as it was necessary to examine the characteristics of "cognitive mechanisms" posited by Siegler and Shipley to interpret their position, it is likewise necessary to examine the four factors offered by Piaget.

The most critical factor of these is equilibration, since it regulates the other three. Piaget and Inhelder (1969) define equilibration as:

> An internal mechanism [which] is observable at the time of each partial construc-
> tion and each transition from one stage to the next. It is a process of equi-
> librium . . . in the sense . . . of self regulation; that is, a series of active compen-
> sations on the part of the subject in response to external disturbances and an
> adjustment that is both retroactive (loop systems or feedbacks) and anticipatory,
> constituting a permanent system of compensations. (p. 157)

Several aspects of this definition are particularly important for the present discussion. First, the equilibration mechanism is an internal, self-regulating one. The impetus for this process is found in the invariant function of adaptation, a biologically given goal of all living organisms. Although the drive to achieve balance may be biological in origin, the source of imbalance and the actual activities used to compensate for that imbalance are attributable to the individual's own constructions, rather than to a biological legacy.

A second key feature of the definition of equilibration is that it invokes the role of assimilative and accommodative processes in its reference to "active compensations." Any behavior "is always grafted onto previous schemes and therefore amounts to assimilating new elements to already constructed structures (innate, as reflexes are, or previously acquired)" (Piaget, 1970, p. 707). Although assimilation permits the integration of new elements into the existing structure, it is accommodation that allows developmental progress through the modification of the structures used in assimilation. Importantly, both processes are activities of the organism, not externally determined mechanisms.

Third, as implied by the reference to "each partial construction" as well as to "each transition from one stage to the next," the processes described operate at both ontogenetic and microgenetic levels. Finally, the reference to both "anticipatory" and "retroactive" compensations implies that perturbations may be initiated by either external or internal conflict. These characteristics of the equilibration process make it clear that the acquisition—or, more properly within Piagetian theory, the *construction*—of knowledge is actively controlled by the individual.

At first glance, the remaining three factors proposed by Piaget as responsible for development (maturation; experience with objects; social experience) might appear comparable to the maturational and learning mechanisms proposed in standard nativist and empiricist theories, respectively. But, because the equilibration process regulates the functioning of these remaining three factors, even these biological and environmental factors must be interpreted within an active-organism framework.

Maturation, for example, "simply indicates whether or not the construction of a specific structure is possible at a specific stage. It does not itself contain a preformed structure, but simply opens up possibilities" (Piaget, 1971, p. 193). Just as maturation provides the child with the biological (physical and physiological) material to use in actively constructing knowledge, so too, the environment provides experiential raw material for growth. This material is not, however, simply given in some prestructured form. Instead, the child uses the environmental aliment in the active, self-driven construction of knowledge.

Piaget's constructivist interpretation of the effect of functioning in the environment is nowhere more obvious than in his discussion of what the child derives from experience with physical objects. The child gains not only "physical knowledge" (knowledge of the properties of objects themselves) derived through the process of empirical abstraction, but also "logicomathematical knowledge" (knowledge about activities or operations performed *on* objects) derived through the process of reflective abstraction. Clearly, logicomathematical knowledge cannot be said to reside in the environment, nor to be presented directly by it, and thus it stands in sharp contrast to the environmentally determined experiences (such as exposure to particular addition problems) emphasized by Siegler and Shipley.

The preceding discussion concerned factors said by Piaget (1964) to cause *development*. Since he recognizes something called "learning" as well, it is relevant to ask what factors are responsible for *it*. Piaget (1970) alludes to the classic learning mechanisms (e.g., reinforcement), but minimizes the impact of the mindless acquisition of information through rote associations: "learning under external reinforcement (e.g., permitting the subject to observe the results of the deduction he should have made or informing him verbally) produces either very little change in logical thinking or a striking momentary change with no real comprehension" (p. 714). For learning to be meaningful, it must take place in the context of understanding, i.e., of assimilation to the child's current cognitive structure. By conceptualizing learning in this way, even exogenously given (i.e., not self-discovered) information must be viewed as dependent upon the knower: "To summarize, learning appears to depend on the mechanisms of development and to become stable only insofar as it utilizes certain aspects of these mechanisms, the instruments of quantification themselves, which would have evolved in the course of spontaneous development" (Piaget, 1970, p. 717).

The differences in approaches may be seen in the way in which each theorist conceptualizes the process of acquiring information from the environment. For Siegler, the first step is one of internalizing information that is in the stimulus, and then acting upon it. For Piaget, the first step is the assimilative process through which that environmental aliment may be filtered. In analyzing young children's failures on the balance beam problem, for example, Siegler (1981) suggests that the child has failed to *encode* the two relevant dimensions simultaneously (i.e., distance from the fulcrum and weight). If those two dimensions could be encoded, he hypothesizes, then the child could combine them correctly in solving the problem. Thus, it is a failure to encode that is at the heart of the child's difficulty. For Piaget, however, the failure to encode both dimensions simultaneously is the *consequence* of a fundamental cognitive immaturity in the child. That is, the child is unable to coordinate dimensions simultaneously because of the limits of the current logical system: "all learning, even empiricist learning, involves logic. This is true in the sense of an organization of the subject's action as opposed to immediate perception of the external data" (Piaget, 1970, p. 715).

Empirical data concerning the consequences of logical level on all phases of perceiving and storing information, as well as on the progression of current logical structure, have been reviewed in detail elsewhere (Liben, 1981), and thus are not repeated here. It is, however, important to reiterate that the empirical data alone cannot resolve these issues because these data are necessarily interpreted within a theoretical framework. For example, interpretations of the empirical data from "training studies" (see, e.g., Beilin, 1971a, 1971b; Brainerd, 1973, 1978; Kuhn, 1974; Liben, 1981; Overton, 1976; Overton & Newman, 1982; and Strauss, 1972, 1974) provide an especially striking illustration of the radically different conclusions that may be drawn from the identical data set, depending on one's theoretical orientation.

In short, although Siegler and Shipley take a "wait and see" attitude pending more empirical data with respect to whether or not "development" and "learning" are ultimately attributable to the same cognitive mechanisms, they themselves invoke externally given input as causal mechanisms. Associationistic learning has primacy in their approach. In contrast, in Piagetian theory even "learning" is hypothesized to take place in the context of the individual's own constructive processes. Thus, for Piaget, developmental processes are central, and learning is derived.

Development and Learning: Conflict or Congruence?

Having discussed the relationship between development and learning *within* each of the two theoretical approaches, it is possible to return to the cross-theory issues raised initially in this chapter. Do the two theories offer the same kinds of explanations for the phenomena of cognitive development?

While the concepts of "learning" and "development" appear in both Siegler's and Piaget's approaches, it has been argued that each theorist uses the concepts differently in the interpretation of what is ultimately responsible for cognitive change. The argument has been that for Siegler, cognitive growth is, in the end, attributable to externally provided experiences that change associations, a process that appears to be close to what is traditionally meant by *learning*. In contrast, Piaget sees cognitive growth as ultimately attributed to the constructive, self-regulatory processes that might be called *development*.

If one contrasts the fundamental processes of the two theories against one another, that is, "development" in Piaget's theory against the "learning" of Siegler's approach, they are surely *not* congruent concepts. They are not congruent, because they focus on radically different processes—internal, constructive, and self-regulating versus external, preformed, and passive. Neither can they be interpreted as conflicting because while they have different foci, neither precludes the other. How, then, *can* the relationship between the two be characterized?

One possibility is that the two are complementary, with each applicable to somewhat different contents. Indeed, Siegler and Shipley (this volume) suggest that their approach is especially well-suited to studying "the development of skills in classrooms" and that "we may learn a great deal about cognitive change processes by including the acquisition of academic skills within the purview of cognitive development" (p. 106).

It is not, however, simply a "schooled" versus "unschooled" boundary along which the applications of the two theoretical approaches divide. The externally motivated mechanisms studied by Siegler are relevant for particular *types* of school instruction, that is, for instruction which is aimed at the child's acquisition of pre-formulated pieces of information (as in rote memorization of the multiplication tables). The internally regulated mechanisms addressed by Piaget are applicable to school instruction that is aimed at having children discover principles. The curriculum described by Strauss (this volume), as well as other curricula designed by educators working within a constructive framework (e.g., Forman & Kuschner, 1978; Kamii & DeVries, 1978) exemplify this kind of instruction. In short, although the two foci do appear to be applicable to different domains, it is the *type* of learning process, rather than the context in which it is learned, that divides the domains of application of the two theoretical approaches.

Yet another way to relate the different foci of Siegler and Shipley and Piaget is by fitting them into the broader level of what Lakatos (1978) refers to as *scientific research programs*. Using Lakatos' concept of alternative scientific research programs, Overton (1985) argues that one class of theories—those falling within the organismic approach—gives scientific legitimacy to both competence and performance constructs, whereas another class of theories—those within the mechanistic approach—focuses on observable (performance) entities only. Because organismic theories allow for both formal and contingent explanations, whereas mechanistic theories rely upon contingent explanations only, the former may be conceptualized as encompassing the latter. Insofar as Siegler's approach is, as argued here, essentially a mechanistic one, it can likewise be viewed as understandable and hence subsumed within the Piagetian approach, although the reverse would not hold.

When viewed from this perspective, it becomes clear that information processing *cannot* be viewed as a tight rendition of Piagetian theory. Thus, the characterization of the information-processing approach as providing: "the microscopic level of analysis that . . . fills in the details that the Piagetian approach does not provide'' (Sternberg, 1984, pp. xiii-ix), can be considered true *only* insofar as one recognizes that such details pertain to a very restricted subset of the concepts within Piagetian theory.

In summary, the approaches of Piaget and Siegler may be distinguished on the basis of the relevant domain of application and with respect to their umbrella scientific research programs. The domains differ in the sense that whereas Piaget's work is more applicable to understanding the ways in which children acquire knowledge in a self-regulated, constructive manner, Siegler's work is more applicable to understanding the ways in which children absorb information presented to them. The research programs differ with respect to the types of causal factors they invoke. Most importantly, at least as now developed, even the so-called developmental processes offered within Siegler's approach remain fundamentally externally driven, and associationistic rather than self-generated.

SUMMARY AND CONCLUSIONS

First, it was argued that a gross content analysis of the classic *Handbook* of developmental psychology (Mussen, 1983) does not provide support for the assertion that Piagetian theoretical and empirical work have been displaced by information processing. More importantly, a conceptual analysis of Siegler's recent work suggests that there are very fundamental differences between his approach and Piaget's. These differences are evident in the derivation, function, and content domains of "unities" of development offered by the two approaches. They are also evident in the mechanisms that are postulated to be at the core of cognitive progress: in Siegler's work these mechanisms are fundamentally externally derived, passive, and associationistic, while in Piagetian theory they are fundamentally internally driven, active, and constructive.

The final section of the chapter was addressed specifically to the theme of the present volume, that is, to the relationship between development and learning. Although each theoretical system begins with different definitions of these terms, it was argued that these definitional differences are not as critical as it might first appear, because in both approaches, still more fundamental processes are postulated as *causes* of cognitive progress. A closer examination of these causes in Siegler's work led back to the earlier discussion of "cognitive mechanisms," in which it had been concluded that the mechanisms ultimately invoked to account for progress were externally driven. An examination of the analogous causes in Piagetian theory (i.e., equilibration, maturation, experience with objects, and social experience) led to the conclusion that even those factors that might appear to be biologically or environmentally determined are actually internally driven and constructive because of the overriding control of the equilibration process.

If the question about the relationship between development and learning is interpreted as a question about the relationship between the developmental processes posited by Piaget versus the learning processes posited by Siegler, it is clear that the two cannot be considered congruent. Given that the two are not mutually exclusive, however, they need not be interpreted as in conflict. Alternative relationships between these two theoretical approaches were examined.

It was argued that from the perspective of the domains of application, the two may be considered to be complementary systems, with Siegler's conceptualization being narrowly applicable to understanding the child's acquisition of information that is presented in a prestructured format, and with Piaget's conceptualization being broadly applicable to the child's self-construction of knowledge. From the perspective of scientific programs of research, the two may be viewed as incorporating different kinds of explanation: contingent in Siegler, and both contingent and formal in Piaget. From this perspective, the Piagetian approach may be viewed as more inclusive than Siegler's.

Before closing, it must be noted again that the current chapter focuses on only one particular information-processing approach. Whether or not this analysis may be generalized to other information-processing approaches is itself a controversial issue. Kail (1985), for example, has argued that information-processing theorists diverge in important ways, while Beilin (1983, 1985a) has argued that those working within the information-processing tradition subscribe to fundamentally similar core constructs. Further discussion of the dimensions on which these research programs may be compared is contained in the Epilogue.

In summary, although the contingent explanations of the kind formulated by Siegler contribute in important ways to our understanding of pieces of the child's cognitive development, information-processing approaches of this kind are *not* tight formalizations of Piagetian theory. Rather than displacing the Piagetian approach, they—like learning theory before them—provide an alternative approach for characterizing cognitive development.

ACKNOWLEDGMENTS

I am grateful to Roger Downs, Jean Gascon, David Feldman, Rochel Gelman, Robert Kail, and John Macnamara, who provided extremely valuable and honest comments on an earlier draft of this chapter, and especially to Willis Overton and Harry Beilin, who not only provided such comments, but whose own work has been invaluable in my continual struggle to understand Piagetian theory. None of these colleagues should, however, be held responsible for, nor assumed to agree with the interpretations offered in this chapter.

REFERENCES

Atkinson, R., & Shiffrin, R. (1968). Human memory: A proposed system and its control processes. In K. Spence & J. Spence (Eds.), *The psychology of learning and motivation* (Vol. 11, pp. 89–198). New York: Academic Press.

Baylor, G. W., & Gascon, J. (1974). An information processing theory of aspects of the development of weight seriation in children. *Cognitive Psychology, 6,* 1–40.

Beilin, H. (1971a). Developmental stages and developmental processes. In D. Green, M. Ford, & G. Flamer (Eds.), *Measurement and Piaget* (pp. 172–197). New York: McGraw-Hill.

Beilin, H. (1971b). The training and acquisition of logical operations. In M. Rosskopf, L. Steffe, & S. Taback (Eds.), *Piagetian cognitive-development research and mathematical education* (pp. 81–124). Washington, DC: National Council of Teachers of Mathematics.

Beilin, H. (1983). The new functionalism and Piaget's program. In E. K. Scholnick (Ed.), *New trends in conceptual representation: Challenges to Piaget's theory?* (pp. 3–40). Hillsdale, NJ: Lawrence Erlbaum Associates.

Beilin, H. (1985a). Current trends in cognitive development research: Toward a new synthesis. *Cahiers de la Fondation Archives Jean Piaget,* Geneva.

Beilin, H. (1985b). Dispensable and indispensable elements in Piaget's theory: On the core of Piaget's research program. In T. S. Evans (Ed.), *Genetic epistemology: Yesterday and today* (pp. 107–125). New York: City University of New York.

Brainerd, C. J. (1973). Neo-Piagetian training experiments revisited: Is there any support for the cognitive-developmental stage hypothesis? *Cognition, 2,* 349–370.

Brainerd, C. J. (1978). The stage question in cognitive-developmental theory. *The Behavioral and Brain Sciences, 2,* 173–213.

Dean, A. L., Chabaud, S., & Bridges, E. (1981). Classes, collections, and distinctive features: Alternative strategies for solving inclusion problems. *Cognitive Psychology, 13,* 84–112.

Fischer, K. W. (1980). A theory of cognitive development: The control and construction of hierarchies of skills. *Psychological Review, 87,* 477–531.

Forman, G., & Kuschner, D. (1978). *The child's construction of knowledge.* Monterey: Brooks Cole.

Gagné, R. M. (1968). Contributions of learning to human development. *Psychological Review, 75,* 177–191.

Gascon, J. (1969). *Modele cybernetique d'une seriation de poids chez les enfants.* Unpublished master's thesis, University of Montreal.

Gelman, R., & Gallistel, C. R. (1978). *The child's understanding of number.* Cambridge, MA: Harvard University Press.

Gottlieb, G. (1983). The psychobiological approach to developmental issues. In P. H. Mussen (Ed.), *Handbook of child psychology* (Vol. II, pp. 1–26). New York: Wiley.

Hanson, N. R. (1958). *Patterns of discovery.* London & New York: Cambridge University Press.

Hilgard, E. R. (1956). *Theories of learning* (2nd ed.). New York: Appleton-Century-Crofts.

Inhelder, B., Sinclair, H., & Bovet, M. (1974). *Learning and the development of cognition.* Cambridge, MA: Harvard University Press.

Kail, R. V., Jr. (1985). Why does thinking develop? The information-processing answer(s). *Contemporary Psychology, 30,* 611–612.

Kail, R. V., Jr., & Hagen, J. W. (1977). *Perspectives on the development of memory and cognition.* Hillsdale, NJ: Lawrence Erlbaum Associates.

Kamii, C., & DeVries, R. (1978). *Physical knowledge in preschool education.* Englewood Cliffs, NJ: Prentice-Hall.

Klahr, D., & Wallace, J. G. (1976). *Cognitive development.* Hillsdale, NJ: Lawrence Erlbaum Associates.

Kuhn, D. (1974). Inducing development experimentally: Comments on a research paradigm. *Developmental Psychology, 10,* 590–600.

Kuhn, T. S. (1962). *The structure of scientific revolutions.* Chicago: University of Chicago Press.

Lakatos, I. (1978). *The methodology of scientific research programmes: Philosophical papers* (Vol. 1). Cambridge: Cambridge University Press.

Laudan, L. (1977). *Progress and its problems: Towards a theory of scientific growth.* Berkeley, CA: University of California Press.

Lewis, M. (1983). Newton, Einstein, Piaget, and the concept of self: The role of the self in the process of knowing. In L. S. Liben (Ed.), *Piaget and the foundations of knowledge* (pp. 141–177). Hillsdale, NJ: Lawrence Erlbaum Associates.

Liben, L. S. (1981). Contributions of individuals to their development during childhood: A Piagetian perspective. In R. M. Lerner & N. A. Busch-Rossnagel (Eds.), *Individuals as producers of their development: A life-span perspective* (pp. 117–153). New York: Academic Press.

Liben, L. S. (in press). Conceptual issues in the development of spatial cognition. In J. Stiles-Davis, M. Kritchevsky, U. Bellugi (Eds.), *Spatial cognition: Brain bases and development.* Hillsdale, NJ: Lawrence Erlbaum Associates.

Macnamara, J. (1984). All about sums. *Contemporary Psychology, 29,* 136–137.

Montangero, J. (1985). The evolution of an evolutionary theory of knowledge: A developmental approach to Piaget's theory. In T. S. Evans (Ed.), *Genetic epistemology: Yesterday and today* (pp. 22–38). New York: City University of New York.

Mussen, P. H. (Ed.). (1983). *Handbook of child psychology.* New York: Wiley.

Ornstein, P. A. (1978). *Memory development in children.* Hillsdale, NJ: Lawrence Erlbaum Associates.

Overton, W. F. (1976). Environmental ontogeny: A cognitive view. In K. F. Riegel & J. A. Meacham (Eds.), *The developing individual in a changing world* (pp. 413–420). Chicago: Aldine.

Overton, W. F. (1984). World views and their influence on psychological theory and research: Kuhn-Lakatos-Laudan. In H. W. Reese (Ed.), *Advances in child development and behavior* (Vol. 18, pp. 191–226). New York: Academic Press.

Overton, W. F. (1985). Scientific methodologies and the competence-performance-moderator issue. In E. D. Neimark, R. De Lisi, J. L. Newman (Eds.), *Moderators of competence* (pp. 15–41). Hillsdale, NJ: Lawrence Erlbaum Associates.

Overton, W. F., & Newman, J. L. (1982). Cognitive development: A competence-activation/utilization approach. In T. Field, A. Huston, H. Quay, L. Troll, & G. Finley (Eds.), *Review of human development* (pp. 217–241). New York: Wiley.

Perry, W. D. (1970). *Forms of ethical and intellectual development in the college years: A scheme.* New York: Holt, Rinehart & Winston.

Piaget, J. (1952). *The child's conception of number.* New York: Norton.

Piaget, J. (1964). Development and learning. In R. Ripple & V. Rockcastle (Eds.), *Piaget rediscovered* (pp. 7–19). Ithaca: Cornell University Press.

Piaget, J. (1970). Piaget's theory. In P. Mussen (Ed.), *Carmichael's manual of child psychology* (pp. 703–732). New York: Wiley.

Piaget, J. (1971). Comments on developmental stages and developmental processes. In D. Green, M. Ford, & G. Flamer (Eds.), *Measurement and Piaget* (pp. 192–194). New York: McGraw Hill.

Piaget, J. (1985). *The equilibration of cognitive structures.* Chicago: University of Chicago Press.

Piaget, J., & Inhelder, B. (1969). *The psychology of the child.* New York: Basic Books.

Siegler, R. S. (1976). Three aspects of cognitive development. *Cognitive Psychology, 8,* 481–520.

Siegler, R. S. (1981). Developmental sequences within and between concepts. *Monographs of the Society for Research in Child Development, 46*(189).

Siegler, R. S. (1983). Information processing approaches to development. In P. H. Mussen (Ed.), *Handbook of child psychology* (Vol. I, pp. 129–210). New York: Wiley.

Siegler, R. S. (1986). Unities across domains in children's strategy choices. In M. Perlmutter (Ed.), *Perspectives for intellectual development: The Minnesota Symposia on Child Psychology* (Vol. 19, pp. 1–48). Hillsdale, NJ: Lawrence Erlbaum Associates.

Siegler, R. S., & Robinson, M. (1982). The development of numerical understandings. In H. W. Reese & L. P. Lipsitt (Eds.), *Advances in child development and behavior* (pp. 241–312). New York: Academic Press.

Siegler, R. S., & Shrager, J. (1984). A model of strategy choice. In C. Sophian (Ed.), *Origins of cognitive skills* (pp. 229–293). Hillsdale, NJ: Lawrence Erlbaum Associates.

Sternberg, R. J. (Ed.). (1984). *Mechanisms of cognitive development.* New York: Freeman.

Strauss, S. (1972). Inducing cognitive development and learning: A review of short-term training experiments. *Cognition, 1,* 329–357.

Strauss, S. (1974). A reply to Brainerd. *Cognition, 3,* 155–185.

6

Educational–Developmental Psychology and School Learning

Sidney Strauss
Tel-Aviv University School of Education

This chapter describes a middle-level model of educational–developmental psychology that allows investigators to have their work informed by developmental psychology and, at the same time, to have their research impact upon education theory and practice. The model presented views developmental and educational psychology as two sides of the same coin, with both sides informing each other. Aspects of this model also deal with development and learning.

I have three parameters in mind when using the term *middle level*. The first is the length of time over which cognitive change takes place. I begin by describing what it isn't. It is not long-term ontogenetic development that takes place over a span of 4 or 5 years, as in the Piagetian stages. It is also not short-term change that could occur in a matter of minutes, as in the case of learning studies. Middle-level change occurs over days, weeks, or months, yet it is developmental in that it involves a reorganization of knowledge.

The second parameter is the level of abstraction of the content we intend to teach. This has implications for our ability to change the content in question via intervention. On the one hand, we have general cognitive structures whose development we are unlikely to influence, whereas on the other we have very specific knowledge that we might be able to change, but it is not general and, hence, trivial knowledge for school learning. Middle-level content can be influenced by instruction, yet it is sufficiently general so that it has impact beyond itself (Feldman, 1971).

The third parameter is the model's location on a scale of developmental theory to educational practice. I do not have clear benchmarks for deciding what *theory* is and what *practice* is, but I take the position that theory is general and abstract where situation–specific content varies within the broad framework of the theory's prescriptions. Educational practice is generally situation–specific. In the model I am describing, one consciously attempts to be in the middle between practical educational work and developmental theory. In this view, educational practice informs and is informed by an educational–developmental model which, in turn, informs and is informed by developmental theory.

The work I have been doing in this area has been most influenced by two traditions: those of Piaget and Vygotsky. As for Piaget's psychogenetic model, the method of analyzing concepts and their developmental relations is structuralist in its inspiration, and the role of conflict as a source of development is an important ingredient of the model. As for Vygotsky's sociohistorical model, relations between children's spontaneous common sense, and formal school-learned concepts are central to Vygotsky's work; they occupy my attention as well. In addition, my work has been informed by instructional techniques whose purpose is to move children along a developmental trajectory by means of social transactions between an adult expert and a novice child. My thinking and research about children's developmental change and the social system that augments it bears a large resemblance to work done in the area of the zone of proximal development (Rogoff & Wertsch, 1984; Vygotsky, 1978).

In the remainder of this introduction I lay out and elaborate some of the developmental assumptions of the middle-level model—in particular those pertaining to multiple representations and the role of symbol systems in development—and some educational aspects of the model.

Developmental Assumptions of the Model

A given in the middle-level educational–developmental model is the assumption that children have multiple representations of their knowledge about the world, be it the logical, mathematical, physical, or social world (cf. Bamberger, 1982). These representations have their own developmental courses that, in turn, influence each other at different points and in different ways in the course of their evolution. School instruction, teaching practice, and curriculum development that structure what, and to an extent how children learn should be deeply informed by this quality of multiple representations of experience.

I have found the distinction between spontaneous and scientific (school-learned) concepts made by Vygotsky to be a helpful way to think about the multiple representations I claim to be basic to educational–developmental psychology. (For an important elaboration of this distinction, see Feldman, 1980). Spontaneous concepts are described by Vygotsky as being unconscious, non-reflective, originating in children's personal experiences, nonsystematic, and not in need of instruction to be constructed mentally. An example of this kind of concept is children's understanding of temperature and heat. Children directly experience objects at different temperatures. They play with water in their bathtubs or at the sink and in those situations they may add hot water, thus making it warmer or they may add colder water, making it colder. Children also know that water being heated on the stove makes it hotter and that ice cubes added to water cool it off. As we see, this spontaneous knowledge of temperature, whose origins are in children's personal experiences with the physical world, are not terribly systematic.

School-learned concepts are thought by Vygotsky to be conscious, reflective, originating in the classroom (or in an informal educational setting), systematic, and in need of instruction to be learned. Once again, I use the concepts of heat and temperature as examples to clarify matters. Here, thermal equilibrium (two objects at different temperatures and in contact with each other eventually arrive at the same temperature via heat exchange), or the quantification of temperature in degrees and heat in calories are examples of school-learned concepts. It is difficult to imagine how children could construct these concepts from experiences with physical reality without having instruction. They are the concepts that are created in laboratories and libraries, are passed from generation to generation through instruction as part of our cultural heritage, and form the basis for what we teach in our schools and universities.

In my educational work, I have added another dimension to this categorization of concepts: the nature of the symbolic system in which these concepts are presented by the experimenter and represented by children. Consider, for example, presenting children with the following situation: Two cups of equal amounts of same-temperature water (say, hot) are poured into a third, empty container. We ask them to tell us what the temperature of the mixed water is and they generally tell us that it is the same temperature or it is hotter than the water in the original cups. Here the children are given an everyday situation where the question is presented qualitatively (hot) and via an ordinal scale (hotter, colder) and they represent it qualitatively via an ordinal scale (same, hotter).

Now let us take the exact same task but instead of asking qualitative questions we ask questions in numerical terms. We tell the children that the water in both cups has been measured with a thermometer to be 60°C and, after pouring the water into the third, empty cup we ask them to tell us the temperature of the mixed water. Here the question is asked in numerical terms and the measuring instrument is based on an interval scale. As we see, children represent this question numerically and understand (incorrectly) that the numbers are to be added.

The point I am making here is that there is an additional layer of complexity in the classification of spontaneous and school-learned concepts, namely, the symbolic system in which the problems are presented and represented. In the case I just presented, spontaneous concepts are qualitative and school-learned concepts, when the content is science, are often presented via their numerical descriptions. These symbolic systems have their own characteristics and they, too, have developmental courses (Gardner, 1983).

I would like to slightly extend the notion of qualitative and numerical symbolic systems via a viewpoint that resembles Carnap's (1966). He argues that the differences between qualitative and numerical concepts are not differences in nature, but differences in the language (symbolic systems) we use to describe them. Neither our observations of phenomena of nature nor the phenomena themselves are qualitative or numerical; instead, the language we use to describe these phenomena can be considered qualitative or numerical. Our temperature task is a case in point. The exact same task was presented twice; in both cases water was poured from two cups into a third, empty cup. The physical phenomenon in both tasks was identical. What makes one task qualitative and the other numerical is the language we use when we present the task. The developmental course of solutions to these two tasks, then, represent the mental evolution of children's grappling with the same conceptual content that is clothed in different symbol systems.

Until now I have discussed Vygotsky's positions about spontaneous versus school-learned concepts. I now briefly present how they are connected, and in Vygotsky's perspective, their relationship is etched in their developmental origins and courses. Vygotsky views spontaneous and school-learned concepts as two sides of a single process of concept development. But to say that they are a single process does not mean that they are identical. Instead, Vygotsky argues that spontaneous and school-learned concepts have different origins (personal experience in the case of spontaneous concepts and the classroom experiences in the case of school-learned concepts). They also have different developmental courses. He writes about the two kinds of concepts developing in reverse directions with spontaneous concepts developing upwards and the development of school-learned concepts proceeding downwards, and he creates a lovely image of each clearing the way for the other. Today, the former is called *data driven* and its processing would be bottom up and the latter is called *theory driven* and its processing would be top down.

The general view presented by Vygotsky is one of dynamic development with intertwining connections made between these two kinds of concepts. Both spontaneous and school-learned concepts have their own developmental paths yet, because they are two sides of the process of conceptual development, their development and functioning influence each other's evolution. I take a similar position in this chapter and use the concepts of temperature and the arithmetic average both as illustrations of these ideas and as a means to describe the middle-level model of educational–developmental that is based on these and other developmental considerations.

Educational Aspects of the Model

It was over 50 years ago that Vygotsky (1934/1962) made a pronouncement that could serve us well today:

To devise successful methods of instructing the schoolchild in systematic knowledge, it is necessary to understand the development of scientific concepts in the
child's mind. No less important than this practical aspect of the problem is its
theoretical significance for psychological science. Yet our knowledge of the entire
subject is scanty. (p. 82)

Few have said it better, 50 years ago or today but, unfortunately, our knowledge
of the entire subject still remains scanty.

Vygotsky went on to pose two questions: "What happens in the mind of the
child to the scientific concepts he is taught at school? What is the relationship
between the assimilation of information and the internal development of a scientific concept in the child's consciousness?" (p. 82). I understand these two
questions to have several parts. The first is: What do children understand of the
scientific concepts they are taught in school? The second is: Are there any
general rules describing how children alter the teacher's (curriculum's) concepts?
A third question is: Does learning scientific concepts, as taught in school, alter
children's everyday, common sense, spontaneous understanding of the same
concepts? The fourth question reverses the third by asking if children's common
sense, spontaneous understanding influences the way they learn the scientific
concepts taught in school? I attempt to answer some of these questions in this
chapter.

The position I take here is that children develop multiple representations of
events, but schools generally reward those who succeed with one of them:
school-learned knowledge that is presented via formal, abstract notations, or
symbol systems. To a great extent, curriculum developers and teachers either
ignore children's everyday, common sense knowledge, or they attempt to supplant it. Rather than ignoring or attempting to remove children's everyday,
common sense understandings of their world, we can work with them as a means
to help organize the more abstract, formal representations of the same or different events. In this way we can have them engage and inform each other, with
each supplementing the other.

These considerations can be taken into account in curriculum development,
but they must be informed by work on normative development and transitions.
Without a clear understanding of developmental landmarks of children's normative, common sense understanding of specific concepts (that are taught in
school), we will not be in a position to insightfully determine the sequence and
timing of instruction for the same concepts.

Similarly, without a model of how development takes place, we will be hard-
pressed to decide how to foster progressive developmental transitions, which is
one of the goals of education. This is, of course, the question of questions and
developmental theories have come up with different models of how novel knowledge is constructed. In the coming sections I show how two models of conceptual
change have been exploited in training children to come to more accurate and

correct understandings of the content of interest: cognitive conflict and analogy training. What underlies both models is the idea that one uses knowledge that children have already constructed to help them reorganize inadequate knowledge in the same or other domains.

In addition, a middle-level model of educational–developmental psychology should include a way to decide what kind of content we want to conduct research on and develop curriculum units about. Two criteria for making such a decision are that the content will be taught in school and that it requires instruction to be learned (as in the case of reading, for example) or understood correctly (as in the cases to be discussed in this chapter of temperature and heat, and the arithmetic average, as we see in the present chapter).

Generally, the choice of what is to be taught in the schools has to do with the significance of the concepts in question for a valued discipline of which they are a part (e.g., the concepts of heat and temperature for physics) and/or their generality across domains (e.g., the concepts of the arithmetic average). These are the concepts I have used to make my ideas about learning and development concrete: (a) the physical concepts of temperature and heat, and (b) the statistical concept of the arithmetic average.

TEMPERATURE AND HEAT

The work done on the development of the concepts of temperature and heat, which I now describe, was a joint effort by a team of investigators at Tel-Aviv University (see Strauss, Orpaz, & Stavy, 1977) and the curriculum materials were developed by Stavy, Bar, and Berkowitz within the framework of MATAL: the Tel-Aviv University Elementary School Science Project. I now point out four phases we have identified in curriculum development: (a) assessing the normative development of the concepts of interest for the curriculum unit, (b) training for the difficult concepts, (c) the translation of the findings from the first and second phases into a curriculum unit, and (c) the evaluation of the curriculum unit's effectivess.

The Development of the Concepts of Temperature and Heat

One way of characterizing the differences between temperature and heat is that the former is an *intensive* physical quantity whereas the latter is an *extensive* physical quantity (Carnap, 1966). An intensive physical quantity remains unchanged despite changes in its amount or extensive quantity. To illustrate once again with the task already presented, imagine that we have two containers of water each of which has same-temperature cold water. When we mix the water from the two containers the temperature will remain cold despite the change in the amount of water. In this example, temperature, being an intensive physical quantity, remained unchanged even though the water increased in its extensive quantity (i.e., its amount of heat). Other examples of intensive physical quantities are sugar–water concentrations, viscosity, hardness, and density.

In a recent study, Strauss et al. (1977) investigated the development of children's reasoning about the concepts of temperature and heat. Varying amounts of water were heated by equal and unequal numbers of candles in order to test children's developing understandings of ratio comparisons (e.g., the direct function, inverse function, and proportions). Also, varying amounts of water at the same and different temperatures were mixed, as in the aforementioned example. A review of the findings on the development of children's understandings of these combinations are found in Strauss and Stavy (1982).

For the purposes of illustration, I consider how children at different ages understood the concept of intensive physical quantity (i.e., when same-temperature water was mixed). In one variant of the task just described, two cups (A and B) with water that the experimenter called "cold water that is the same temperature" are poured into a third, empty cup (C) and the child is asked whether the water in cup C is the same temperature as when it was in cups A and B. Very young children from approximately ages 3 to 5 or 6 often judge correctly that the water was the same temperature "because they were the same temperature before and all you did was pour them together." Older children, from ages 5 through 8, produce *incorrect* judgments on the *same* task and judge that the water in cup C is twice as cold because "it has twice the amount of water." Still older children through age 12 produce *correct* judgments and justify them much like the very young children did. The explanation offered for this finding (Strauss & Stavy, 1982) is that the very young children do not attend to the amounts of water (i.e., their extensive quantity); older children do attend to these amounts and judge temperature, an intensive quantity, as if it were an extensive physical quantity; whereas the oldest children separate intensive and extensive physical quantities and apply the respective nonadditivity and additivity appropriately.

This general phenomenon where an initially correct judgment is replaced by an incorrect judgment which, in turn, is replaced by a correct judgment has been termed *U-shaped behavioral growth* and has been documented in a number of cognitive domains (Strauss, 1982).

Another way to represent this same concept of intensive physical quantity is via a numerical representation. For example, we can present children with water in two containers and measure their temperature with a thermometer. Let's say the temperature recorded in each cup was $10°$ C. The water from the two cups is then poured into a third, empty cup and the children are asked to tell us the temperature of the mixed water. The overwhelming majority of children through age 13 answer that the mixed water's temperature was $20°$ C instead of the correct answer of $10°$ C (Strauss et al., 1977). Here it is clear that the children are adding numbers as if the addition models the joining of extensive physical quantities.

These data are interesting in their own right because they address important issues in developmental theory (see Strauss & Stavy, 1982). However, our educational purposes also commit us to gain some understanding of how progressive cognitive development occurs so that we can be informed about how to help children overcome conceptual difficulties they may be encountering. One way to accomplish this is through training studies so as to pick up the developmental complexities in conceptual change.

Conflict Training

The purposes of the second training phase of curriculum development is to devise and test ways of helping children overcome the above mentioned difficulties that were detected in the first phase. This is done with an eye toward incorporating these methods into the curriculum unit itself. Although there are many ways to carry out such work, I concentrate here on the method of inducing cognitive conflict as a means to accomplish the aforementioned.

In the case just provided, there was a conflict between children's qualitative, common sense understandings of temperature and of their understanding of the school-learned number system as they apply it to temperature. Part of the conflict may be due to a confusion on the part of the children between joining and adding (Carnap, 1966; Cohen & Nagel, 1934; Hempel, 1952). Notice that in the case of intensivity tasks, water is being physically joined or combined. Hempel (1952) introduced a symbol for physical joining or combining, a small circle, instead of the plus sign. Hence, $A \circ B$ designates, in our case, mixing water from one cup with water from another cup. In the case of extensive quantity, the arithmetic analogue is "+". The general principle of additivity, with respect to any magnitude, M, can be expressed:

$$M(A \circ B) = M(A) + M(B).$$

The reason for this distinction is that there are two types of additivity: (a) the physical operation of joining or mixing objects; and (b) the arithmetic operation performed on numbers. One does not add lengths or weights. Rather, one adds numbers that represent lengths of lines or weights of objects. Arithmetic operations of addition can be appropriately performed on numbers that represent measures of extensive physical quantities. In other words, arithmetic operations of addition model the physical joining of extensive physical quantities. It may be the case that children attempted to apply this model to numerical intensive physical quantity tasks, thus producing incorrect judgments on them. But, once again, we note that these very same children produced correct judgments when the same task was given but where qualitative language was used.

We measured the effects of conflict training between children's qualitative and numerical representations of intensive physical quantity. The conflict, of course, was between judgments produced by an individual child. This type of conflict, which has been sometimes been termed *organizational disequilibrium conflict,* has been shown to be effective in inducing cognitive change (Snyder & Feldman, 1977; Strauss & Ilan, 1975. For a review of conflict training techniques whose purposes were to induce progressive cognitive advance, see Strauss, 1972). The main reason given for why this type of conflict has been effective is that the child him or herself offers contradictory judgments that result from thought organizations he or she has constructed. This is in contrast to the source of conflict coming from authorities (such as teachers and experimenters) who contradict what children are thinking.

Children from ages 7 to 11 were confronted with contradictions between their own judgments on qualitative and numerical tasks and were asked what they thought about it. One sign, although not a decisive one, that children's qualitative and numerical representations of temperature are different, was that many of the children at all ages found it difficult to understand that the qualitative and numerical versions were the same task asked in different ways. And this despite the fact that we used the same cups and water and even pointedly said, "Now let's take the same cold water and measure its temperature. Here we have cold water at 10° C and here we have cold water at 10° C."

After discussion, children understood that the tasks were the same. We found three age-related responses to the conflict. The first type was found among the youngest children (the 7- and some 8-year-olds) who did not even recognize that a conflict existed and argued that cold water when mixed with cold water remains cold and that the same water when measured to be 10° C and mixed turns out to 20° C. Or as many children stated, "It's different when you have numbers."

The second type of response was found among somewhat older children (8- and 9-year-olds); their response was to change their correct qualitative judgment to an incorrect one by arguing that cold water when mixed with cold water at the same temperature becomes colder. This, of course, puts them in a double bind because they now argue in the qualitative version that the mixed water is colder whereas the numerical equivalent leads to hotter water (20° C being hotter than 10° C). Here we see a drop in performance that results from one representational system that carries with it a set of rules (in this case additivity of numbers being prominent) overriding another representation whose symbol system is different. In this example, the experience-bound common sense notion of temperature as an intensive physical quantity is overridden.

The third response to contradiction was found among the oldest children (many 10-year-olds) who changed their incorrect numerical answers to correct ones (10° C ○ 10° C = 10° C). This seems reasonable enough, but think for a moment about how this comes about. Why should children change their predispositions to add numbers? Why should they recognize that their arithmetic is modeling the wrong physical quantities? I have claimed elsewhere (Strauss &

Stavy, 1982) that in the aforementioned case, a change in children's incorrect answers come about when they consult their correct qualitative understanding of the problem. That is, they must first pay attention to the fact that it is water that is being poured and temperature that is being asked about, and that temperature is not additive. This knowledge is necessary to change incorrect numerical solutions to correct ones. Now we see the interesting developmental phenomenon that the numerical representation that overrode the performance in the qualitative representation (in the second response) becomes reorganized by that very qualitative representation.[1]

The aforementioned study tells us two things. First, it indicates that our technique was successful in inducing conceptual change and it could possibly serve as a model for other experiments involving conflicting qualitative and numerical representations. This point is important for decisions about sequencing within curriculum units. Second, we learned about how children at different ages and with different patterns of reasoning were affected by the training intervention. This point is important for the timing of experiences in curriculum development. In other words, we saw that most 10-year-old children resolved the conflict in a way that led to a correct understanding of both the qualitative and numerical aspects of the tasks. This is a clue for us that a curriculum unit, that attempted to include activities that would exploit the natural conflict between these two ways of representing the environment, should be introduced to classrooms where the children are at least 10-years-old. These two points lead us to the third phase of curriculum development: the design of the curriculum unit itself.

Curriculum Design

Here we have the problem of translating the research results into a curriculum unit. Before discussing how this has been done, I would like to note that a curriculum unit entitled "Temperature" was developed at MATAL—The Tel-Aviv University Elementary School Science Project in 1974 by Stavy, Bar, and Berkowitz. Underlying the unit was the notion that if children have experiences centering on the concept of temperature via verification procedures (such as

---

[1]As an aside in the history of science, it took 150 years from the time that Galileo invented the thermometer until scientists could separate heat from temperature. For an interesting discussion of the history of the differentiation of heat and temperature, see Wiser (in press) and Wiser and Carey (1983). The reason they were able to make that separation was that Black in the mid-18th century had developed a model that made that distinction. But this distinction was not made on the basis of the numerical data generated from using the thermometer; rather, the distinction was made when Black constructed a model of physical reality. Koyré (1968) and Kuhn (1977) have argued forcefully that the relations between theory and measurement are a one-way route. It is rare that theory and conceptual change occur due to results of experimental measurement, and it is generally the case that theory change brings measurement change in its wake.

measuring the temperatures of water with thermometers), improved understanding of the concepts will ensue. For example, if children using a thermometer measure the temperature of water in two containers to be 10° C, and the water is then mixed into a third, empty container and it, too, is found to be 10° C, this verification of the intensive physical quantity should lead to a better understanding of the temperature concept. The actual result in the classroom was that many children thought the thermometer was broken because it was always "stuck at 10° C."

An informal assessment indicated that the children who were taught this unit did no better in solving these temperature tasks than children who received no formal instruction about this concept. In other words, instruction that involved both manipulating materials and assessing their effects was not effective in advancing these children's conceptualizations about temperature. We argue here that a curriculum unit that encourages children's activities and verification experiences, if not based on a thorough understanding of the development of children's competences about the concepts in question, should not be expected to be successful as a teaching instrument.

Armed with this different way of thinking about curriculum development and given our research findings on the development of children's qualitative and numerical understandings of the temperature concept, Stavy, Bar, and Berkowitz attempted to do what we claimed must be done in the third phase (i.e., translate the findings from research into a revised curriculum unit). A typical classroom in Israel has 35–40 children, so whatever unit is constructed must take into account the fact that it is unlikely that a teacher will have an opportunity to pose the problem of conflicting judgments on an individual basis. This means that the conflict should be provoked via questions raised in activities of the curriculum unit that lead children to confront their contradictions, in discussions between children or, preferably, both.

An example of how this was accomplished is illustrated in Fig. 6.1. This figure consists of four pages of a worksheet booklet that was constructed by Jona Collman in such a way that page 1 could be folded back so that the qualitative scale would be aligned with the numerical scale on page 2. The example in the figure is for the mixing of water at unequal temperatures; however, there were also other activities that involved mixing water whose initial temperatures were the same (i.e., intensive quantity tasks).

Notice in the figure that the children were first requested to make a judgment about the temperature that results from mixing equal amounts of hot and cold water and were then requested to make a similar judgment about the mixing of water that was hot and measured to be 90° C and water that was cold and measured to be 10° C. This was done to get the qualitative and numerical representations engaged. Next they were asked if the two questions were the same or not. This was included to get the children to overcome the problem that we had found in our research, namely, many children did not even recognize that

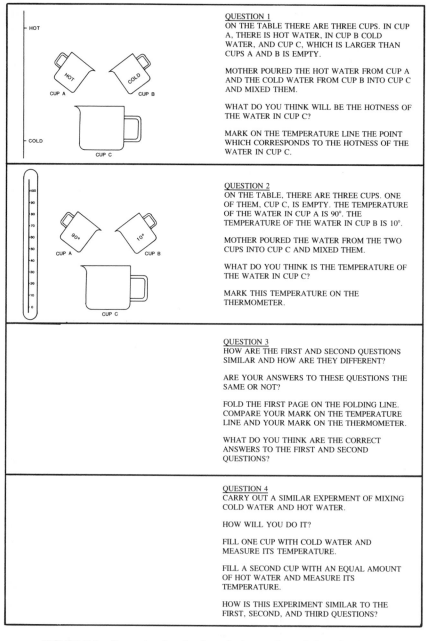

FIGURE 6.1. Example of revised curriculum unit worksheet (on intermediate temperature). Note. This four-page worksheet booklet was constructed so that page 1 could be folded back so that the qualitative scale was aligned with the quantitative scale on page 2.

the qualitative and numerical tasks were the same except for the language being used to describe them. They were then asked to compare their answers by folding page 1 over onto page 2 and to note if there were discrepancies. This was done to indicate to the children the fact that their judgments differed when the tasks were presented qualitatively and numerically. The query about which is the correct answer is a way to have the conflict between judgments made obvious.

The above is an attempt to indicate how research findings from developmental psychology can inform curriculum design. The example given was one of several that attempted to induce cognitive conflict between children's qualitative and numerical representations of the results of mixing same-temperature and different-temperature water. However, it is not enough to note the close relation between results of developmental experiments and the construction of curriculum materials. Because even well-constructed curriculum materials pass the test of being well thought out but are not successful in teaching the concepts of interest, as we saw in the first curriculum unit on "Temperature," this suggests that we need an evaluation of the results from the revised curriculum unit, the subject of the fourth phase of curriculum development.

Evaluation

The results of such an evaluation are found in detail in Stavy and Berkowitz (1980). Seventy-seven children, all of whom were 10 years old, were given pretest items that included mixing equal and unequal amounts of water at the same and different temperatures. This was designed to establish a baseline for placing the children into one of three groups: (a) those who were administered the revised curriculum unit under normal Israeli classroom conditions, (b) those who were given conflict training on an individual basis (i.e., the experimenter gave the conflict training to the individual child), and (c) those who were in a control group. All of the children were given a pretest and two posttests. The first posttest was given immediately after training (except for the control group that had no training) and the second posttest was given 1 month after the first posttest.

The results were that: (a) all of the children were statistically equivalent on their pretest understandings of the qualitative and numerical versions of intensive physical quantities tasks, and tasks measuring the results of mixing water at different temperatures; (b) the classroom-trained and individual-instruction children who learned from the curriculum unit improved their understanding of the numerical aspect of both the intensive quantity and intermediate temperature tasks from the pretest to both posttests; and (c) the control-group children did not improve significantly from the pretest to both posttests. In short, the findings were that the curriculum unit was effective in inducing progressive cognitive change.

To recapitulate, we have shown that curriculum development and developmental psychology can inform each other in such a way that both benefit. The first phase of curriculum development requires basic research into how the concepts in question develop over a wide age range. The second phase requires training studies at different ages so that we can detect how children resolve conflicts: In the case we presented, the cognitive conflicts were those that arose between the two symbol systems used to understand the temperature concept. The third phase involves translating the results of the first two phases into curriculum design. We showed how specific activities in the revised unit on "Temperature" included tasks that were informed by what we had learned from our initial developmental research. Note that the sequence of classroom activities and their timing were determined by that research. The fourth phase pertained to evaluating the effects of the curriculum unit on children's conceptual development when the unit was taught in a regular classroom. It should also be noted that the tools for evaluating the cognitive achievements were actually developed in the first (research) phase. Our results were that the curriculum developed through these four phases was effective.

THE ARITHMETIC AVERAGE

*The Lord must have loved the average man because he made more
of them than the others''.*
        —Attributed to a British bishop in the late 19th century.

This section has two parts that pertain to the first two phases of curriculum development as it is viewed within the educational–developmental psychology perspective: (a) the phase where we investigate the normative development of children's understanding of the concept of interest, the arithmetic average in the present case, and (b) the training phase.

The Development of the Arithmetic Average

One of the motivations for the present example of how one can connect developmental psychology and education grew out of an inability to answer questions raised in our studies on the development of the concept of temperature. To remind the reader, there we examined how children understood what happened when we mixed water from two cups where the water was initially at the same or different temperatures.

Some mixing tasks were presented numerically (e.g., 70° C, 10° C). In the cases of mixing water that was initially at different temperatures and equal amounts, the correct solution to such tasks is to average the initial temperatures of the water. We found that until approximately age 14, children had great difficulty solving these tasks. Furthermore, tasks that required calculating the weighted average (where the amounts of water were unequal) were not solved correctly by any of the children. What we did not know was if those children who solved these tasks incorrectly did not know how to calculate the average, if they knew how to make such a calculation but did not know that that was appropriate for the case of temperature, or if they had conceptual difficulties understanding what the average is. One purpose of the present study was to determine which of these alternatives held. A clue that there may be conceptual difficulties comes from non-developmental work on the concept of the average where it was shown that college students had conceptual difficulties with the weighted average (Mevarech, 1983; Pollatsek, Lima, & Well, 1981). In order to answer our initial question, we set out to assess the development of children's concepts of the average.

Another motivation from the middle-level model of educational–developmental psychology for researching the concept of the average is that it is simply ubiquitous. Whenever and wherever there are numerical descriptions of objects, events, and processes one invariably encounters the average. The extraordinary range of areas covered by this concept gives it importance and, being a general concept applied across a wide range of domains, it fulfills one of the requirements proposed in the introduction for what should be included as content for educational–developmental work.

The average is calculated by merely adding the values to be averaged and dividing this sum by the number of values that were summed. Perhaps the simplicity of the procedural side of its calculation makes the average appear to be straightforward and simple. Our study shows that, quite unlike the procedural side, the development of children's understanding of the *properties* of the average is neither straightforward nor simple. In order to recognize why this is so, we have to go beyond the procedural side and concentrate on the average's properties.

Because there is nothing in principle that is different about the concept of the average than other concepts we have investigated, the method for testing its development in children should be similar to the others. As a consequence, we chose the following route to test it: First, we analyzed this concept into some of its properties and attempted to find organizational relations that held between them. We then constructed tasks to measure each of these properties, and having done so, we administered the tasks to children over a wide age range. Finally, we analyzed the data in search of both developmental paths for each of the properties and types of reasoning patterns that develop over time, these patterns reflecting mental organizations children have constructed about the properties.

We arrived at seven properties of the average: (a) the sum of the deviations around the mean is zero, (b) the average is located between the extreme values, (c) the average is influenced by values other than the average, (d) the average does not necessarily equal one of the values that was summed, (e) the average can be a fraction that has no counterpart in physical reality, (f) when calculating the average, a value of zero, if it appears, may be added, and (g) the average is representative of the values that were averaged.

I only present our experimental data for the first property, that the sum of the deviations around the average is zero. Let us begin with an example of this property. A simple example comes from the average of the numbers 1 and 3. The average is 2. Now, we must calculate the deviations from the average and we do this by subtracting each number from the average. The first number was 1 and the average was 2, so ($1 - 2 = -1$). We make the same calculation for the second number we averaged, 3, and when we do that we find that its deviation from the average is $+1$ ($3 - 2 = 1$). The property we are exemplifying here is that the sum of the deviations around the average is zero, which means that were we to add these deviations, they should sum to zero. In our example, we add -1 and $+1$ and arrive at zero.

This property is easy enough to demonstrate via examples such as the one just provided, but it is my experience that it is not an easy property to grasp when we go beyond the demonstrations. Once children (and adults) are provided with an example such as the one just given, they have few difficulties calculating other examples to demonstrate the property; however, there is a distance between being able to demonstrate such a property and understanding just why it is that the sum of the deviations around the average equals zero.

The study I report now is based on a master's thesis by Efraim Bichler (Strauss & Bichler, in press). In our study to assess the development of children's reasoning about the properties of the average, we asked five questions about the property in question. One of them, which I call the cards task, was: "The children in a class brought picture playing cards to school. They put all of their cards into a pile and then passed them out to every child so that each one got the same number of cards. When they did that it turned out that each child got 4 cards. Afterwards, each child got back all of the original cards he brought to school. The teacher then divided the class into two groups: those who had more than four cards and those who less than four cards. The children who had more than four cards gave their extras to the teacher. The teacher then passed out the extras to the children in the other group and she passed them out so that each child in the group would have four cards. When she did this, did she have any cards left? Did she have too few to hand out to the children? Why do you think so?" The basic idea here is that the number of cards that were extras (above the average) equalled the number of cards missing in the group that had less than four cards (below the average) and the teacher had none left (zero) when she finished passing out the extras (adding those above the average to those below the average).

A total of 80 middle-class children were tested with four age groups and 20 children per age group. The mean ages of the four groups was 8, 10, 12, and 14 years with equal numbers of boys and girls per age group.

The findings were that 10%, 10%, 10%, and 30% of the 8, 10, 12, and 14-

year-olds, respectively produced correct judgments for the five tasks. The dominant justification offered for the correct judgments was that because we passed out the cards the first time and everyone received equal numbers, the same should happen when we pass them out the second time. This is a rather practical solution and it is perfectly adequate, although it does not indicate whether the children understood the property. A second justification was that when passing out the cards, the surplus should equal the deficit and several children even stated the principle behind the property. The last justification did not occur with regularity until age 14. For incorrect judgments, the dominant justification was, "It depends." When this justification was probed further we learned that children meant something like: "I do not have enough data. Were I to know how many children and/or cards there were, I could tell you if the teacher was left with any extras, but since I don't know the exact number, I can't tell you."

These findings indicate that even by age 14 there is a rather significant percentage of children who do not solve the questions tapping this property. If children had such difficulties when the questions were asked qualitatively, it seems reasonable to assume that they will have even more difficulties understanding the property when it is presented numerically. I reiterate here: the children could solve the procedural side but they could not understand its significance.

One of the purposes of the first phase of the middle-level model is to determine the nature of the normative development for the content of interest. A second purpose is to find areas where children have difficulties grasping the content. I have just done this for the concept of the arithmetic average. In the second phase of the model, attempts are made to help children overcome these natural difficulties via training.

Analogy Training

In the present case we used analogy training as the technique to induce progressive cognitive change. As Miller (1979) argued, an analogy taken in its broadest definition is any expression of similarity or resemblance. The use of analogy as a method for inducing progressive cognitive change rests on the assumption that analogies function as a tool of thought, and that they are a source of generating an understanding of domains yet unknown. Children and adults have mental models that have been constructed for a base domain and are mapped on to (analogies are drawn to) other domains as an aid to structure them. Often these mappings are inappropriate and lead to confusions (see, e.g., Clement, 1981). This suggests three points: analogies are a tool of thought for constructing new knowledge; mapping knowledge from one domain to another where the mapping is inappropriate may be a powerful source of resistance to understanding a domain in instructional situations; and analogies can be used as an instructional tool to help children (and adults) restructure their understanding of a domain.

The middle-level model suggests additional reasons for using analogy as a training technique. The analogy part of analogy training is both one of the objects of the study and its vehicle. As for its being an object of the study, we have a pragmatic interest to know if we can induce progressive cognitive advance via analogy training. The idea of it being a vehicle has several parts: (a) it can be a developmental tool: through analogy training we can determine if understanding the property follows a developmental course; (b) it can be a diagnostic tool: we can determine if children at initially identical/similar levels move to the same or different points along the developmental course, and we can determine the nature of the difficulties children encounter in understanding the concepts presented in the instruction, these resistances indicating that we are possibly up against mental organizations; (c) it can be an instructional tool: through careful analysis, we can determine effective instructional techniques so that teachers who have a handle on the developmental course children progress through can assist children negotiating their way through that course; and (d) it can be a training tool for teachers: teaching teachers to be aware of the transactions between them, as experts, and the children, as novices, could be very helpful in sensitizing teachers to developmental issues that arise in instruction in schools.

The middle-level model also places emphasis on multiple-knowledge representations. By and large, research on analogies has been between different school-learned knowledge. For example, Gentner and Gentner (1983) summarized analogies between an atom and the solar system, both of these concepts being examples of school-learned knowledge. I would like to suggest that in addition to studies where we attempt to teach for analogies between different school-learned knowledge, one can also teach analogies between different kinds of knowledge (e.g., spontaneous, common sense knowledge, and school-learned knowledge).

I would like to present the results of a study that uses analogy as its technique to instruct children to understand the significance of the property that the sum of the deviations around the average equals zero. The work is being conducted as a master's thesis by Ariella Salinger. The guiding principle behind the instruction was that it should make use of children's already existing common sense knowledge that could be properly applied to the property at hand and that they had not thought to use. It was thought that this existing knowledge, to be effective for instruction, should be grounded in everyday experiences and well-understood. In our case, the training was based on using everyday, common sense knowledge as an analogy for the numerical representation of the property.

We tested children's understanding of the property in question via three tasks: (a) building a sand castle, (b) cards, and (c) numerical tasks. For the sand castle task, we asked children what they do when building a sand castle at the beach and most began their story with levelling the area where the castle was to be built. For those who did not begin their story with that part, we asked them if it would be appropriate to begin by levelling the sand and all agreed that it would be. They were then asked what it meant to level the sand and either spontaneously or through a short discussion they came to the understanding that it entails filling the areas that were below the level with the sand that was above it and that when this was done, there was no sand above or below the level. The cards task was the one just presented. The numerical task involved presenting children with numbers: 1,1,2,3,5,5,5,7,7. The children were to work out the average ($36/9 = 4$), separate those numbers that had more than the average from those that had less, calculate the differences between each number and the average, and add these differences.

The three tasks are structurally similar in that in all three cases we have an average problem of the property that the sum of the deviations around the mean equals zero. The sand castle problem's symbolic content is qualitative and it is part of children's everyday knowledge where the physical content (sand) is for all intents and purposes continuous. The cards task is qualitative and part of children's everyday knowledge where the physical content (cards) is discrete. The numerical task's symbolic content is numerical and the knowledge it calls on is school-learned knowledge.

The study included 84 children, half of whom were 8-year-olds and half were 11-year-olds. There were two treatment groups: (a) the analogy-training group that was given a pretest, training, and a posttest, and (b) the control group that was given a pretest and a posttest. Our study's data analysis is just underway, but there are some broad findings of relevance to this chapter that can be reported. In the pretest we found that all of the children solved the sand castle task correctly, 36% of the 8-year-olds and 67% of the 11-year-olds solved the cards task correctly, and none of the children solved the numerical task correctly.

In the instructional situation, we began with the cards task to determine the child's understanding of the property. All children were then given the sand castle and the numerical tasks. For those children who solved the cards task correctly, we asked if they saw a similarity (analogy) between that task and the sand castle task. All children understood the similarity either spontaneously or after a very short discussion where the interviewer asked several leading questions. After that similarity was clarified, the experimenter presented the numerical task and the children were asked to work out the arithmetic operations that would show us the principle behind the property. With some assistance, most of these children could work out the problem. They were then asked if there was a similarity between the sand castle problem, the cards task, and the numerical task. Many children spontaneously understood the nature of the similarity. Of those who did not, a short discussion with leading questions on the part of the experimenter led to an understanding of the similarity.

Of those children who solved the cards task incorrectly, all argued that they could not know if the teacher had any cards left when she passed them out or, as we mentioned earlier, they said, "It depends." These children were given the sand castle task, which they all solved correctly. When they were asked if there was any similarity between that task and the cards task, some could spontaneously understand the similarity whereas others could not, even after the experimenter asked leading questions and even indicated what that similarity is. When those who did and did not understand the analogy were given the numerical task, only some of those who understood the sand castles and cards analogy correctly solved the numerical task.

When we looked at change that occured between the pretest and posttest for children's understanding of the numerical task, it was found that for the 8- and 11-year-olds, respectively, 23% and 10% of the control group and 75% and 60% of the analogy-training children changed from an incorrect to a correct understanding of the numerical representation of the property.

Overall, what happened in the analogy training was that it was helpful for children who understood during the training that the sand castle and cards tasks were analogous. Most of these children were able to successfully understand the numerical task that, prior to the training, was not solved correctly. Of the children who did not solve the numerical problem correctly during the training session, most did not understand the analogy between the sand castle and the cards task. They focused on the content differences (e.g., continuous sand vs. discrete cards) that tended to obscure the underlying structural analogies. In other words, what does not map in the analogy can occupy center stage in some children's understandings and can render the structural analogies difficult to grasp.

In addition to the aforementioned, a picture of tutoring is emerging from our study. It appears that: (a) there is a reciprocity in the ways that the teacher and child pace and organize their interactions; (b) both enter the instructional situation with different concepts about the content to be taught, yet when instruction begins, the teacher created a shared language and conceptual framework; and (c) the main task of instruction is to transfer the responsibility of understanding the concepts from the adult to the child and props are used by the adult to help manage that transfer.

To sum up the presentation of my work on the concept of average, I offered a structuralist analysis of the nature of the concept of the average that yielded the properties and formed the basis for the initial research on the development of these properties and their interrelations. The instructional approach I took used the tool of analogy as a vehicle to teach the property in question where structurally identical tasks were presented. These tasks differed in their symbolic content (qualitative and numerical) and the kind of knowledge children bring to bear on the tasks (spontaneous and school-learned). The technique for teaching the understanding of the numerical representation of the property was to build on the structurally same knowledge that children had already constructed for that property via the sand castle problem that has different symbolic content (qualitative) and knowledge (spontaneous). The nature of building this bridge was via analogies and that training technique was successful in inducing cognitive advance.

SUMMARY AND CONCLUSIONS

The main purpose of this chapter was to show how developmental psychology and education can be seen as complementing and informing each other. I began with the idea that children have multiple representations of their world and that one way to understand them is to through the prism of Vygotsky's work where he distinguishes between spontaneous and school-learned knowledge. To this I added the symbol systems (qualitative and numerical) that also have their developmental courses. I argued that the world is organized a priori neither qualitatively nor numerically but that the qualitative and numerical renderings we give the world are the result of languages we use to interpret it.

I claimed that the development of spontaneous and school-based knowledge have their own evolutionary course and that when put in touch with each other at different points in each one's trajectory, they influence each other differently. One example of this was the development of the qualitative and numerical understandings of the concept of temperature. What we saw was that conflicts between the two representations of the same task were resolved differently at different points in each one's trajectory.

The general picture that emerges from our educational–developmental work is that children have characteristic ways of constructing their spontaneous, common sense concepts about their world and that these mental constructions do not necessarily mesh with the school-learned knowledge about the same concepts. In the cases where they don't, we can expect difficulties in children's understanding these concepts when they are taught in school. Working out the places where common sense knowledge and school-learned knowledge do not go hand-in-hand seems a good place to look for theoretical and conceptual insights for those interested in educational–developmental psychology.

I briefly contrasted Vygotsky's sociohistorical model with Piaget's psychogenetic model and now slightly elaborate this comparison. There are three main differences between these models. First, Vygotsky saw school-learned, scientific knowledge as being historical and as interacting with children's common sense, spontaneous knowledge whereas Piaget saw them as being essentially separate. Second, the sources of cognitive development were different: Vygotsky viewed the interpersonal and social, external, aspects of human interaction as being the primary source of mental evolution, whereas Piaget's system had the sources of cognitive development as being internal, intrapersonal. And third, the role of language in children's cognitive development was different. For Vygotsky the symbolic system played a major role in giving form to children's cognitions and cognitive change whereas Piaget saw language as being a reflection of children's underlying cognitive (operational) structures and not an instrument for cognitive change. (For a review of these three points, see Strauss, in preparation).

It is obvious that each view has much to offer educational–developmental psychology, despite their apparently profound differences. I believe it is important to attempt to find a way to reconcile them. I confess to having trouble trying to work out how Piaget's characterization of mental structures gets put into practice in school settings. Similarly, although Vygotsky's model is more in tune with what happens in schools, I find the lack of a structural analysis in Vygotsky's work to be a fundamental problem when mapping out children's progress through thought organizations. I am not one for papering over cracks that separate different approaches to developmental theory (Strauss, in press) but I think that the sociohistorical and psychogenetic approaches are not so deeply divided that in integrating model is impossible. A recent attempt to do just that has been made by Bearison (1986).

I have attempted to sketch an outline of what a middle-level model of educational–developmental psychology might include. As far as the content of research and development in educational–developmental psychology goes, I suggested that, first and foremost, we should be working on subject matter that is taught in schools. Subjects that are not taught in schools, although they may be interesting, have a low priority for educational research and development. On similar grounds, I also suggested that we should study material that generally requires instruction to be learned (as in the case of reading for example) or understood correctly (as in the cases of temperature and heat, and the arithmetic average, as I showed in this chapter). In this view, concepts such as conservation, which have captured the hearts and minds of developmental psychologists, are not good candidates for educational-developmental psychology because they are concepts that do not need instruction to be understood correctly.

I then went on to say that one of the areas where educational–developmental psychologists might be doing theoretical, conceptual, and empirical work is in how children's everyday, common sense, spontaneous knowledge interacts with their school-learned knowledge. I also suggested that these interactions should be studied where we keep in mind the symbolic system in which these kinds of knowledge are clothed.

These two kinds of knowledge may be about the same task, as in the case of the development of children's common sense and school-learned knowledge about temperature. To remind the reader, we put children's everyday understandings of intensive physical quantity in contact with their numerical representations of the same concepts. The tasks were identical but the knowledge and symbolic systems called upon were different. These two kinds of knowledge can also be about the same concepts but where different tasks are used, as in the case of teaching children about the property of the arithmetic average that the sum of the deviations around the mean equals zero. Here we put children's everyday qualitative understanding of the effects of levelling sand on the beach in touch with their numerical representation of this property. The same property clothed in different knowledge and symbol systems was assessed via different tasks.

The sketch of the model also included four steps for conducting developmental research and developing curriculum units. The first step involves research to get normative data about the development of children's concepts of the subject matter in question. This kind of research gives us normative data about sequential development that informs us about the sequence of the content in instructional materials. It also indicates the places where children have difficulties in grasping the concepts correctly, and where they don't.

In the second phase of curriculum development we conduct training studies to help children overcome the natural difficulties discovered in the first phase. One needs to know how development is energized because it allows us to plan how to foster progressive cognitive development. Two techniques were investigated: cognitive and analogy.

Using the former for the concept of temperature, we pitted children's conflicting understandings (which arose from different underlying symbolic representations) about temperature, and found out how conflicts were resolved at different ages, and when the conflict was correctly resolved. The results of such studies provide us with information about the timing of introducing instructional materials into the classroom. The implications of this kind of research for educational practice and developmental theory show that the educational–developmental model occupies a middle level where it can go in both the direction of educational practice and developmental theory.

The second kind of training study, analogy training, is not an adversarial kind of training, pitting one kind of representation against another. Instead, it is based on the idea that some of the children's concepts are difficult to dislodge. Rather than trying to put them into conflict with each other, we can borrow some of the children's already existing common sense concepts and use them as a demonstration of the more formal school-based concept. This can often be a common sense concept that the child would not have thought of as being appropriate for solving the task at hand. This sort of training was demonstrated in our attempt to teach a property of the arithmetic average via the analogous situation of the levelling of sand on the beach.

The third phase is the translation of the research findings into curriculum materials. I presented one example of how this translation can take place in the case of temperature. Such a translation is fraught with enormous difficulties, but is not insurmountable.

The fourth step involves evaluating the effects of the curriculum unit on children's conceptual development when the unit is taught under regular classroom conditions. As I stated previously, the tools for making that assessment are developed in the first phase, when the educational–developmental psychologist conducts research to assess normative development of the concepts to be taught in the school.

What have presented here is an account of how education, learning, and development can be pursued without distorting the aims and interests of either developmental psychology or education. It is a preliminary account; however, it includes a sketch of the issues one has to deal with when attempting to make developmental psychology more clearly in tune with what and how children learn and develop both in and out of school.

ACKNOWLEDGMENTS

This is Working Paper Number 40 of the Tel-Aviv University Unit of Human Development and Education. I would like to thank David Henry Feldman, Tamar Globerson, Lynn Liben, and Iris Levin for very helpful comments on an earlier version of this chapter.

REFERENCES

Bamberger, J. (1982). Revisiting children's drawings of simple rhythms: A function for reflction-in-action. In S. Strauss (Ed.), *U-shaped behavioral growth* (pp. 191–226). New York: Academic Press.

Bearison, D. J. (1986). Transactional cognition in context: New models of social understanding. In D. Bearison & H. Zimiles (Ed.), *Thinking and emotions: Developmental perspectives* (pp. 129–146). Hillsdale, NJ: Lawrence Erlbaum Associates.

Carnap, R. (1966). *Philosophical foundations of physics.* New York: Basic Books.

Clement, J. (1981). *Analogy generation in scientific problem solving.* Proceedings of the third annual meeting of the cognitive science society. Berkeley, CA.

Cohen, M. R., & Nagel, E. (1934). *An introduction to logic and scientific method.* New York: Harcourt, Brace, & World.

Feldman, D. H. (1971). Map understanding as a possible crystallizer of cognitive structures. *American Educational Research Journal, 8,* 485–501.

Feldman, D. H. (1980). *Beyond universals in cognitive development.* Norwood, NJ: Ablex.

Gardner, H. (1983). *Frames of mind.* New York: Basic Books.

Gentner, D., & Gentner, D. R. (1983). Flowing waters or teeming crowds: Mental models of electricity. In D. Gentner & A. L. Stevens (Eds.), *Mental models* (pp. 99–129). Hillsdale, NJ: Lawrence Erlbaum Associates.

Hempel, C. G. (1952). *International encyclopedia of unified science, Vol. 2, No. 7: Fundamentals of concept formation in empirical science.* Chicago: University of Chicago Press.

Koyré, A. (1968). *Metaphysics and measurement: Essays in the scientific revolution.* London: Chapman & Hall.

Kuhn, T. S. (1977). *The essential tension.* Chicago: University of Chicago Press.

Mevarech, Z. R. (1983). A deep structure model of students' statistical misconceptions. *Educational Studies in Mathematics, 3,* 415–428.

Miller, G. A. (1979). Images and models, similes and metaphors. In A. Ortony (Ed.), *Metaphor and thought* (pp. 202–250). Cambridge, England: Cambridge University Press.

Pollatsek, A., Lima, S., & Well, D. (1981). Computation or concept: Students' understanding of the mean. *Educational Studies in Mathematics, 12,* 191–204.

Rogoff, B., & Wertsch, J. V. (Eds.). (1984). *Children's learning in the zone of proximal development.* San Francisco: Jossey-Bass.

Snyder, S. S., & Feldman, D. H. (1977). Internal and external influences on cognitive developmental change. *Child Development, 48,* 937–943.

Stavy, R., & Berkowitz, B. (1980). Cognitive conflicts as a basis for teaching quantitative aspects of the concept of temperature. *Science Education, 64,* 679–692.

Strauss, S. (1972). Inducing cognitive development and learning: A review of short-term training experiments I. The organismic developmental approach. *Cognition, 1,* 329–357.

Strauss, S. (Ed.). (1982). *U-shaped behavioral growth.* New York: Academic Press.

Strauss, S. (Ed.). (in press). *Ontogeny, phylogeny, and historical development.* Norwood, NJ: Ablex.

Strauss, S., & Bichler, E. (in press). The development of children's concepts of the arithmetic average. *Journal of Research in Mathematics Education.*

Strauss, S., & Ilan, J. (1975). Length conservation and the speed concept: Organizational disequilibrium training between concepts. *Journal of Educational Psychology, 67,* 470–477.

Strauss, S., Orpaz, N., & Stavy, R. (1977). *The development of children's concepts of heat and temperature.* Unpublished manuscript, Tel-Aviv University.

Strauss, S., & Stavy, R. (1982). U-shaped behavioral growth: Implications for theories of development. In W. W. Hartup (Ed.), *Review of child development research* (Vol. 6, pp. 547–599). Chicago: University of Chicago Press.

Vygotsky, L. S. (1962). *Thought and language.* Cambridge, MA: MIT Press.

Vygotsky, L. S. (1978). *Mind in society: The development of higher psychological functions.* Cambridge, MA: Harvard University Press.

Wiser, M. (in press). The differentiation of heat and temperature: History of science and novice-expert shift. In S. Strauss (Ed.), *Ontogeny, phylogeny, and historical development.* Norwood, NJ: Ablex.

Wiser, M., & Carey, S. (1983). When heat and temperature were one. In D. Gentner & A. L. Collins (Eds.), *Mental models* (pp. 267–297). Hillsdale, NJ: Lawrence Erlbaum Associates.

7 Going for the Middle Ground: A Promising Place for Educational Psychology

David Henry Feldman
Tufts University

It is by now a commonplace that Piaget was not greatly interested in the affairs of education, this despite two important books on the topic (Piaget, 1948, 1970). Piaget's epistemological concerns were much broader than the practical problems that teachers face daily when implementing curricula and managing a classroom. Piaget did have a healthy distaste for traditional forms of pedagogy, and his written work on education was reformist if not downright radical. Perhaps because of his deep commitment to the value and importance of individual control and direction, Piaget was in fact skeptical of formal instruction altogether during the early years. It is not surprising, then, that his work was readily taken up by reformist elements in western education and became assimilated to the "open" education or "informal education" movement that was the legacy of Deweyan progressive education of the 1930s and 1940s (Kohlberg & Mayer, 1972). In practical terms, this tended to mean that Piaget was used to further buttress already existing assumptions about how education should proceed. Rather than taking the Piagetian framework as a serious challenge to educational thought, Piaget's authority was invoked without using his actual epistemological framework. It was as if open educators had already laid down their principles of education and then, ex post facto, discovered that Piaget could be interpreted to endorse those principles. Piaget's "to understand is to invent" became a favorite catch phrase of the 1960s reformists. So long as one did not look at the work of Piaget too closely, this extra push from the world's leading developmentalist was welcome. Throughout, however, there were those who were uncomfortable with this all too facile use of Piaget's framework, who saw that in certain respects it was a distortion of Piaget's work to use it this way. Indeed, the more seriously

Piaget is studied, the more questionable is the adoption of his work as a model for education.

In this chapter I consider two complementary Piaget-inspired attempts to put educational psychology on a more solid footing. The first of these, that of Sidney Strauss and his colleagues, is my primary assignment because I have been asked to discuss his chapter in this volume. The second is my own work, which is similarly motivated in many ways. My purpose is to compare these two approaches to establish a "middle ground" theory for educational psychology. Perhaps the best reason for putting the two approaches together and comparing them is that, taken together, they seem to do a much better job of making a case for the importance of such a middle ground theory for educational psychology than either does alone.

PIAGET AND EDUCATIONAL PSYCHOLOGY

As is clear to anyone who understands Piaget's framework, his basic focus was on a set of universal changes in the mental apparatus: cognitive restructurings that occur in all children in all cultures over the course of development. Piaget was looking for the common elements, the shared processes that make each of us a member of the human family, and the shared changes in these processes that give us a common basis in experience. Although learning specific content areas may color the process of change, they do not affect it in any important way. Indeed, this commonality is fundamental to the concept of universality; if specific experiences were critical to development, then the chances are that such changes would not be universal. For the Piagetian, all human beings tend to form certain common systems for interpreting the world that are impervious to variations in experience. These issues are by now well known in developmental circles, although less among educational psychologists. (Bereiter, 1970, 1982; Feldman, 1971, 1980, 1981a, 1982; Kohlberg, 1970).

For education, the implications of this point of view of mental development are basically that children will develop by themselves, whether there are teachers, schools, curricula, libraries, or computers. In effect, education is irrelevant to development, at least development of the fundamental structures of thought. It is not surprising, then, that developmental frameworks like Piaget's have been largely ignored by educational psychology. As Hawkins (1974) wrote:

> The developmentalist scheme is inadequate to the deepest and most central concerns of education. It is inadequate because it buries under a metaphor just that level of interaction between "development" and "learning" without which our species would lack its more distinctive characteristics. (p. 237)

For more than half a century educational psychology has been dominated by its parent discipline, experimental psychology, which has left the field with a strange quality. Prestige and significance were attached to work that had the purity of the psychology laboratory, although its impact on educational practice has been minimal. And a good thing too because the work was rarely about education. Fortunately, teachers and curriculum people recognized that whatever the educational psychologists were doing, it had little to do with them, so each field more or less went about its business and business was good. Except of course for the embarassing fact that in principle the field of educational psychology exists in order to be of service to education.

Strauss' Middle Ground Framework

Into this stable but unsatisfactory breech have come Strauss and his colleagues, whose approach to research is as refreshing as it is different from traditional educational psychology. Grounding his work in Piagetian theory and the writings of Russian developmentalist Vygotsky, Strauss proposes that there are indeed universal, inevitable changes in children's thinking over time, but that there are also important changes that come about through the conscious efforts of those who attempt to transmit knowledge. These two sets of changes intersect and influence each other in ways that profoundly affect the educational process.

Strauss adds a third dimension to the process of change, and this is the particular symbol system through which information is transmitted and interpreted. For example, the same information about temperature can be represented qualitatively "it is very hot" or quantitatively "it is 205°." For certain purposes, the qualitative representation is the more appropriate or easier to work with, and for other purposes the quantitative representation is more suitable. A child must learn these symbol systems, their rules and procedures, as well as the other aspects of the problem at hand.

The critical set of relationships to comprehend, Strauss argues, is among these three dimensions: (a) the spontaneously developing, everyday concepts that are based on common experience; (b) formal, school-based knowledge about the same phenomena; and (c) the symbol systems that can be used to represent information about this phenomenon and others. The latter two dimensions are not *developmental* in the sense that Piaget originally meant the term, but are perfectly consistent with Vygotsky's more inclusive developmental framework. In any case, the effort in Strauss' empirical and conceptual research on science education is to take into account what is going on in all three areas of children's understanding, and to devise ways to use each of them to assist the child in mastering specified curriculum content. This way of using Piaget's theory accepts the validity of universal development, development that is not affected by intervention, but adds to it other dimensions of development that are crucially affected by what is presented by others. Strauss departs from Piaget to some extent when he allows, a la Vygotsky, that even the universal developmental changes themselves may be affected by the other two dimensions. This new integration is becoming a more widely held position among developmentalists (cf. Brown & Ferrara, 1985; Cole, John-Steiner, Scribner, & Souberman, 1978; Wertsch, 1985), and Strauss has anticipated this trend in his work.

Middle-Level Theory. For Strauss, a middle-level theory has several assumptions. His first criterion is that change, to be described as middle level, must neither be very long (several years) nor very short (a few hours), but should deal with progress that takes place over weeks, months or, perhaps most appropriately, over semesters. The second criterion is that the theory deal with bodies of knowledge that are neither so abstract or general that they are impervious to change, on the one hand, nor so specific as to be trivial (nonsense syllables would be an extreme case, but perhaps Strauss also means learning to spell or to memorize capitols of countries). Finally, middle-level theories should fall somewhere between broad developmental theorizing and educational practice. This criterion is intended to position the investigator to avoid being bogged down by the detail that occupies teachers day to day, or the more general characteristics of universal developmental change, which is helpful as a backdrop for education but insufficient to really guide it.

As with a number of contemporary developmentalists (Brown & Ferrara, 1985; Cole et al., 1978; Wertsch, 1985), Strauss follows Vygotsky, who seems to have begun formulating a middle-level model of his own more than 50 years ago (Vygotsky, 1934). In particular, Strauss sees his work as dealing with Vygotsky's notion of "zone of proximal development." This is an intriguing concept of responsiveness to instruction that Vygotsky proposed as an alternative to IQ-like estimates of children's intelligence.

At the heart of Strauss' approach is the idea of multiple representations of knowledge, an idea also inspired by Vygotsky's distinction between spontaneous and scientific concepts. For Vygotsky, these were simultaneously evolving systems that could complement each other if understood properly. Spontaneous concepts were picked through the child's casual contacts with the world, his or her efforts to comprehend what and how things worked without explicit guidance from those more sophisticated. An example is the child's idea of cause and effect in transformation tasks such as conservation. Piaget of course spent much of his career examining such concepts.

In contrast, scientific concepts came directly from society, and in particular from school. These concepts simply would not be acquired by the growing child without direct intervention by teachers or other adults. Examples of such concepts would be the idea of a collective, or exploitation of the masses (or to use examples more congenial to a westerner, the ideas of democratic participation or principles of freedom). The term *scientific* is somewhat misleading for these concepts; *cultural knowledge* would perhaps capture them better. In any event, the distinction is clear enough. For the former set of concepts, simply being alive and circulating around the environment is sufficient for the concepts to be constructed. For the latter, some conscious effort and intention on the part of the society is not only necessary, it must take place in effective form if the concepts are to be acquired. How well the two sets of concepts work together determines the child's "zone of proximal development."

In addition to Vygotsky's spontaneous and scientific concepts, Strauss adds a third dimension, that of the symbol system through which most scientific concepts are learned. It makes a difference, Strauss argues, if information is carried through a precise numerical system, versus a more informal verbal system, versus a representation in graphic form. These vehicles for carrying information, themselves bodies of knowledge about which a child must learn from the culture, are thus more in the scientific than spontaneous category. They influence how well and what the specific character of scientific knowledge will be for the child.

Empirical Research. The interplay among the three dimensions of concept formation—spontaneous, scientific, and symbolic—is what Strauss believes has been ignored in educational psychology. He is of course right about this, but to study such interplay is no small challenge. And it is to meet this challenge that Strauss' empirical work is aimed. Some of that work is reported in the chapter that appears in this volume and the reader can judge how well it achieves its stated objectives. In my opinion it does so rather well, although one has the feeling at times that the problems were chosen more for their tractability for research purposes than for educational importance. This seems fair enough when trying to establish a paradigm, although it does run the risk of repeating the same mistake made by the educational psychologists who selected learning problems more for their laboratory value than because anyone cared about whether or not children learned the material. This qualification stated, it is nonetheless true that Strauss and his colleagues have done an impressive amount of good empirical work on concepts that are relevant, if not of burning interest, to science education.

In his research, Strauss shows that the child who seeks to master the material taught in natural science courses often brings to the task a history of spontaneous learning that is rarely attended to systematically in the classroom. From this point of departure, Strauss builds a set of four phases to his research technique. These four phases, interestingly, come close to summarizing four different programs of funding currently offered in the Learning and Instruction branch of the National Science Foundation. For grant proposals in this country to be successful there must be a choice among (a) studying the basic developmental pattern of acquisition of certain concepts, (b) intervention or instructional efforts to teach various subject matter content, (c) creation of experimental curriculum units or packages, or (d) evaluation studies.

In what is perhaps the most important research implication of the Tel Aviv approach, Strauss has shown that an adequate program of research must include all four components. Indeed, the importance of taking all of these components into account at the outset of the project is emphasized. In the course of the research, each of these components is informed by and in turn informs the construction of the others. The process is much more like juggling four balls simultaneously than like moving sequentially through a checklist of precisely stated objectives.

Current funding criteria tend to stress the importance of having both conceptual analysis and procedural strategies well worked out in advance, to prove that the investigator has thought analytically and thoroughly before going on the public dole. In fact, as Strauss shows convincingly, the analytic work should be of an entirely different kind. Analysis of the concepts of the curriculum content, a search of the literature, and collection of teacher lore about what techniques might be used to transmit the content, will lead to good models of curriculum construction and refinement of evaluation techniques. When the project begins it would be folly to try to have everything specified in advance. In fact, the most important justification for the work is that answers to questions about all four issues will emerge from the process in a cybernetic, iterative, self-correcting sort of manner. Perhaps this is another reason why educational psychology research has tended to be so insipid. All of the life has to be drained out of a project for it to be eligible for government money. The willingness to stop and follow up on interesting surprises and unexpected twists is discouraged.

I am of course overstating all of this for emphasis. But not by much. What makes Strauss' work so vital and so important is also what makes other work less so. He has had the courage to take on the real challenge of doing educational psychology research, and very few others have had this kind of courage or commitment. Indeed, as I have just tried to argue, there are institutional and professional pressures to do just the opposite. Doing the kind of work that Strauss and his colleagues do is time consuming, expensive, and requires more than the usual ability to delay gratification. Yet there seems to be no viable alternative. Doing work of real significance for education requires large commitments of resources over several years. Few have been willing or able to pay such a high price for such relatively modest gains. Strauss and his group have been willing to do so because they are not condescending toward their applied objectives. Most of them have taught in schools or have been responsible for curriculum development projects. Not underestimating the enemy is one of the first rules of war.

Producing one reasonably finished curriculum unit is an exceedingly time consuming process. Strauss' group has prepared units about heat and temperature and the arithmetic average; each took the intense efforts of a team of researchers more than 5 years to complete. How many times have efforts of this scope or sophistication been undertaken in this country? If nothing else were to come of the Tel Aviv group's work, the sobering truth about the difficulty of doing good curriculum development work would be contribution enough. But I believe that much more will come of it, in fact already has. Methodology is central, however, to whatever use is made of the work of Strauss and his colleagues. And the method that is used in this research strikes me as carefully wrought, well thought out, and appropriate to the problems of schools. Especially the last quality has been missing in much previous research in educational psychology.

Content. Strauss' middle-level model makes no assumptions about the wisdom of curriculum content, leaving that matter to the policy makers. After all, this is a value decision and not a scientific one. The model assumes that those responsible for teaching subject matter would like to do it better and that the task of the researcher is to learn from the teacher how classrooms really work, and in turn to show the teacher how to be more successful at transmitting important material. Thus, the existing curriculum is the starting point and anchor of Strauss' research model. Anything that pulls the focus too far away from this epicenter in any direction is counterproductive. And yet, the very poles of general theory and classroom practice between which the model is placed are the source of techniques and concepts that will provide needed information about how to improve students' learning.

It is, however, too facile to say that because it neither falls into the micro world of the daily classroom activity nor the macro world of the grand developmentalist, that a middle-level model has been constructed. Were these two "worlds" to anchor the two ends of a conceptual continuum, then Strauss' work might represent an intermediate-level model. But I would argue that Strauss' model does not fit neatly between these two and that in fact, Strauss has committed what Carl Bereiter (1970) has referred to in a related context as a "category error". Both the curriculum and developmental models are actually process models, whereas Strauss' is a content-based one. For process, Strauss actually draws upon both cognitive-developmental (conflict) and learning/information processing theories (analogy) to drive his learning studies. Thus the middle-level model is not so much an alternative theoretical position as it is a pragmatic willingness to use the best available knowledge without being seduced into buying any particular theoretical prescription. It is an applied stance in the best sense of the term. The crucible for deciding what is valuable is what will work in the actual setting.

The fact that Strauss and his co-workers have been as successful as they have in improving student achievement is testimony to the ingenuity and perseverence of the research team. But in truth there was only the barest beginning of a guide from theorists like Piaget, Vygotsky, and others for them to follow as they constructed their research techniques and developmentally based experimental curricula based on developmental theories. The major implication from Strauss' work is that good theoretical models of classroom learning are in very short supply.

Another Middle Ground Theory

In my own effort to establish a middle-ground theoretical space for educational psychology, I have been motivated by goals similar to Strauss'. Indeed, his important article on cognitive–developmental theory (Strauss, 1972) helped guide my work in this area. Here is how I expressed the need for a middle-ground theory in an article written for the educational research community (Feldman, 1981a):

> One of the most important debates about education in recent years began (and unfortunately ended) with the first issue of the journal *Interchange* in 1970. The debate was between Carl Bereiter and Lawrence Kohlberg (Bereiter, 1970), and it was over the issue of what constituted the proper focus of educational research and educational practice. Bereiter argued, to no one's surprise, that education ought to be concerned about things that can be changed, modified, or influenced in a direct way by educators. Kohlberg (also to no one's surprise) argued that Bereiter's focus was too myopic and atomistic, too mechanical and controlling, and urged instead that educators become attuned to the natural processes of change that occur in children. Education, Kohlberg asserted, should facilitate the child's spontaneous attempts to make sense of the world. Bereiter's approach could perhaps be characterized as an "outside to inside" strategy, while Kohlberg, like his mentor Piaget, chose an "inside to outside" approach. I tried to enter this short-lived debate myself in 1971 when I published a paper in *AERJ* which tried to offer ground on which both Bereiter and Kohlberg could stand (and not be facing each other at 20 paces). This conceptual middle ground was to have had the critical feature of Bereiter's approach, a significant role for educators, as well as Kohlberg's heart's desire that the educational process emphasize developmental changes that were naturally occurring. I had in mind that there are certain processes of instruction and certain aspects of curriculum that, on the one hand, are broader than Bereiter's association games and drill and practice and yet, on the other hand, are more specific than the universal developmental stages discussed by Kohlberg, which all children are supposed to achieve. (p. 21)

In many respects my vision of what educational psychology should look like is similar to Strauss'. We concluded independently that both microscopic laboratory-type learning studies and global frameworks were equally inadequate and we both saw that something more distinctively educational in nature should be the field's focus. Not surprisingly, we both began to look for some conceptual solutions that would fill the bill. Here is where our two approaches diverged rather sharply. Strauss, being involved more in the educational applications, took the reasonable step of accepting typical curriculum content as its starting point.

Although concepts of heat and temperature are not always taught in science classes in every school, they often are. Strauss' other research focus, the arithmetic average, may be a mainstay of the school curriculum, but is nonetheless fundamental to much scientific reasoning. It does not take a great deal of rationalizing to see how content such as these fulfills the Vygotskian notion of ''scientific'' knowledge at the same time as they clearly have aspects that are part of a broader spontaneous set of understandings a la Piaget. Staying close to the real world of the classroom Strauss has chosen to study the development of knowledge areas that have a perfectly legitimate claim to inclusion in normal school curricula.

Because my approach to the problems of educational psychology was primarily theoretical and less practice-oriented, the content of my formulation is less clearly related to actual curricula. I propose a rapprochement between the fields of developmental and educational psychology by expanding the criteria by which bodies of knowledge could properly be considered developmental; a goodly number of such bodies of knowledge were presumed to be relevant to school learning (Feldman, 1976, 1980, 1981a, 1981b). From Strauss' point of view, my proposals probably still remain too far removed from day to day practice, my theory too general and abstract to be of direct use to curriculum makers or instructional designers. We both saw Piaget's developmental theory as too general to be of use to educators, but although Strauss' strategy was to try to infuse practice with a responsible rendering of Piagetian theory, my solution to the problem was quite different. I sought to expand the theoretical framework by simply claiming that the developmental territory was much more vast than even Piaget had thought.

Interestingly, the problem with this idea of expanding the notion of development is that it can be taken to an extreme, so that it loses its unique character (cf. Bereiter, 1982; Brainerd, 1981; Feldman, 1981a, 1981b). In responding to my proposals for an expanded view of developmental domains in *Beyond Universals in Cognitive Development,* for example, both Bereiter (1982) and Brainerd (1981) tried to argue that, by my criteria, the content they had been studying was just as developmental as Piaget's, thus blurring the distinction I was trying to make between learning and development. This is not at all what I (or Piaget or Vygotsky) had in mind, but it brings to focus the problem of where to draw the line. In my own framework, the line separating development from learning was drawn where qualitative, structural, stagelike transformations take place in orderly sequence. These are difficult criteria to specify systematically, which helps in part to explain why it was possible for critics like Bereiter and Brainerd to take them and run. Still, I did and do maintain that a vital distinction must be made between developmental analysis, which is broader than the accumulation of facts and symbols, and learning analysis, which attempts to specify the micro sequences of changes in small-scale knowledge entities. The distinction perhaps could be expressed as the difference between characterizing the criteria for excellence of a master poet or master computer programmer and characterizing the specific items in the memory of the same poet or programmer. The distinction between learning and development need not be a hard and fast one, but the flavor of the distinction should be clear.

My framework, the "universal to unique continuum," sketches a series of regions of developmental theory space in which various developmental "domains" are placed (see Fig. 7.1). The continuum specifies a universal set of domains of knowledge and skill in the Piaget tradition, as well as several additional sets of domains that are not universally acquired. These non-universal domains are neither spontaneously acquired nor mastered by all children in all cultures. Moving along the continuum from universal to unique, the regions mark bodies of knowledge that fewer and fewer individuals acquire. Cultural domains of knowledge are the closest to the universal Piagetian domains in that they represent bodies of knowledge that are expected to be universally acquired within a given culture. Although their acquisition is not universal across cultures, all individuals within a particular culture are expected to achieve a certain level of mastery of these valued domains. Examples of cultural domains include reading, writing, understanding maps, managing money, and understanding one's political system.

The next region on the continuum represents developmental domains that are based on the mastery of a particular discipline. Examples of these kinds of domains are chess, dance, aviation, medicine, carpentry, and law. Unlike cultural domains, where virtually everyone is expected to be proficient with certain kinds of knowledge or skills, discipline-based domains are the province of a much smaller segment of the population. With discipline-based domains the individual is also much freer to choose a particular domain to study. These domains, by virtue of being more specialized, also allow individuals to share a distinctive way of thinking about the nature of the particular field.

Still less frequently attained are bodies of knowledge I have identified as "idiosyncratic." Most of these domains are probably subareas of a discipline: They represent one's specialty—the particular work one chooses to master in a particular way. It is the opportunity to focus on a circumscribed set of problems and to develop a characteristic approach or understanding that makes this kind of mastery idiosyncratic. One kind of example is the study of particular subareas of a discipline by adults (e.g., patent law, repairing Maseratis, studying Middle English literature). Another kind of idiosyncratic development is that of the child

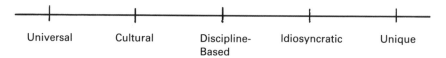

FIGURE 7.1. Developmental regions from universal to unique.

prodigy, when there seems to be an extremely strong, quick, and complete connection between an individual and a particular domain.

Finally, at the far end of the continuum there are unique achievements within domains. These represent new organizations of fields that have never before been accomplished in quite the same way. Such reorganizations or unique contributions are extremely infrequent; although many of us may aspire to making unique and lasting contributions to our fields, few actually manage to do so.

All of the regions of the continuum, whether they represent bodies of knowledge acquired by large segments of the population or ones uniquely impacted upon by a single individual, are nonetheless developmental domains. Developmental domains are ones that are characterized by a series of stagelike transformations, starting with the novice level and moving toward expert, master, or preeminent contributor. The shifts in quality of performance within developmental domains must be subject to transition mechanisms that are themselves developmental (i.e., that involve reorganization and qualitative advance between levels).

The major claim of the universal to unique framework is that there are numerous developmental domains to be studied and compared in addition to the universal ones that Piaget was interested in. Most of these nonuniversal domains would not be acquired beyond the minimal levels, and in many cases not at all, without systematic efforts by the society and without the availabilty of specific cultural resources to help bring about progress. In other words, most developmental domains require education for mastery. Thus, my middle ground is populated by whole bodies of knowledge that students may aspire to master or which their cultures require them to master. In either case, systematic educational efforts are required for this to occur. My way of using Vygotsky was to incorporate his point that society pushes development as much as nature drives it spontaneously, but does so in quite a different way from Strauss.

For Strauss, it is in the interplay among spontaneous, scientific and symbol system concepts that the middle ground is to be found. In this one sense, his framework is more process oriented than mine. He does not really seek to alter the content of any of his three dimensions: spontaneous development, instruction, and the acquisition of symbol systems all proceed as the relevant theorists have proposed. What Strauss proposes to do which is novel is to pay attention to how one dimension affects and is affected by each of the others: In this complex set of influences and counter influences the process of development is revealed. Strauss seeks to identify and control some of the encounters of these three dimensions with the aim of being more effective in transmitting the curriculum content specified by the school authorities. For example, the use of *conflict* in Strauss' research is explicitly intended to bring two of the dimensions into juxtaposition; this is what creates the conflict—with a little help from the teacher, of course. In the case of heat and temperature conflict, Strauss pitted the student's qualitative, common sense understanding of temperature with their understanding (or lack of it) of how numerical concepts are applied to the same situation. Through discussion and instruction, the students' two systems were brought into productive conflict, and then the children were helped to resolve the conflict by moving to the next level of understanding of the problem at hand.

But note that unlike the spate of conservation training studies of a decade ago, Strauss' technique does not attempt to transform any of the various developmental trajectories that it uses. This is not quite true, of course, because it is hoped that spontaneous development will be reformed to some extent by the directed conflict of the instructional technique. Fundamentally, however, the middle ground in Strauss' model is the interplay among existing different developmental systems. It takes curriculum content as given, it takes symbol systems as given, and it takes spontaneous development as given, then works with all three to bring about progress for the student. Theoretically, then, Strauss' model is quite different from mine. Whereas Strauss attempts to direct attention to intersections among existing systems, I have tried to show common structural properties and common transition mechanisms across several domains that until now have not been conceived of as developmental.

The universal-to-unique model takes a more theoretical stand, and tries to draw attention to the possibility that much of curriculum should be reconceptualized in terms of developmental principles, rather than the learning principles that have been traditionally applied. These have been either informal or pragmatic on the one hand, or based on laboratory learning theory based on the other. Developmental domains are simply different ways of thinking about content, casting content as stages or levels of organized knowledge arranged into sequences from novice to master, with the common principles being the transition processes that help students move from one level to the next. It may well be that among the transition processes that could help move students from stage to stage and level to level, the techniques that Strauss and his colleagues have tried might be utilized. In truth, there is relatively little known about just what kinds of experiences contribute to developmental change, and Strauss' work is a contribution toward that goal. But the critical assumption for Strauss is that the encounter among universal, scientific, and symbol systems knowledge is how development proceeds. This is very likely to be at least partially true, but it tends to downplay the unique and distinctive qualities of each domain of knowledge, an issue highlighted by the universal-to-unique framework.

Thus two approaches—Strauss' and universal-to-unique—are not in conflict, but tend to emphasize different aspects of the process of developmental change. Universal-to-unique does not deal directly with the interaction among dimensions of development, whereas Strauss' middle-ground theory does not deal with questions of the appropriateness of various forms of knowledge when looked at within a coherent developmental perspective. Both sets of issues are important, and neither in itself represents an adequate effort to build a middle-level model.

Perhaps the two approaches, taken together, might more closely approximate such a model. As it stands, Strauss' model is inadequate with respect to content. The problems chosen to study seem arbitrary, or if not arbitrary, chosen more for their suitability for research purposes than for any relevant curriculum reason. The improvements in learning of the subject matter are welcome, but hardly major or crucial. The universal-to-unique model, on the other hand, has no clear prescriptions or even clear predictions about how to facilitate development in the various domains, but it does point in the direction of how to understand many bodies of knowledge better. It also suggests a framework within which fields may be classified and analyzed with respect to their place in the school curriculum, in the society at large, or in specific applications. This is quite a different purpose from that of Strauss' middle-level model, but one that seems to me to be entirely consistent with it.

The most distinctive feature of both Strauss' and my work in educational psychology is that we both see educational psychology and developmental psychology as reciprocally related. Our common viewpoint is that both the traditional field of educational psychology on the one hand, and developmental psychology on the other, have had a sterile quality that can be overcome to some extent by putting the two fields into greater contact with one another. In our respective ways, Strauss and I have been trying to bring about such contact, although to be sure we are not the only ones to have done so. Jerome Bruner, Lawrence Kohlberg, and others have had substantial impact on the two fields over the years, but the fact remains that the problem of establishing a viable educational/developmental psychology remains largely unsolved. It is toward a solution of the problem of reconceptualizing educational psychology that the work of Strauss, and to some extent my own work, is aimed. We have both chosen to approach the task by trying to create some middle-ground area for the hybrid field to occupy, and this seems an appropriate place to begin a field and end a chapter.

ACKNOWLEDGMENTS

The work reported here was supported by grants from the Spencer Foundation, The Andrew W. Mellon Foundation, and the Jessie Smith Noyes Foundation. I am indebted to Lynn S. Liben and Lynn T. Goldsmith for their very helpful and constructive suggestions on earlier drafts. I also wish to thank Sidney Strauss for many hours of stimulating discussion that were much more interesting than writing this chapter.

REFERENCES

Bereiter, C. (1970). Educational implications of Kohlberg's cognitive-developmental view. *Interchange, 1,* 25–32.

Bereiter, C. (1982). Structures, doctrines, and polemical ghosts: A reply to Feldman. *Educational Researcher, 11,* 22–25.

Brainerd, C. J. (1981). Stages II: A review of *Beyond universals in cognitive development. Developmental Review, 1,* 63–81.

Brown, A. L., & Ferrara, R. A. (1985). Diagnosing zones of proximate development. In J. V. Wertsch (Ed.), *Culture, communication and cognition: Vygotskian perspectives* (pp. 273–305). New York: Cambridge University Press.

Cole, M., John-Steiner, V., Scribner, S., & Souberman, E. (Eds.). (1978). *Mind in society: The development of higher psychological processes by L. S. Vygotsky.* Cambridge, MA: Harvard University Press.

Feldman, D. H. (1971). Map understanding as a possible crystallizer of cognitive structures. *American Educational Research Journal, 8,* 482–501.

Feldman, D. H. (1976). The child as craftsman. *Phi Delta Kappan, 58,* 143–149.

Feldman, D. H. (1980). *Beyond universals in cognitive development.* Norwood, NJ: Ablex.

Feldman, D. H. (1981a). Beyond universals: Toward a developmental psychology of education. *Educational Researcher, 10,* 21–31.

Feldman, D. H. (1981b). The role of theory in cognitive developmental research: A reply to Brainerd. *Developmental Review, 1,* 82–89.

Feldman, D. H. (1982). A rejoinder to Bereiter. *Educational Researcher, 11,* 26–27.

Feldman, D. H. (1986). *Nature's gambit: Child prodigies and the development of human potential.* New York: Basic Books.

Hawkins, D. (1974). *The informed vision: Essays on learning and human nature.* New York: Agathon.

Kohlberg, L. (1970). Reply to Bereiter's statement on Kohlberg's cognitive-developmental view. *Interchange, 1,* 40–48.

Kohlberg, L., & Mayer, R. (1972). Development as the aim of education. *Harvard Educational Review, 42,* 449–496.

Piaget, J. (1948). *To understand is to invent.* New York: Penguin Books.

Piaget, J. (1970). *Science of education and the psychology of the child.* New York: Orion Press.

Strauss, S. (1972). Inducing cognitive development and learning: A review of short-term training experiments. I: The organismic developmental approach. *Cognition, 4,* 329–357.

Vygotsky, L. S. (1934). *Thought and language.* Cambridge, MA: MIT Press.

Wertsch, J. V. (Ed.). (1985). *Culture, communication and cognition: Vygotskian perspectives.* New York: Cambridge University Press.

8

Bandwidths of Competence: The Role of Supportive Contexts in Learning and Development

Ann L. Brown
Robert A. Reeve
University of Illinois

INTRODUCTION

Learning and Development

How do children learn? How are new modes of thought developed? Most would agree that these are the guiding questions of a developmental cognitive psychology. The relation between learning and development has always been controversial, however, and many contemporary developmental theorists avoid taking a clear stance on this issue, a fact that reflects the current state of flux of developmental theory. But all the traditional positions can be recognized today in somewhat disguised form, i.e., (a) that learning and development are unrelated, (b) that learning and development are identical, (c) that learning precedes development, and (d) that development precedes learning.

Some have interpreted the orthodox Piagetian position as adhering to the first position, that learning and development are unrelated. Vygotsky (1978) certainly classified Piaget's early writings as examples of an independence position and the tenor of the introductions to the Genevan work on Learning and Cognitive Development (Inhelder, Sinclair, & Bovet, 1974), by both Piaget and the authors, suggests that they were aware of the claim of a separate and "secondary" status for the concept of learning. The opening line is, "It may seem surprising that Genevan developmental psychologists have seen fit to write a book on learning" (p. 1). The term *learning*, however, was interpreted very much in terms of a reinforcement theory, Piaget's "learning in the strict sense (sensu stricto), rather than learning in the broader sense (sensu lato) which embraces cognitive development as a whole" (Piaget, 1959). On the basis of this definition, Piaget could equally well be classed as regarding learning and development as inseparable (sensu lato). When making claims about any theoretical position on the centrality of learning to development, it is essential that one clarifies the concept of learning being espoused. Guthrie, Hull, Spence, and Tolman, all had theories of learning, sorting out the differences between them, however, occupied the talents of whole generations of experimental psychologists.

The most explicit version of the "learning equals development" position is the Skinnerian stance, eloquently expressed by Baer (1970), who claimed that the concept of development was redundant; improvement with age is merely the sum of past learning. Perhaps not so readily recognized as a member of this camp are extreme versions of universal novice theories of immaturity, and simple forms of novice to expert shift explanations of development (for criticisms, see Brown, 1982; Brown & DeLoache, 1978; Carey, 1985). A position that holds that development is the result of the acquisition of expertise, without recourse to developmental constraints, would be a clear example of learning being equal to development.

Another recognizable position is that learning is prerequisite to development. Skills-hierarchy approaches that postulate the acquisition and automization of subskills leading to, or even affording, a restructuring at higher levels are examples of this theoretical ideal type (Gagné, 1962).

And finally, probably the most commonly expressed position (at the level of textbooks) is that development is prerequisite for learning. Examples of this include maturational theories, certain simplified stage theories, and notions of readiness in general.

The aforementioned examples are meant to illustrate that it is perfectly reasonable to hold any permutation of the learning/development issue and, at least implicitly, developmental psychologists do. Many also believe that a combination of these approaches characterizes human development (Case, 1985; Fischer, 1980), and this was certainly the position taken by Vygotsky (1978). In this chapter we concentrate on central aspects of Vygotsky's theory of learning and development, most notably the concept of a "zone of proximal development."

The Zone of Proximal Development

Vygotsky's central interest was in the evolution of cognitive processes, in growth and change rather than "fossilized," or automated processes of static state cognition. Even if one's goal is to understand adult cognition, this does not imply studying cognition in stasis. On the contrary, it is necessary to "alter the automatic, mechanized, fossilized character of the higher forms of behavior and turn it back to its source through experiment [to permit] dynamic analyses" (Vygotsky, 1978, p. 64). Vygotsky's "experimental–developmental" method was designed so that "one can, under laboratory conditions, provoke development" or "create a process of psychological development" experimentally (Vygotsky, 1978, p. 61). Given this emphasis on developing processes of thought, it is not surprising that Vygotsky had a special interest in children's learning, where one can observe cognitive processes "undergoing change right before one's eyes." For Vygotsky, developmental analysis was central to psychological investigation, not a peripheral offshoot having to do with the specialized study of children.

Vygotsky intended the notion of a zone of proximal development to capture the widely recognized fact, then and now, that "learning should be matched in some manner with the child's developmental level" (Vygotsky, 1978, p. 85). But he went farther, by arguing that one cannot understand the child's developmental level unless one considers two aspects of that level: the *actual developmental level* and the *potential developmental level*. "The zone of proximal development is the distance between the actual developmental level as determined by independent problem solving and the level of potential development as determined through problem solving under adult guidance, or in collaboration with more capable peers" (Vygotsky, 1978, p. 86). The actual developmental level is the result of "already completed developmental cycles." When a child's ability, or competence, is assessed on some static, independent test, this measure reflects the child's actual level of development; and this is true whether the measure is a standardized test or the laboratory experiment familiar to developmental psychologists.

An example of a static test of actual developmental level would be the estimate of an average 5-year-old's performance on a particular task purportedly measuring a particular cognitive process. Many researchers stop here; this is certainly the primary method of testing children if articles in the major developmental journals are representative of the field. But what if one does not stop here, and like Piaget in his clinical interviews, one "offers leading questions" or, like Vygotsky, one demonstrates "how the problem is solved" or "initiates the solution and the child completes it"—in short what if the child "barely misses an independent solution of the problem" (Vygotsky, 1978, p. 85) and is helped by a supportive environment to achieve a greater level of competence. As Vygotsky (1978) posed the problem:

> Suppose I investigate two children upon entrance into school, both of whom are ten years old chronologically and eight years old in terms of mental development. Can I say that they are the same age mentally? Of course. What does this mean? It means that they can independently deal with tasks up to the degree of difficulty that has been standardized for the eight-year-old level. If I stop at this point, people would imagine that the subsequent course of mental development and of school learning for these children will be the same, because it depends on their intellect. Of course, there may be other factors, for example, if one child was sick for half a year while the other was never absent from school: but generally speaking, the fate of these children should be the same. *Now imagine that I do not terminate my study at this point, but only begin it.* These children seem to be capable of handling problems up to an eight-year-old's level, but not beyond that. Suppose that I show them different ways of dealing with the problem. Different experimenters might employ different modes of demonstration in different cases: some might run

through an entire demonstration and ask the children to repeat it, others might initiate the solution and ask the child to finish it, or offer leading questions. In short, in some way or another I propose that the children solve the problem with my assistance. Under these circumstances it turns out that the first child can deal with problems up to a twelve-year-old's level, the second up to a nine-year-old's. Now, are these children mentally the same? (pp. 85–86, italics added)

Vygotsky argues that what children can do with the assistance of others is "even more indicative of their mental development than what they can do alone" (Vygotsky, 1978, p. 85), a point to which we return.

The zone of proximal development marks boundaries of competence within which a child can navigate with and without aid. At the lower boundaries are those "fruits" of "developmental cycles already completed," a conservative estimate of the child's status. At the upper bound are the estimates of just emerging competences that are actually created by the interactions of a supportive context. By considering both levels of the spectrum, one has a better estimate of a child's potential and, in addition, by observing the process of change as it occurs microgenetically one learns a great deal about development (Brown, 1982).

The zone of proximal development permits us to estimate the child's "immediate future and his dynamic developmental state" (Vygotsky, 1978, p. 90). It is important to note, however, that what the child can do now in social interaction becomes, in time, part of his or her independent repertoire. Social interaction creates zones of proximal development that operate initially only in collaborative interactions. But, gradually, the newly awakened processes "are internalized, they become part of the child's *independent developmental achievement*" (Vygotsky, 1978, p. 90). What is the upper bound of competence today becomes the springboard of tomorrow's achievements.

Because Vygotsky concentrated primarily on social contexts for creating competence, he placed a heavy emphasis on imitation as the well-spring of learning, arguing that a "full understanding of the concept of the zone of proximal development must result in reevaluation of the role of imitation in learning" (p. 82). To this end, Vygotsky pointed out that a person can imitate only that which is within his or her developmental level; the point is made clearly in the following obvious example:

> For example, if a child is having difficulty with a problem in arithmetic and the teacher solves it on the blackboard, the child may grasp the solution in an instant. But if the teacher were to solve a problem in higher mathematics, the child would not be able to understand the solution no matter how many times she imitated it. (Vygotsky, 1978, p. 88)

In common with current language development theorists, Vygotsky believed that knowing what a child is ready to imitate is knowing a great deal about the child's underlying competence.

But imitation is not the only driving force of progress. Vygotsky also emphasized such socially directed activities of a more knowledgeable other as providing prompts to a more mature solution, directing leading questions, forcing the
child to defend or change his or her theory, and so on. In this respect, Vygotsky
had much in common with early (contemporary to him) Piagetian theory (*The
Language and Thought of the Child*, 1926, and *Judgment and Reasoning in the
Child*, 1928) where it was also argued that the development of logical thought is
enhanced by the need to defend one's ideas to actual or imagined audiences. The
notion of supportive contexts creating new levels of competence can include
contexts other than the overtly social.

Chapter Outline

A basic theme of this chapter is the concept of bandwidths of competence, or
zones of proximal development created in contexts that vary in degree of support. These contexts can be overtly social as in the case of adult or peer assistance (see the next section) or only covertly so in the case of modifications in
thinking in response to an imagined or internalized audience. We also argue that
children create their own zones of competence by working recursively on their
own theories (see section titled Children as Creators of Their Own Zones of
Competence). In the fourth section, we discuss how developmental psychologists, sometimes unwittingly, create supportive contexts to reveal and perhaps
even accelerate development. Two themes that run throughout the chapter are:
(a) the importance of studying processes in change, of observing cognition over
time, or microgenetic analyses espoused by both Vygotsky and Genevan psychologists, and (b) the overriding concept of supportive environments for learning. Finally we argue that a consideration of zones of proximal development at
the very least permits us to consider the central issue of learning and development in a somewhat different light.

SOCIAL INTERACTIONS AS CONTEXTS
FOR LEARNING

The Genesis of Individual Thinking in Social Settings

The claim that individual thought processes might have their genesis in social
interactions is not unique to Vygotsky; in his early work, Piaget also considered
the role of social experience in development. In particular, Piaget regarded peer
interaction as an ideal forum for helping children "decenter" their thinking from
one particular egocentric perspective and consider multiple perspectives; such
social settings also provide incentives to coordinate opposing egocentric views,
and hence arrive at a more mature sociocentric consensus. Faced with a group of

peers who not only fail to accept one's own views but hold opposing opinions of their own, the child must compromise. In the process of compromising, the group produces a solution that is more mature than each individual effort. The conflict arising from group disagreement creates disequilibrium and the resulting adjustment to this state is a primary cause of cognitive development.

In his early work, Piaget stressed that a great deal of development was mediated by just such social interactions (see Doise, Mugny, & Perret-Clermont, 1975, for recent Genevan work on social interaction, and Forman, 1982, for a discussion). In addition, Piaget (1926) claimed that we internalize such interactions to form the basis of individual cognition, especially in the case of logical thinking:

> The adult, even in his most personal and private occupation, even when he is engaged on an inquiry which is incomprehensible to his fellow-beings, thinks socially, has continually in his mind's eye his collaborators or opponents, actual or eventual, at any rate members of his own profession to whom sooner or later he will announce the result of his labours. This mental picture pursues him throughout his task. The task itself is henceforth socialized at almost every stage of development . . . the need for checking and demonstrating calls into being an inner speech addressed throughout to a hypothetical opponent whom the imagination often pictures as one of flesh and blood. When, therefore, the adult is brought face to face with his fellow beings, what he announces to them is something already socially elaborated and therefore roughly adapted to his audience. (p. 59)

In the middle part of this century, American social psychologists interested in group dynamics also became concerned with the group as a learning context for individual cognition. For example, Bales (1950) argued that individual problem solving and group problem solving are necessarily similar, as the one (individual) is born of the other (social). Bales (1950) stated that ''Individual problem solving is essentially in form and in genesis a social process: thinking is a re-enactment by the individual of the problem-solving process as he went through it with other individuals'' (p. 62).

Similarly, Kelley and Thibaut (1954) put forward a theory of internalization similar to Vygotsky's when they suggested that an individual:

> acquires his thought and judgmental habits largely through interaction with other persons. It is by no means entirely fanciful to suppose that he 'internalizes' certain problem-solving functions that are originally performed for him by others. For example he may internalize a 'critic' role in the sense of learning to apply to himself the same standards and rules of critical evaluation that another person has previously manifested in interaction with him. (p. 738)

Vygotsky, however, went further and argued that not only do individual thought processes have their genesis in social interaction but that individual mental processes share organizational properties in common with the social situations from which they were derived. It follows that variations in the social interactions to which a child is exposed would have important consequences for the development of certain forms of thinking, hence the importance given by neo-Vygotskians to such crucial interactions as those between peers, siblings, parent and child, and teacher and child, the primary socialization agents of the young (Rogoff & Wertsch, 1984).

Internalization of Executive Control

What kinds of social interactions, likely to occur in groups, are important processes for individual thinking? Those who have been concerned primarily with adults have stressed the internalization of executive control, critical thinking, Socractic dialogue ploys, or metacognition—whatever your theoretical bias would lead you to call activities that create and revise, oversee, question, elaborate, and control premises, arguments, and problem solutions (Brown, Bransford, Ferrara, & Campione, 1983). For example, Dashiell (1935) came very close to discussing executive control when he described the six shared group activities that a participant might internalize as part of personal cognition:

(1) motivation by some felt difficulty, (2) analysis and diagnosis, (3) suggestion of possible solution or hypothesis, (4) the critical tracing out of their implications and consequences, and perhaps (5) an experimental trying out, before (6) accepting or rejecting the suggestion. (p. 1131)

Shaw (1932) also noted that one major function of the group was that it acts as a form of executive to its individual members. For example, the initiator of a suggestion will reject his or her own plan only one third as often as will other members of the group. The group members function together to reject inadequate plans that escape the notice of individuals working alone. Bales (1950) describes the central role of such executive routines as (a) asking for, giving, repeating, and clarifying information; (b) asking for and giving directions; and (c) asking for and suggesting ideas or plans for possible lines of action. Thus, a major function of the group is that it makes overt many of the executive critical functions that are usually hidden when an individual works alone. Kelley and Thibaut (1954) suggest this essential role of critic and evaluator, first learned in interpersonal settings, becomes internalized as a set of self-regulatory skills, all favorite Vygotskian concepts.

   The internalization of executive control, or the transition from other-regulation to self-regulation (Brown & French, 1979; Wertsch, 1979), has also been a major focus of developmental psychologists studying mother–child dyads. One of the most commonly reported examples of this type of interaction is mother–child dyads working on the construction of wooden block puzzles (Wertsch,

1979). The following is a sample of a videotaped interaction between a mother (M) and her 2½-year-old daughter (C):

1. C: Oh (glances at model, then looks at pieces pile). Oh, now where's this one go? (Picks up a black cargo square, looks at copy, then at pieces pile.)
2. M: Where does it go in this other one (the model)? (Child puts black cargo square back down in pieces pile, looks at pieces pile.)
3. M: Look at the other truck (model) and then you can tell. (Child looks at model, then glances at pieces pile.)
4. C: Well (looks at copy, then at model).
5. C: I look at it.
6. C: Um, this other puzzle has a black one over there. (Child points to black cargo square in model.)
7. M: Um-hm.
8. C: A black one (looks at pieces pile).
9. M: So where do you want to put the black one on this (your) puzzle? (Child picks up black cargo square from pieces pile and looks at copy.)
10. C: Well, where do you put it there? Over there? (Inserts black cargo square correctly in copy.)
11. M: That looks good.

Wertsch argued that this is an example of the mother serving a vital regulatory function, guiding the problem-solving activity of her child. Good examples of the mother assuming the regulatory role are statements 2, 3, and 9, where the mother functions to keep the child on task and to foster goal-relevant search and comparison activities. This protocol represents a mid-point between early stages, where the mother and child speak to each other, but the mother's utterances do not seem to be interpreted by the child as task relevant, and later stages, where the child assumes the regulatory functions herself, with the mother functioning as a sympathetic audience. Detailed observations of adult executive control come from such divergent situations as those of language acquisition (Greenfield, 1984; Scollon, 1976), picture book reading (DeLoache, 1984; Ninio & Bruner, 1978), memory tasks (Rogoff & Gardner, 1984), story telling (McNamee, 1981), reading comprehension (Au & Kawakami, in press; Palincsar & Brown, 1984), and number games (Saxe, Gearhart, & Guberman, 1984), as well as block play.

Shared Task and Goal Structures

Especially with very young children, social interactions do not always serve to highlight executive control of action patterns in a clearly defined problem space. In order to be sensitive to the gradual transfer of the executive role, the child must have a quite sophisticated concept of what the task is. Often, however, children and adults share very different concepts of the goal structure of the problem, and what appears to be joint activity on a common task is much more akin to parallel play: Adult and child interact with the concrete task but share little in the way of a common goal; indeed, they may often fail to share a common attentional focus.

Under such circumstances, either the adult or the child must begin an interaction by catching the attentional focus of the other. Excellent examples of these preliminary goal setting activities have been recorded by Rogoff observing adults' interactions with her twins (Rogoff, Malkin, & Gilbride, 1984). Adults attempt to elicit mutual gaze with 4- to 7-month-old twins by such common attention getters as "did you see that?" "what happened?" "lookit," and so on, just as 4-year-olds do with 2-year-old playmates (Shatz & Gelman, 1973). But as Rogoff et al. (1984) point out, this orchestration of shared attention does not always proceed strictly from adult to child as the children themselves actively involve themselves in situations that allow learning to occur. "Together the adult and child calibrate the appropriate level of participation by the child" (p. 43). One example of the child controlling the interaction appears when the 9-month-old boy twin catches sight of an attractive toy, a Bugs Bunny Jack-in-the-Box, while playing. He pushes it toward the adult and continues to pat the top until the adult is drawn into the game and works the mechanism for the baby. After the Jack has popped out, the adult tries to draw the child's attention to another game, but the baby "fidgets and whines." As the adult persists in the alternate game, the baby "grabs the box again, whining louder." This struggle of wills continues until the baby "raises his hands over his head in frustration and fatigue!" The adult capitulates and turns the handle of the desired box, asking sympathetically, "Is that what you wanted?" The toy is activated; the baby smiles; pulling the toy toward him, now calm (Rogoff, 1982).

Rogoff provides a variety of examples of the child as the participant who determines which toy will be selected; the baby initiates the action, the adult follows his lead. In the example just given, the baby seems to have been determined to play with the Jack-in-the-Box, not settling for the adult's attempts to interest him in other games. The baby was active in choosing the toy and seeking participation in its use. It would be erroneous to characterize the child's part in such interactions as the passive recipient of others' goals and instructions.

In general, however, the child's goal structure is the one that undergoes the major adaptation because it is usually the adult who has a clearly defined goal in mind; this is particularly true when the adult is engaged in deliberate teaching of academic-like skills. A major role of the "expert" in such situations is to get children to change their conception of the task in favor of a more strategic, economic, or academically sound approach. Wertsch (1984) has argued that one of the major changes that children undergo in the zone of proximal development is that they accept a qualitatively different interpretation of the goal of the joint activity. It is the expert's role to define an appropriate goal, to segment the task into manageable subunits, to arrange interactions at the child's level, and to change her demands in keeping with the child's growing expertise. This implicit teaching role is more clearly seen in activities that are similar to academic learning settings, when the child is playing a game with number correspondence (Saxe et al., 1984), reading (Palincsar & Brown, 1984), or story telling (McNamee, 1981). In other situations that are more clearly play-like, the adult's role can be much more like that of an equal, engaged in parallel play or often taking the lead of the child.

The Centrality of Instruction

One common feature of the type of interactive situations in which children often find themselves is that adults adopt, either implicitly or explicitly, a teaching function. It is this natural instructional role that is a mainstay of development. As Wertsch (1984) points out, the Russian word *obuchenie* actually means the "teaching–learning process," and it is this symbiotic function that is central to Vygotsky's theory (see Wertsch, 1984, for a detailed discussion). *Obuchenie* "creates the zone of proximal development," it

> rouses to life, awakens and sets in motion a variety of internal processes of development in the child. At this point, these processes are still possible for the child only in the sphere of interaction with surrounding people and in the sphere of collaboration with peers. But these processes, which constitute the course of internal development, then become the internal property of the child himself or herself. (Vygotsky, 1962, p. 450)

It is important to note that the teaching function of interactional situations need not be explicit, or be the central agenda of the activity. We have already seen that a group problem-solving setting is said to provide a learning forum for its members, even though the guiding activity is successful problem solution, regardless of individual contributions or the potential for personal development. Similarly, many of the situations examined by those interested in the zone of proximal development are informal apprenticeship settings where the teaching function is a minor part of the total activity. Typical of learning in informal settings is a reliance on *proleptic teaching* (Brown & Campione, 1984; Rogoff & Gardner, 1984; Wertsch & Stone, 1979). *Proleptic* means "in anticipation of competence" and in the context of instruction refers to situations where novices are encouraged to participate in a group activity before they are able to perform unaided, the social context supporting the individual's efforts. The novice carries out simple aspects of the task while observing and learning from an expert, who serves as a model for higher level involvement.

In many cultures, children are initiated into adult work activities such as weaving (Greenfield, 1980, 1984), tailoring (Lave, 1977), marketing (Lave,

Murtaugh, & de la Rocha, 1984), and so on without explicit formal instruction (Cole & Bruner, 1971; Cole & Scribner, 1975). The expert members of the group have as their main agenda the task of weaving, tailoring, and the like and are only secondarily concerned with initiating the novice, or overseeing the progress of the apprentice. It is the adult who takes on most of the responsibility for getting the task done with the child participating as a spectator, then a novice responsible for very little of the actual work (Laboratory of Comparative Human Cognition, 1983). As the apprentices become more experienced and capable of performing more complex aspects of the task, aspects that have been modeled by adults time and time again, they are ceded greater and greater responsibility until they become experts themselves. Within these systems of tutelage, novices learn about the task at their own rate, in the presence of experts, participating only at a level they are capable of fulfilling at any point in time.

The main features of informal proleptic instruction are very different from formal schooling. In informal learning situations the group has responsibility for getting the job done, or at least an illusion of joint responsibility is maintained. Children join in, often on their own initiative or with seemingly little pressure from the adults; they participate only at the level they are currently able to perform, or just beyond. They are rarely allowed to fail because errors are costly to production of a concrete product, the major task at hand. Everyone has the same, clearly defined agenda, the name of the game is known to all, the goal is clear. The adults (experts, mastercraftsmen) model appropriate behavior and occasionally guide novices to increasingly more mature participation. There is rarely any demand for solo performance on the part of children, indeed it is often difficult to measure any child's individual contribution because everyone is participating at the same time. Children perform well within their range of competence; rarely are they called on to perform beyond their capacity; the adults do not expose the children's ignorance, but jointly benefit from their increasing competence. Above all, such teaching is implicit; a Zinacanteco woman (expert weaver), asked how girls in her society learn to weave, claimed that they learn by themselves! (Greenfield, 1984).

Although adults in apprenticeship systems may not be aware of their instructional function, closer examination certainly reveals that they do teach, and the teaching style they adopt has a readily identifiable structure. Greenfield (1984; see also Wood, 1980; Wood & Middleton, 1975), in examining common features of informal instruction in language acquisition and in weaving, identifies six common elements to the two informal learning situations: (a) the degree of aid, or scaffolding, is adapted to the learner's current state; (b) the amount of scaffolding decreases as the skill of the learner increases; (c) for a learner at any one skill level, greater assistance is given if task difficulty increases, and vice versa; (d) scaffolding is integrated with shaping, i.e., local correction and aid are given in response to the child's current performance; (e) the aid or scaffolding is eventually internalized, permitting independent skilled performance; and finally

(f) in both the language and weaving contexts, the teachers appear to be generally unaware of their teaching function.

The instructional role, however, can sometimes be quite explicit and this has been the general rule in American studies of mother–child, teacher–child interactions, for the mothers/teachers have been set to teach the child explicitly by the experimental context. But even given the change from an implicit to explicit teaching role, Greenfield's six elements describe the proleptic teaching role quite well (see Au & Kawakami, in press; Brown & Palincsar, in press; Palincsar & Brown, 1984; Tharp et al., 1984). To illustrate, we give one example of mother–child interaction (Saxe et al., 1984) and one of teacher–child dialogues (Palincsar & Brown, 1984).

Saxe et al. (1984) examined mothers as they attempted to teach their 2½ to 5-year-old children a number reproduction game. The goal was to match pennies with cookie monsters; a number of cookie monster pictures (set sizes 3, 4, 9, and 10) was placed on a board and the child's task was to select from a set of 15 the same number of pennies, put them in a cup and take them to the mother. The mothers introduced and controlled the task differently as a function of the starting competence of the child. Mothers of low-ability children began with a single array subgoal, such as, "count the cookie monsters." With higher level children, however, they began with statements such as, "You have to get the same number of pennies as there are cookie monsters," and indirect requests intended to help focus the child on the need to achieve a numerical representation of one of the arrays without specifying the means for doing this. In short, the mothers adjusted their degree of aid to the learner's current status.

Mothers also adjusted their degree of aid as a function of task difficulty (e.g., increasing set size, by giving more direct assistance and more explicit prompts). Some mothers of high-ability children referred back to previous easy set sizes in order to guide their children. Mothers also organized the task differently as the child became more competent. In addition, they responded locally to each individual move on the part of the child; they shifted down to a goal directive simpler than, and subordinate to, the previous higher one if the child produced an inaccurate count and shifted up to a superordinate, less explicit, directive if the child had succeeded. Just as did the weavers in Greenfield's studies, the mothers provided scaffolding and shaping for their child's efforts. They adjusted the goal structure (superordinate or subgoal) to the child's level, shifting it up or down depending on the child's attainments and the perceived task difficulty.

Next, we consider one example from our own work of an explicit attempt to make instruction in the schools more like the natural tutoring procedures of proleptic teaching (Brown & Palincsar, in press; Palincsar & Brown, 1984). Junior high-school poor learners, with particularly depressed reading comprehension scores, were taken from their traditional formal reading instruction and placed in a reciprocal teaching environment (Brown & Palincsar, 1982, in press; Palincsar & Brown, 1984). In reciprocal teaching, students of varying levels of competence and an adult teacher take turns "being the teacher," that is leading a dialogue on a segment of text they are jointly attempting to understand and remember. The "teacher" responsible for a particular segment of text leads the ensuing dialogue by stating the gist in her own words, asking a question on that segment, clarifying any misunderstandings, and predicting what might happen next. All of these activities are embedded in as natural a dialogue as possible, with the adult teacher and students giving feedback to each other.

Close inspection of these dialogues revealed repeated examples of guided learning (i.e., where the adult teacher provided modeling, feedback, and practice to students at a level that appeared to match the student's current need). As students became better able to perform some aspects of the task, the teacher increased her demands accordingly, until the students' behavior became increasingly like that of the adult model, who in turn decreased her level of participation and acted as a supportive audience.

One example of such an interaction is shown in Table 8.1. This dialogue took place between an expert teacher and a seventh-grade minority student named Charles (IQ = 70, Reading Comprehension grade equivalent = third grade). At the beginning of the training session, Charles was unable to formulate a question. The teacher, estimating that he is having more than usual difficulty with the task, opens her interaction by stating the main idea (statement 2). She continues to lead him, asking for a "why" question (statement 4) but, receiving no response, she resorts to forming a question for him to mimic (statement 6). Even imitating a fully formed question is difficult for Charles (statements 7, 9). Again, on Day 4, the teacher formulates the question (statement 20), but this time she waits until Charles comes very close to an adequate question by himself. As Charles improves, the teacher demands more from him. On Day 4, the teacher does not open by providing the main idea, she probes for it (statement 14) and probes for a question (statements 16, 18), which she corrects (statement 20). Note, however, that although the teacher actually produces the questions on both Day 1 and Day 4, on Day 4 she waits until Charles has contributed most of the elements himself.

As Charles' ability to participate increases even further, the teacher again increases the level of participation that she demands from him. On Day 7, she requests a modification to his question form (statement 23), but he formulated the question (statement 24). By Day 11, she receives two excellent questions, but now demands only one (statement 27), i.e., she requires him to stick to the exact rules of the game. Finally, by Day 15, Charles can perform his part unaided.

Charles and Sara were part of a reading tutorial that met regularly with the same expert teacher. Charles was a particularly weak student at the start, unable to formulate questions at all. Sara, in contrast, began the intervention with a clear notion of the kinds of questions that occur in school—"fill in the blanks." Excerpts from her protocol are shown in Table 8.2. On Day 2, the teacher, who has tolerated "fill in the blanks" questions until this point, attempts to take the student beyond this level (statement 2) and asks for a main idea rather than a

TABLE 8.1
The Acquisition of Question-Asking by a Weak Seventh Grade
Student (Charles)

Day 1:

Text:	The water moccasin, somewhat longer than the copperhead, is found in the southeastern states. It lives in swampy regions. It belongs, as do also the copperhead and the rattlesnakes, to a group of poisonous snakes called pit vipers. They have pits between their eyes and their nostrils which, because they are sensitive to heat, help the snakes tell when they are near a warm-blooded animal. Another name for the water moccasin is "cottonmouth." This name comes from the white lining of the snake's mouth.

 1 S: What is found in the southeastern snakes, also the copperhead, rattlesnakes, vipers—they have. I'm not doing this right.
 2 T: All right. Do you want to know about the pit vipers?
 3 S: Yeah.
 4 T: What would be a good question about the pit vipers that starts with the word "why?"
 5 S: (No response)
 6 T: How about, "Why are the snakes called pit vipers?"
 7 S: Why do they want to know that they are called pit vipers?
 8 T: Try it again.
 9 S: Why do they, pit vipers in a pit?
10 T: How about, "Why do they call the snakes pit vipers?"
11 S: Why do they call the snakes pit vipers?
12 T: There you go! Good for you.

Day 4:

Text:	Spinner's mate is much smaller than she, and his body is dull brown. He spends most of his time sitting at one side of her web.

13 S: (No question)
14 T: What's this paragraph about?
15 S: Spinner's mate. How do spinner's mate . . .
16 T: That's good. Keep going.
17 S: How do spinner's mate is smaller than . . . How am I going to say that?
18 T: Take your time with it. You want to ask a question about spinner's mate and what he does, beginning with the word "how."
19 S: How do they spend most of his time sitting?
20 T: You're very close. The question would be, "How does spinner's mate spend most of his time?" Now, you ask it.
21 S: How does spinner's mate spend most of his time?

TABLE 8.1
Continued

Day 7:

| *Text:* | Perhaps you are wondering where the lava and other volcanic products come from. Deep within our earth there are pockets of molten rock called *magma.* Forced upward in part by gas pressure, this molten rock continually tries to reach the surface. Eventually—by means of cracks in the crustal rocks or some similar zone of weakness—the magma may break out of the ground. It then flows from the vent as lava, or spews skyward as dense clouds of lava particles. |

22 S: How does the pressure from below push the mass of hot rock against the opening? Is that it?
23 T: Not quite. Start your question with, "What happens when?"
24 S: What happens when the pressure from below pushes the mass of hot rock against the opening?
25 T: Good for you! Good job.

Day 11:

| *Text:* | One of the most interesting of the insect-eating plants is the Venus's flytrap. This plant lives in only one small area of the world—the coastal marshes of North and South Carolina. The Venus's flytrap doesn't look unusual. Its habits, however, make it truly a plant wonder. |

26 S: What is the most interesting of the insect eating plants, and where do the plants live at?
27 T: Two excellent questions! They are both clear and important questions. Ask us one at a time now.

Day 15:

| *Text:* | Scientists also come to the South Pole to study the strange lights that glow overhead during the Antarctic night. (It's a cold and lonely world for the few hardy people who "winter over" the polar night.) These "southern lights" are caused by the Earth acting like a magnet on electrical particles in the air. They are clues that may help us understand the Earth's core and the upper edges of its blanket of air. |

28 S: Why do scientists come to the south pole to study?
29 T: Excellent question! That is what this paragraph is all about.

TABLE 8.2
Improvement in Question-Asking by a More Competent Seventh
Grade Student (Sara)

Day 2:

Text:	**How Can Snakes be so Flexible?**
	The snake's skeleton and parts of its body are very flexible—something like a rubber hose with bones. A snake's backbone can have as many as 300 vertebrae, almost ten times as many as a human's. These vertebrae are connected by loose and rubbery tissues that allow easy movement. Because of this bendable, twistable spinal construction, a snake can turn its body in almost any direction at almost any point.

1 S: Snakes' backbones can have as many as 300 vertebrates—almost _ _ _ times as many as humans.

2 T: Not a bad beginning, but I would consider that a question about a detail. Try to avoid "fill in the blank" questions. See if next time you can find a main idea question and begin your question with a question word—how, why, when. . . .

Day 3:

Text:	There are snakes in nearly all parts of the world. Some snakes prefer warm, arid desert areas. Others prefer leafy forests, fields, and woodlands. Some stay in areas near water and are fine swimmers. Then there are several varieties that live all their lives in the sea.

3 S: Can snakes live their whole lives in seas?

4 T: See if you can ask a question using your own words.

Day 4:

Text:	The other kind of camel—the one with two humps—is the *Bactrian.* Its home country is the Gobi Desert of northeastern Asia. The Bactrial has shorter legs and longer wool than the one-humped camel. It also has stronger, more rugged feet. This is important because instead of having sand to walk on, the Bactrian camels live in rough and rocky parts of the world.

5 S: Where is the Bactrian found?

6 T: Good for you.

Day 6:

Text:	When most full-grown spiders want to travel, they have to walk on their eight legs. But some small kinds of spiders, and many young ones, use an easier way. They climb up on bushes, fence posts, or weed stems and spin streamers of silk. When the wind catches the silk and blows it away, each spider tightly holds onto his own streamer. The silk streamer carries him through the air as if it were a parachute or a balloon.

TABLE 8.2
Continued

---

7 S: I think I have another. When it's traveling, what do they compare the spider to?

8 T: An interesting question.

Day 11:

Text:	The young caterpillar's first meal is its own eggshell. Then it eats a leaf and each day eats more and more food. After a few days, the caterpillar becomes too large for its skin. A new skin forms beneath the first one, the old skin comes open and, like a snake, the caterpillar wriggles its way out of the split skin. Then the caterpillar goes on eating leaves or other kinds of food. When the new skin becomes too tight for the growing body, it again splits and comes off. By then the caterpillar is covered by another skin. This eating and shedding goes on for several weeks. The old skin may be replaced by a new one four or five times. Each time the skin is shed, the size and color of the caterpillar change.

9 S: Why does the caterpillar's skin split?

10 T: Excellent question. That was the point of the entire paragraph.

---

detail question. On Day 3, Sara comes up with a main idea question as requested (statement 3), so again the teacher increases her demands by suggesting that, instead of selecting a line from the text, the student summarize in her own words, a process called invention (Brown & Day, 1983) that is difficult for weaker students to handle. For the remainder of the sessions, Sara's questions are classified primarily as inventions. The teacher has been modeling inventions, and the student has followed suit.

Turn now to observations of a regular classroom teacher leading her reading group according to the reciprocal teaching method. In Table 8.3, we see excerpts from the third day of instruction using this method and in Table 8.4 are excerpts from the thirteenth instructional day. The group consisted of one adult teacher and five seventh-grade poor readers.

Because of the larger group size, compared with the tutorial, the students were able to provide modeling and feedback for each other, learning from their peers as well as from their teacher. As the sessions progressed, the teacher was able to hand over a great deal of the work to the students and serve more as a coach than a teacher. An illustration of this change is shown in the contrast between the dialogue samples in Table 8.3, where the teacher is in control and the students interact almost exclusively with her, and that of the later session from the same group, shown in Table 8.4, where the students respond to each other with encouragement from the adult teacher.

Both the Day 3 and Day 13 dialogues attest to the fact that the students and

TABLE 8.3
Reciprocal Dialogue from an Early Session; Study 2, Group 3, Day 3

Text:

> Can Snakes Sting with their Tongues?
> No—snakes' tongues are completely harmless. They're used for feeling things and for sharpening the snakes' sense of smell. Although snakes can smell in the usual way, the tongue flickering in the air picks up tiny particles of matter. These particles are deposited in two tiny cavities at the base of the nostrils to increase the snakes's ability to smell.

1. A: Do snakes' tongues sting?
2. K: Sometimes.
3. A: Correct.
   This paragraph is about do snakes sting with their tongue, and different ways that the tongue is for and the senses of smell.
4. *T: Are there any questions?
5. C: Snakes' tongues don't sting.
6. *T: Beautiful! I thought, boy, I must have been doing some fast reading there because I missed that point. A_____, could you ask your question again?
7. A: Do snakes' tongues really sting?
8. *T: Now, A_____, since you have asked the question, can you find in that paragraph where the question is answered?
9. A: No, snakes' tongues are completely harmless.
10. *T: So we'll try it again. Can you generate another question that you think a teacher might ask?
11. A: What are the tongues used for?
12. *T: Good!
13. L: The sense of smell.
14. *T: Is that correct? A_____, do you disagree? Yes.
15. A: That answer was right, but there are other things that the tongue can do.
16. L: But she only said tell one, she didn't say tell all of them.
17. *T: O.K.
18. B: It is used to pick up tiny particles.
19. *T: O.K. I think that this is an important point. You have the basic concept which is correct, O.K., but what the question really is saying is, is it used for smell? O.K.?
20. B: They are used for feeling things for sharpening snakes' sense of smell.
21. *T: O.K. They are used for sharpening the snakes' sense of smell. Are they used for smelling? That's the point we aren't clear on.
22. L: In my answer I said it is for the sense of smell.
23. *T: This is fine; this is what the technique is all about. What it means is not that you are right or wrong or good or bad. What it says is that we have just read something and have had a disagreement about what it says. We need to work it out.
24. A: My prediction is that they will now talk about the different things about snakes. Where they live, and what they eat and stuff like that.
25. *T: O.K. Good. What do you think they eat?
26. A: Animals.
27. A: Deserts.
28. C: I challenge. Snakes, all of them, don't live in the desert. They live in the woods and in swamp areas.

---

*Indicates turns taken by adult teacher

TABLE 8.4
Reciprocal Dialogue from a Later Session; Study 2, Group 3, Day 13

Text:
> In the United States salt is produced by three basic methods: solar (sun) evaporation, mining, and artificial heat evaporation. For salt to be extracted by solar evaporation, the weather must be hot and dry. Thus, solar salt is harvested in the tropic-like areas along our southern ocean coasts and at Great Salt Lake.

1. C: Name three different basic methods how salt is produced.
2. A: Evaporation, mining, evaporation . . . artificial heat evaporation.
3. C: Correct, very good. My summary on this paragraph is about ways that salt is being produced.
4. *T: Very good. Could you select the next teacher?
   (Student selects another student)

Text:
> The second oldest form of salt production is mining. Unlike early methods that made the work extremely dangerous and difficult, today's methods use special machinery, and salt mining is easier and safer. The old expression "back to the salt mine" no longer applies.

5. L: Name two words that often describe mining salt in the old days.
6. K: Back to the salt mines?
7. L: No. Angela?
8. A: Dangerous and difficult.
9. L: Correct. This paragraph is all about comparing the old mining of salt and today's mining of salt.
10. *T: Beautiful!
11. L: I have a prediction to make.
12. *T: Good.
13. L: I think it might tell when salt was first discovered, well, it might tell what salt is made of and how it's made.
14. *T: O.K. Can we have another teacher?

Text:
> Table salt is made by the third method—artificial evaporation. Pumping water into an underground salt bed dissolves the salt to make a brine that is brought to the surface. After purification at high temperatures, the salt is ready for our tables.

15. K: After purification at high temperatures the salt is ready for what?
16. C: Our tables.
17. K: That's correct. To summarize: After its purification, the salt is put on our tables.
18. *T: That was a fine job, Ken, and I appreciate all that work, but I think there might be something else to add to our summary. There is more important information that I think we need to include. This paragraph is mostly about what?
19. A: The third method of artificial evaporation.

TABLE 8.4
Continued

---

20. B: It mainly tells about pumping water from an underground salt bed that dissolves the salt to make a brine that is brought to the surface.
21. *T: Angela hit it right on the money. This paragraph is mostly about the method of artificial evaporation and then everything else in the paragraph is telling us about that process. O.K. Next teacher.

Text: | For thousands of years people have known salt—tasting it, using it for their lives' needs. Sometimes it has been treasured as gold; other times it has been superstitiously tossed over the shoulder to ward off bad luck. Somehow people and salt have always been together, but never is the tie more complete than when the best people are called "the salt of the earth."

22. C: My question is, what are the best people called?
23. L: The salt of the earth.
24. C: Why?
25. L: Because salt and the people have been together so long.
26. *T: Chris, do you have something to add to that? O.K. It really isn't because they have been together so long; it has to do with something else. Brian?
27. B: (reading) "People and salt have always been together but never has the tie been so complete."
28. *T: Allright, but when we use the expression, "That person is the salt of the earth," we know that means that person is a good person. How do we know that?
29. B: Because we treasure salt, like gold.

---

*Indicates turns taken by adult teacher

teacher were able to engage in a smooth flowing discussion. On Day 3, however, the teacher is very much the pivotal participant. As can be seen in Table 8.3, one session of the silent reading is followed by one extensive dialogue, where the students interact with one another only once (statements 1–3); the remainder of the runs are S–T, S–T, student (S) followed by teacher (T). The students interact individually with the teacher, not with each other. Note also that the entire interaction focuses on one segment of text and on one disputed point—the use of snakes' tongues. Interestingly, other reading groups had problems with this segment, one student reading, "No snake's tongue is completely harmless," instead of the correct, "No—snakes' tongues are completely harmless," thus generating an interesting confusion and occasion for clarification.

The same group is seen again, 10 intervention days later, in the dialogue shown in Table 8.4. Here, four reading–dialogue sets are included in 29 statements, rather than only one as in Table 8.3. Now the majority of the "runs" are student-controlled, with the teacher interspersing praise and encouragement (statements 4, 10, 12) and some management (statements 4, 14, 21). The teacher only intercedes with advice and modeling when a student misses the point and the other students do not catch it (statements 18, 26, 28). The teacher has moved from the pivotal role of responding individually to each child, to a coach who sits in the background, offers encouragement, and occasionally pushes for a better interpretation of the text. The expert provides just the degree of scaffolding necessary for the dialogues to remain on track, leaving the students to take as much responsibility as they can.

In practical terms, the results of the reciprocal teaching intervention were dramatic. The students clearly internalized the types of interactions they had experienced, improving not only in their ability to paraphrase the gist and ask questions of clarification, interpretation, and prediction, but also in their ability to assume the role of teacher, producing their own questions and summaries, and evaluating those of others. In addition, the intervention resulted in dramatic improvements on laboratory, classroom, and standardized tests of comprehension. The participating students progressed from the very poorest performers in the class to the average level set by their normally achieving agemates. But perhaps more important, the child's feelings of personal competence and control improved dramatically, enabling them to go farther and to improve their skills on their own (Brown, Palincsar, & Purcell, 1986; Reeve & Brown, 1985). The teachers also adhered to the six steps described by Greenfield (1984), adjusting their level of control to the child's products and the difficulty of the task. The students gradually internalized the teacher's procedure so that they could perform unaided. Expert teachers perform these adjustments without necessarily being aware of the fine-tuning of the reciprocal interaction in which they are engaged.

Interactions such as these examples of mother–child, teacher–child, expert–novice dialogues have a central place in learning and provide a major impetus to cognitive growth. According to Vygotsky (1978), teaching–learning, or *obuchenie,* creates development, which in turn determines the level at which teaching–learning can be directed. Learning and development are interwoven in a complex spiral pattern, none of the four alternatives mentioned in the introduction fully capture the flavor of this relationship. Certainly, however, such a position is not consistent with either the position that learning and development are unrelated or that they are identical. Instruction creates a zone of proximal development within which learning can occur.

> Learning is not development; however, properly organized learning results in mental development and sets in motion a variety of developmental processes that would be impossible apart from learning. Our hypothesis elaborates the unity but not the identity of learning processes and internal developmental processes. (Vygotsky, 1978, pp. 90–91)

Needless to say, there remain many unanswered questions concerning social interactions as contexts for individual development. Stimulating as Vygotsky's ideas might be, the zone of proximal development is a concept in need of validation. Social interactions do not always create new learning; some parents are surely more effective teachers than others; peer interactions vary enormously, only some creating ideal learning experiences. We need a great deal more research addressing such qeustions as: (a) What kinds of interactions are maximally effective at inducing cognitive growth? (b) Can optimal interactions be orchestrated deliberately? (c) To what extent do social collaborations lead to independent competence? (d) What are the mechanisms underlying internalization? and so on. In short, Vygotsky provided a blueprint for research, but supportive contexts need to be delineated in far greater detail.

Dynamic Assessment

Implicit in the adult–child dialogues we have been considering is the notion of on-line diagnoses. In order to be responsive to the child's "region of sensitivity to instruction" (Wood & Middleton, 1975), the expert must continually define and refine her theory of the child's existing state of learning. As such, the interactions in the zone of proximal development must involve an implicit diagnostic activity.

Vygotsky was also concerned with a more explicit diagnostic function; he had a pressing practical interest in using the concept of a zone of proximal development for diagnostic purposes. As Director of the Institute of Defectology in Moscow, Vygotsky was faced with the practical task of designing educational assessment procedures that could take the place of Western IQ measures, which, as we have seen, he regarded as retrospective estimates of past learning rather than prospective predictions concerning potential developmental trajectories. Therefore, the notion of a zone of proximal development had a central place in Vygotsky's work on assessment, and it continues to play a major role in Soviet clinical diagnoses and remedial training (Egorova, 1973; Vlasova, 1972; Wozniak, 1975; Zabramna, 1971).

For practical reasons then, Vygotsky needed a way of estimating both actual and potential developmental levels, and this is reflected in the passage quoted previously where he gives the example of two 10-year-olds with actual mental ages of 8 years, one of whom can, with the experimenter's help, perform at a 12-year-old level and the other who can perform only at a 9-year-old level. If a practical method could be found where such differences could be measured, Vygotsky believed they would have both diagnostic and instructional significance (Brown & French, 1979; Vygotsky, 1978; Wozniak, 1975).

In the work on the zone of proximal development described so far, the primary interest has been in observing the child's assisted progress in the zone of proximal development created by various forms of social interaction. Rarely have investigators considered the other aspect of Vygotsky's theory, that the fruits of the zone of proximal development created in the interaction will be internalized and become part of the independent repertoire of the child and this change can be measured. One exception is the work of Palincsar and Brown (Brown & Palincsar, in press; Palincsar & Brown, 1984) where independent measures of learning and transfer were taken in addition to estimates of progress within the interaction. But for assessment purposes, one needs to estimate independent progress, i.e., Vygotsky's imaginary 10-year-old who gains 4 years is different from the one who gains only 1. Although both children "failed" in their unassisted attempts to solve the problem, both benefited from instruction, but the first child was far more "ready" to receive instruction than the second. The subsequent careers of spectacular "gainers" (Budoff, 1974) is the central interest of many psychologists concerned with dynamic assessment; the most notable proponent being Reuven Feuerstein (1979, 1980), who also developed his Learning Potential Assessment Device when faced with the practical assessment problem of evaluating children in displaced person camps who had spent years without systematic formal education (Feuerstein & Richelle, 1963). Static standardized ability and achievement tests are even less appropriate for children for whom the assumption of appropriate consistent formal education cannot be held (Brown & French, 1979).

In our own work on diagnostic zones of proximal development (Brown & Campione, 1984; Brown & Ferrara, 1985; Campione, Brown, & Bryant, 1985; Campione, Brown, Ferrara, & Bryant, 1984), we have taken the idea of systematically measuring aspects of assisted learning one step further. Like Vygotsky and contemporary Soviet investigators (Egorova, 1973; Vlasova, 1972), we assess children's independent performance first on variants of a problem to estimate a level at which they cannot perform without assistance and then on other variants, after the interactive sessions. In addition, however, we also measure the degree of assistance a particular child requires during the interactions. For example, a child is set to learn an inductive reasoning problem such as a series of matrices problem similar to the Raven Progressive Matrices test of intelligence (Raven, 1938), or a double classification task (Bryant, Brown, & Campione, 1983), or a series completion task (Ferrara, Brown, & Campione, 1981; Simon & Kotovsky, 1963). Initially, the child performs poorly; she is then given a series of such problem accompanied by a standard set of prompts or hints. The hints are structured in a general to specific sequence with the initial hints being quite nonspecific, "Is this problem like any other you have seen?" "Can you see a pattern?" Subsequent hints, which become more and more concrete and specific, are given as the child needs them. We estimate the amount of help needed on both learning and transfer sessions.

Consider some concrete examples. The problems shown in Fig. 8.1 are matrices type problems. The child's job is to figure out how the missing figure in the lower right corner of each problem should look. A computerized testing situation was developed in which the child could construct the missing figure using a touch-sensitive panel and could receive graduated animated hints from the com-

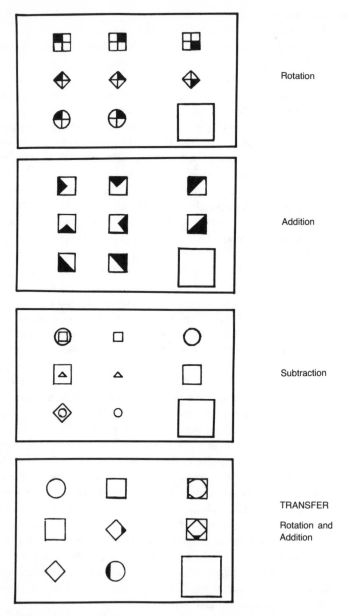

Rotation

Addition

Subtraction

TRANSFER

Rotation and
Addition

FIGURE 8.1. Examples of matrices inductive reasoning problems
(from Campione et al., in press).

puter with the touch of a button (Campione, Brown, Ferrara, Jones, & Steinberg, 1985).

Initially, the children learned each of three rules—rotation, addition (imposition), and subtraction. The top problem in Fig. 8.1 is a rotation problem. In such problems, the left-most figure in each row is rotated 90° to the right to obtain the figure in the center, and that figure is then rotated another 90° to the right to obtain the right-most figure. The second problem in Fig. 8.1 is an addition problem and the third problem a subtraction example. The children were provided with a practice box in which they could try out various manipulations (e.g., rotation) on the various items. If the children could not solve a problem unaided, they requested and received a series of hints from the computer (in one study, or from an experimenter in another). These hints ranged from general to specific, and later hints in the series consisted of an animated demonstration of the rotation, addition, or subtraction movement. The children continued using the practice box, generating solutions and requesting hints, until they could solve two consecutive problems of each type without aid.

Following learning, maintenance and transfer sessions were given. In the first session, the students attempted to solve maintenance problems. These were the same three types already learned to criterion—rotation, addition, and subtraction—but they were presented in a random order. The students had to identify the type of problem, i.e., discover which rule applied, and then construct the correct answer.

On subsequent sessions, both maintenance and transfer items were given, the maintenance items interspersed among novel transfer items. Transfer matrices are illustrated in the fourth problem in Fig. 8.1, they involved a combination of two of the rules learned initially in the context of separate matrix problems. The answer to the example in Fig. 8.1 would involve rotating the left-most figure in each row 90° to the right and superimposing that rotated figure on the one in the middle column to generate the right-most item. Items of this type appear on the adult superior version of the Raven's matrices test.

In a series of such studies, we found that the degree of aid needed to learn and transfer solutions in inductive reasoning domains is an extremely sensitive index of individual differences. Slower and younger children need more aid to reach the same degree of initial learning. As the degree of change from the initial learning situation to the transfer probes increases, ability-related differences also increase. Of greater importance is that learning and transfer efficiency, measured as degree of help given by the adult (or adult plus computer), is a sensitive predictor of long-term improvement within the domain. For example, using a double classification matrices task with 5-year-old children, Bryant, Brown, and Campione (1983) considered the change from static pretest to static posttest that took place after the interactive sessions. Even after the effects of IQ, pretest scores, scores from the Raven Coloured Progressive Matrices (another intelligence test) on the gain scores were statistically removed, a considerable amount of the variance in improvement was attributable to the amount of aid needed to learn and transfer (approximately 20% in each case). Alternatively, if one looks at simple correlations, the best predictor of improvement from the pre- to the posttest was performance on far transfer items, followed by transfer indices and then learning efficiency. It would appear that individual differences in the degree of assistance needed for learning and transfer in interactive sessions is an important predictor of independent improvement within a domain. As such, these indices serve important diagnostic functions over and above that which could be provided by static tests, as Vygotsky predicted.

This diagnostic function would be particularly important if guided learning and transfer assessments such as the aforementioned could be designed to test readiness within common academic subject areas. If a teacher, in addition to knowing a child's static test scores, could also gauge a particular child's readiness to learn in situations such as mathematics or reading, he or she could tailor his or her instruction accordingly. Diagnosis is only important if it leads to remediation (Binet, 1909; Brown, 1985). For this reason, we are currently devising dynamic assessment measures of early mathematic skills as well as extending our work on reading comprehension.

Children as Creators of Their Own Zones of Competence

In the previous section we emphasized the importance of social interaction for creating zones of proximal development; guided by an expert who provides the essential scaffolding, the child progresses to greater levels of first social and then independent competence. But we should not overlook the fact that microgenetic analyses of children working alone suggest that children create and extend their own zones of competence without aid from others. Of course one could argue, as did Piaget and Vygotsky, that even when apparently working alone, the child is interacting with an imagined, internalized audience.

We believe that it would be a mistake to overemphasize the conception of children as other-directed, i.e., always guided in their learning by outside forces. Behaviorist theories were also theories of other-directed guidance, guidance conceived in terms of a variety of external reinforcements that shape behavior, and a simple interpretation of Vygotsky's theory could also lead to an overemphasis on guided learning where parents, peers, and instructors always instigate development. Although these guided learning situations may be interesting and important, we should be careful not to concentrate exclusively on external pressures in knowledge acquisition. Although children are undoubtedly observers and imitators of adult behavior—even if they learn primarily in this fashion—they are also capable of actively orchestrating their own learning. We have seen this is true even for the very young learner in interactive situations, witness Rogoff's example of the 9-month-old initiating the game of Jack-in-the-Box. It is equally important to acknowledge that children learn in situations where there is no obvious guidance, no feedback other than their own satisfaction, and no external pressure to improve or change. In a very real sense they act as little scientists, creating theories-in-action (Karmiloff-Smith, 1984) that they challenge, extend, and modify on their own. The child is not only a problem solver but a problem creator—a metaphor that has much in keeping with scientific thinking.

Some of the best evidence of self-motivated learning comes from situations in which children are observed as they operate on a problem, over considerable periods of time, without external pressure, and seemingly with no motivation other than to improve the theory on which they are working. In this section we illustrate this point by describing some examples of our own work on self-directed learning followed by a discussion of neo-Genevan microgenetic studies of learning (Karmiloff-Smith, 1984; Karmiloff-Smith & Inhelder, 1974–1975).

Errors and Self-Correction

In collaboration with Judy DeLoache, Mary Jo Kane, and Susan Sugarman, we have conducted a series of studies on young children's self-directed learning. We have been particularly interested in error correction procedures as a function of age and task complexity, and in the similarity of the microgenetic progression within and across ages that children seem to undergo when they operate on an interesting problem, producing and correcting errors and solutions on their own volition. Consider first a group of 24 to 48-month-old children videotaped as they engaged in free play with a set of five nesting cups (DeLoache, Sugarman, & Brown, 1985). Although the children saw the cups nested before they began to play, there was no real need for them to attempt nesting themselves; however, they did so, working long and hard in the process, and there were no age differences in the likelihood that they would eventually achieve a correct seriation. There were, however, interesting differences with age in the children's strategies for improving their system.

The most primitive strategy, used frequently by children below 30 months, was *brute force*. When a large cup was placed on a smaller one, the children would press down hard on the non-fitting cup. Variants of brute pressure were twisting and banging, but the same principle held; the large cup will fit into the smaller one if only one can press hard enough.

A second strategy initiated by some of the younger children was that of *local correction*. After placing two non-fitting cups together children removed the top cup and did one of two things: They either looked for an alternative base for the non-fitting cup or tried an alternative top for the original base. Both ploys involved minimal restructuring and necessitate considering the relation between only two cups at any one time. The third characteristic ploy of children below 30 months was to respond to a cup that would not fit into a partially completed set of cups by *dismantling the entire set* and starting again.

Older children (30–42 months) faced with a non-fitting cup engaged in strategies that involve *consideration of the entire set* of relations in the stack. For example, one sophisticated strategy was *insertion;* the children took apart the stack at a point that enabled them to insert the new cup in its correct position. A second strategy, *reversal,* was also shown by older children. After placing two non-fitting cups together, children would immediately reverse the relation between them (5/4 immediately switched to 4/5).

The rapidly executed reversal strategy was not shown by the younger group. Some young children would repeatedly assemble, for example, cups 4–1, starting with 4 as a base and then inserting 3, 2, and 1. Then they encountered the largest cup, that is, 5, and attempted to insert it on top of the completed partial stack, pressing and twisting repeatedly. When brute force failed, they would dismantle the whole stack and start again. Similarly, having assembled 1, 2, 4, and 5 and then encountering 3, the younger children's only recourse was to begin again.

Although there are clear age differences in the efficiency with which the children strived to achieve a seriated stack, note that even the very youngest children persisted at the task, corrected their own errors, and made progress toward a goal, without any obvious external pressure to do so; that is, they formulated and tested their own theories-in-action.

It would appear that this form of progression, from brute force and local correction to a consideration of the problem as a whole, is a general acquisition mechanism. For example, a very similar trend is seen in older children (4–7 years) attempting to construct a railway circuit (Brown, in press; Karmiloff-Smith, 1979b). Children are shown cardboard pieces of track that, if assembled correctly, will make a railway circuit for a small toy train. They are then shown a more complex version, and, given tracks, asked to make one like that themselves. One solution is to alternate the straight and curved pieces. Another is to put together four curved pieces into arches at the top and bottom and join each arch with two straight pieces. These correct constructions are shown as (a) and (b) in Fig. 8.2. The children are left alone to complete the circuit.

Many of the youngest children begin by placing any randomly selected piece next to any other and hence end up in a position that cannot possibly lead to solution. Examples are shown in panels (c) and (d) of Fig. 8.2. Of interest is what the children do now. Even the youngest persist in their efforts, but their strategies change with age and experience in a way quite analogous to the stacking cups task just described.

The first line of attack is the *brute force* approach; the children try to make the track fit by firmly pushing them together to close up gaps. This is followed by *local correction,* the children remove the last few pieces and try to fix them but

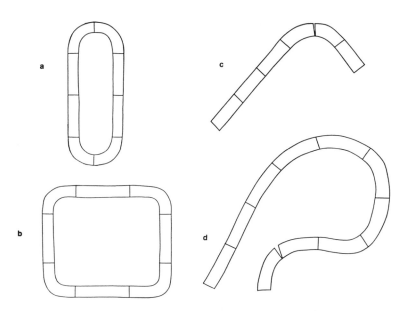

FIGURE 8.2. Examples of correct and incorrect assemblies of the rail circuit task.

ignore the rest of the construction that is equally in need of work. The third stage is the one where the children, seeing the trouble they are in, *disassemble the entire construction,* and start again, even though part of the construction could be salvaged. These early strategies are essentially identical to those developed by much younger children as they attempt to seriate nesting cups.

The more mature strategies on the railway task also parallel those developed to deal with the cups assembly task. These strategies involve viewing the *construction as a whole,* thus enabling the children to rearrange only those pieces that need rearranging, leaving correct sections intact. Often the corrections involved the strategic *reversal* of already joined pieces, or *insertion* of a critical straight (curved) piece. Finally, some efficient learners actually dismantled a perfectly workable system and reconstituted a new version, pointing out that there were several solutions to the one problem. This developmental progression was seen both across ages (macrogenetic change) and within an age group (microgenetic change) when children were given a long time to work on the problem (Karmiloff-Smith, 1979b). It was also seen when children were asked to fix up disasters created by other children; and hence the level of problem difficulty could be kept constant across ages (Brown, in press).

Similar microgenetic trends can be seen if one considers much older children (12 years old) revising their own written compositions. An early correction strategy is again *local correction,* trying to fix up one local error even though the entire production is much in need of revision. This is followed by the *disassembly* ploy, where, realizing the need for massive revision, the child jettisons his whole initial efforts and starts again, even though parts are salvagable. Finally, with practice at revising, the child comes to master the type of activities that result from a *consideration of the product as a whole, inserting* needed clarification and *reversing* the order of existing segments. Although the analogy with the 2-year-old nesting cups is somewhat far-fetched, the similarity in the microgenetic pattern is intriguing.

For all of these examples, we can ask, *why do the children bother?* Implicit in the situations is the *goal:* that the cups should be seriated, a workable railway should be constructed, an acceptable composition should be written, and so on; but the children, remain free to leave the field whenever they like. But they persist; they persist even in the face of frustration; they persist for long periods of time; they persist, correcting their own errors time and time again. Perhaps even more impressive evidence of this persistence and self-control comes from studies by Karmiloff-Smith (1979a, 1979b, 1984) in which young children are seen correcting and perfecting their productions even after a perfectly adequate solution has been reached. Reorganization and improvement in strategies are not solely responses to failure, but often occur when the child has quite adequate functioning procedures but seeks to improve them. It is not failure that directs the change, but success—success that the child wishes to refine and extend. We illustrate this point with one example from Karmiloff-Smith.

Theories in Action

In a landmark paper, Karmiloff-Smith and Inhelder (1974–1975) examined children, from 4 to 9 years of age, as they played with a set of balancing blocks. Their task was to play with the blocks and balance them on a narrow metal rod fixed to a long piece of wood (see Fig. 8.3). These were no normal blocks, however. Standard blocks had their weight evenly distributed, and the correct solution was to balance them at the geometric center. Weight blocks had the weight of each "side" varied either conspicuously (by gluing a large square block to one end of the base rectangular block) or inconspicuously (by inserting a hidden weight into a cavity on one end of the rectangular block).

At first, the children made the blocks balance by *brute trial and error* using proprioceptive information to guide action. Behavior was purely directed at the goal of balancing. This ploy was obviously successful; the children balanced the blocks. In this sense they had met the goal set them, the blocks all balanced; they could stop at this point. But they did not stop here even though by some criteria they had "finished" the game; they had met the goal of achieving balance. Without any external pressure to do so, they set about testing and revising theories to uncover the rules governing balance in the miniature world of these particular blocks. Their initial theories involved incomplete rules that produced

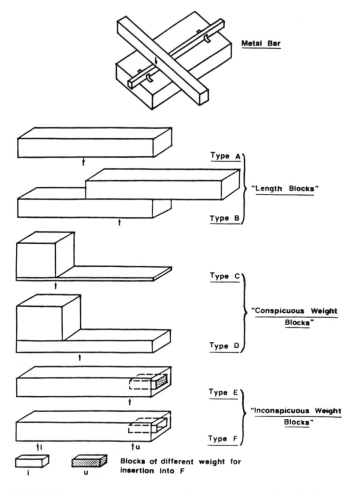

FIGURE 8.3. Examples of the block types used by Karmiloff-Smith
and Inhelder (1974–1975).

errors. A common early theory was to concentrate exclusively on the geometric
center and attempt to balance all blocks in this fashion. This works for standard
unweighted blocks but not for weighted blocks of either kind. Here the theory did
not result in balance, so the weighted blocks were discarded as exceptions
("impossible-to-balance"), even though the child had previously been able to
balance them all.

After this theory was well established and working well for unweighted
blocks the child became discomfited by the number of, and regularity of, the
impossible-to-balance set. A new juxtaposed theory was then developed that

incorporated the conspicuous weight blocks. For these, the children compensated for the weight that was obviously added to one end and adjusted the point of balance accordingly. Inconspicuous weight problems still generated errors; they looked identical to the unweighted blocks and were, therefore, subjected to the dominant geometric center rule. When they did not conform to the theory they were discarded as anomalies that were "impossible-to-balance." The children's verbal responses reflected these juxtaposed solutions, with exclusive length justifications given for unweighted blocks and weight justifications given for conspicuously weighted blocks.

After establishing and practicing the juxtaposed theory, the young theorists were again made uncomfortable by the remaining exceptions to their own rules and began to seek a rule for them. In so doing, a reorganization was induced that resulted in a single rule for all blocks. The children paused before balancing any block and roughly assessed the point of balance. Verbal responses reflected their consideration of both length and weight, e.g., "You have to be careful, sometimes it's just as heavy on each side and so the middle is right, and sometimes it's heavier on one side." After inferring the probable point of balance, only then did the children place the block on the bar.

The progression from procedures that fail to procedures that work, shown in the stacking cups and railway track examples, can be explained in terms of goal-directed learning, the child wishes to correct errors. But in the blocks example, the pressure to work on adequate partial theories to produce more encompassing theories is very similar to what occurs in scientific reasoning. Like scientists, it is essential that children first gain control of simple theories in their quest for a more complex and more adequate theory. Karmiloff-Smith and Inhelder (1974–1975) refer to this as creative simplification:

> The construction of false theories or the overgeneralization of limited ones are in effect productive processes. Overgeneralization, a sometimes derogatory term, can be looked upon as the creative simplification of a problem by ignoring some of the complicating factors (such as weight in the block study). This is implicit in the young child's behavior but could be explicit in the scientist's. Overgeneralization is not just a means to simplify but also to unify; it is then not surprising that the child and the scientist often refuse counterexamples since they complicate the unification process. However, to be capable of unifying positive examples implies that one is equally capable of attempting to find a unifying principle to cover counterexamples. (p. 209)

Progress comes only when the inadequate partial theory is well established and the learner is free to attempt to extend the theory to other phenomena. In this way, the theorists, be they children or scientists, are able to discover new properties that in turn make it possible for new theories to be constructed.

There can be little doubt that children, even very young children, do work unaided on their own theories, creating and extending their own levels of competence and sophistication as they do so. Note, however, that these self-directed improvements would not be apparent if one were to maintain the tradition of considering only one-shot, static estimates of the child's competence. Indeed, Karmiloff-Smith has emphasized that cross-sectional age trends are often indistinguishable from microgenetic changes within a child over relatively short periods of time (Karmiloff-Smith, 1979a, 1979b, 1984; Karmiloff-Smith & Inhelder, 1974–1975). To estimate a child's current cognitive status, one must be very careful in the type and extent of performance one captures in order to estimate competence. An added complexity is that just as similarities in processing, such as revealed in the nesting cups and railway track examples, do not necessarily result in identical end products, identical end products do not necessarily implicate the same underlying processes. Evidence of early competence does not necessarily imply an equivalence in the underlying cognitive processes that are used to solve easy and difficult versions of the same task (Thornton, 1982); modified versions of traditional tasks may not be conceptually equivalent to traditional tasks (cf. Dean, Chabaud, & Bridges, 1981). By the same token, similar performances on a single task should not be taken as evidence for similar cognitive processing in two different age groups. Again, a microgenetic approach is the more likely method to reveal similarities and differences in process and product alike. The notion of zones, or bandwidths of competence through which the child navigates, with or without assistance, could be a more fruitful metaphor for theory development than that of a static, frozen, snapshot in time that predominates in the developmental literature.

TASK ENVIRONMENTS AND SUPPORTIVE CONTEXTS

Demonstrating Cognitive Precosity

Developmental psychologists also collaborate with children to reveal bandwidths of competence by providing contexts that vary in the support they provide for learning. Indeed, a predominant interest of developmental psychologists in the past few years has been the game of demonstrating that contrary to theory X, Y, or Z, preschool children have much more competence than was supposed (see Gelman, 1978; Gelman & Brown, 1986, for reviews). This controversy for Piagetians centered around the transition from preoperational thought to concrete operations said to "occur" between 5 and 7 years of age (roughly), and for learning theorists of several persuasions, it also took the form of questions concerning a putative 5-to-7 shift (White, 1965). Disputed were such issues as whether a qualitative shift occurred between non-mediated learning in the preschooler to mediated learning in the older child (Kendler & Kendler, 1962; Zeaman & House, 1963). Similarly, a shift from absolute to relational learning was also under contention (Brown & Scott, 1972; Kuenne, 1946; Reese, 1968). For those interested primarily in memory development, the controversy concerned the existence and extent of strategic processes prior to the onset of formal schooling (Brown, 1975; Brown & DeLoache, 1978; Wellman, Ritter, & Flavell, 1975).

In all of these domains, researchers had considerable success demonstrating preschool competence, and the methods they used were similar. The guiding principle was to look for evidence of cognitive precosity, not only in the traditional laboratory tasks, but also in situations where preschool competence could most readily be shown. To considerably oversimplify the comparative literature, the two major techniques used to expose early competency have been (a) to *strip away* all but the most essential elements of the task in order to reveal its cognitive demands in the simplest possible form and (b) *to situate the experiment in the familiar,* i.e., in task settings compatible with preschoolers' interests and knowledge.

A combination of these two techniques marks the better cross-cultural experimental work (Laboratory of Comparative Human Cognition, 1983) and also reveals early competence in preschool children. For example, Shatz (1978) argued cogently that earlier (or later) competence in communicative situations can readily be accounted for by the excess baggage of the task. In unfamiliar situations, with arbitrary stimuli, where the children must expend considerable cognitive effort identifying the items and comprehending the nature of the game, they appear unable to communicate adequately with a peer. In situations where the game is familiar, the information to be conveyed is meaningful and, therefore, cognitive "capacity" is freed for the communicative aspect of the task, the younger children look far more reasonable; they communicate well. Flavell and his colleagues (Flavell, 1977; Salatas & Flavell, 1976) have also shown that complexity and familiarity are important factors leading to a diagnosis of egocentricism in children. Similarly, Gelman and her colleagues (Gelman, 1978, 1983; Gelman & Baillargeon, 1983; Gelman & Gallistel, 1978) have made this point quite graphically for several "concrete" operational tasks. And many investigators have shown the importance of complexity and familiarity in revealing or disguising the memorial sophistication of small children (Brown & DeLoache, 1978; Deloache, 1980, 1984; Perlmutter & Myers, 1979; Sophian, 1986; Wellman & Somerville, 1982).

We illustrate this research trend with a glance at the history of one problem-solving task, first examined in rats, and then extended to more and more child centered versions of the basic problem (Crisafi & Brown, 1983). The task, originally a Hullian (Hull, 1952) classic, was said to measure inferential reasoning (Maier, 1936), although not by Hull. It involved the ability to combine two separately learned pieces of information to reach a goal. A schematic version of the original Hullian maze is shown in Fig. 8.4. For example, a hungry rat would be placed at box B and trained to run to G, the goal, for food. In a second

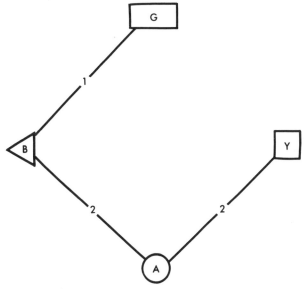

Schematic Version of the A–B–G Problem

FIGURE 8.4. Schematic version of the A–B–G problem based on Hull (1952).

separate part of the study, the rat, now thirsty, would be placed at A and trained to run to either B or Y where it would find water. In the final stage of the study, the rat would be placed in A. If thirsty, it would run with equal probability to B or Y, the water sources; if hungry, it would run only to B, the connecting route to G, the food box. The fact that rats could piece together this information was taken as evidence of a simple form of inferential reasoning, the ability to piece together two separately learned items of information to reach a goal.

Maier (1936) extended this paradigm to more elaborate mazes suitable, he thought, for work with both rats and children. The actual details of Maier's studies need not concern us here. Suffice it to say that the problem he developed to test the subject's inferential skill involved a maze like the one illustrated in Fig. 8.5. The maze was child-size (an identical rat size maze was available for rats), and consisted of darkened runways through which the child was expected to complete routes to reach goal boxes in a similar inferential pattern to the Hull studies. Children below 6 did not fare well in this estimate of their maze running abilities; as can be seen in Fig. 8.6, it is not until well into the school years that children perform as well as rats! The fact that running in a darkened maze in a basement laboratory may be a task setting suitable to no organism, but better suited to rats than preschoolers, was not open to a great deal of debate in the early years of child psychology.

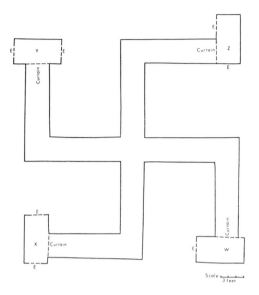

FIGURE 8.5. Schematic version of the A–B–G problem used by Maier (1936).

Things improved considerably in the 1960s, when there was considerable upsurge of interest in children's learning in paradigms originally developed for the study of rats, pigeons, and monkeys (Stevenson, 1970; White 1970). As an example of the better work of that period, Kendler and Kendler (1967) adapted the basic Hullian task for use with children. They used an apparatus similar to that shown in the top half of Fig. 8.7. It consisted of an automatic box with three distinctively colored panels, each of which could be covered by a plain aluminum outer panel. At the outset of the learning situation, only the two outside panels of the box were opened. The child learned to press a button on the red side to obtain a marble and to press a button on the blue side to get a steel ball. After learning these responses to criterion, the side panels were closed and the center panel was opened. Now the child learned to deposit one of the items, for example the marble, into a slot in the center panel so that a toy charm would be dispensed. The order of acquisition of the two problem parts proved to be immaterial. On the critical test trials, all three panels were opened for the first time, and the child was asked to make the toy charm come out as quickly as possible. A correct response required that the child combine the information regarding which item obtained the charm (the marble) with the information concerning its location (the red side). In a series of studies using this task, the Kendlers found that only 6% of the kindergarteners tested could solve the problem unaided, a result that has been replicated many times by many investigators.

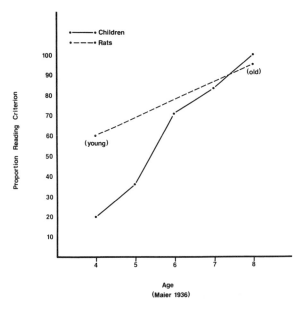

FIGURE 8.6. Data from rats and children in Maier's A–B–G maze (Maier, 1936).

Crisafi (1980) attempted to make the task more hospitable for very young learners by introducing familiar objects and already-known connections between locations and tokens, ploys that had resulted in increased rates of learning in cross-cultural studies (Cole, Gay, Glick, & Sharp, 1971). In Crisafi's first task (shown as B in Fig. 8.7), the child learned to find a penny or dime in a purse or a piggy bank and then learned that the insertion of the correct coin into a gumball machine produced a gumball. The inference task required combining the correct item, for example the penny, and its location, the purse, to get a gumball. The objects in this task were chosen to be familiar and the relations among them to be consistent with the child's previous experience (pennies are found in purses and are used to operate gumball machines). The second task (shown as C in Fig. 8.7) demanded the same solution. It involved a specially designed truck that dumped a candy when a grey token (located in either a milk container or a saucepan) was inserted. These objects were also familiar and attractive, but the relations among the constituent elements were novel. Crisafi's third task was similar to the automated box apparatus designed by the Kendlers and just described. The objects and relations were aribtrary and unfamiliar. The logical structure of the three tasks is shown in Table 8.5.

Thus, the three versions of the task were designed to form an easy-to-hard sequence of three instantiations of the same rule. The difficulty of the presumed

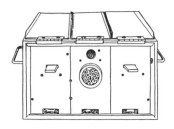

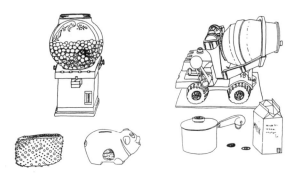

FIGURE 8.7. Three versions of the A–B–G problem used by Crisafi and Brown (1983).

sequence was confirmed. The ability of 2-year-old subjects to combine the two pieces of information was dramatically influenced by the familiarity and compatibility variables. Unaided inferential solutions were shown by 89% of the children on the gumball task, 67% on the truck task, and 0% on the automated box task. Obviously, 2-year-olds are capable of this simple form of inferential reasoning under optimal circumstances. Armed with these learning environments, ranging from easy to difficult analogues of the same problem, Crisafi and Brown (1983) were able to aid very young children to transfer the solution to the more difficult versions.

The moral of this brief history is, of course, the dramatic change in psychologists' estimates of the cognitive capacity of the preschool child faced with a simple inferential reasoning task. Note that the database is not in question, children below 5 do have extraordinary difficulty solving Kendler and Kendler's (1967) version of the task and we have no doubt, although we have not tested it ourselves, that they would prove somewhat recalcitrant maze runners! This well-established fact is as much a part of our picture of children's learning as is their precosity in solving gumball and truck versions of the problem (Crisafi & Brown,

TABLE 8.5
Design for Combining Information Tasks

Task Structure:	Container– Subgoal Relation (A–B, x–y)	Subgoal–Goal (B–G)	Combining Test (A–B–G)
Task Varient			
Familiar Objects:			
1. Know Rela- tions (Gumball Machine)	bank–penny purse–dime	penny–gumball machine → gumball	bank → penny penny → gumball
2. New Relations: (Truck)	carton–white but- ton pan–grey button	white button– truck → candy bean	carton → white button white button → candy bean
Unfamiliar Objects:			
3. New Relation (Box-Auto- mated)	red panel–marble blue panel–ball bearing	marble–center panel → M & M	red panel → mar- ble marble → M & M

1983). There is no doubt that cognitive activities revealed in supportive contexts may be obscured in unfamiliar task formats that are perhaps more suitable for other species of learners (Maier, 1936). Similarly, differences in efficiency such as those displayed on the gumball and automated version of the task by 3-year-olds, but not by 6-year-olds, are an important aspect of the learning profile that differentiates age groups. Again, it is bandwidths of competence across and within settings that reveal age differences, rather than static estimates of "capacity" on a single task variant appropriate to a restricted age range.

What Does it Mean to Call a Context Supportive?

Findings such as those just mentioned, that very young children have the competence to perform logically, strategically, operationally, and so on, on very simple task formats are fairly representative of the recent developmental literature and are the kind of evidence that has been used to call into question general notions of stages of development. But what do such findings really tell us? What are we doing, as experimenters, when we render a task suitable for 2-year-olds, or unschooled *Kpelle* (see Cole et al., 1971). In many demonstrations of early competence, there is a suspicion of circularity in the arguments proposed to explain the phenomena; if the contextual support manipulations work, then that task instantiation is judged suitably indigenous for preschoolers or unschooled others; if the manipulation does not work, then the context is judged unsuitable for revealing competence that we now assume to be "there", somewhere! Clearly what is needed is some a priori analysis of what is manipulated when we induce early competence and a detailed specification of the difference between earlier and later forms of competence.

Why does the 3-year-old fail on the task versions readily solved by the 6-year-old? Various theorists have argued that the memory load is too high, that the younger child's processing capacity is overburdened, or that the task is incompatible with the child's existing knowledge base. Any or all of these may be true, but we need some systematic method of determining what we mean by increased memory load or overburdened processing capacity, and we need some systematic way of mapping the knowledge base. Some attempts at systematic a priori analyses exist already. For example, Case, extending the theory first exposed Pascual-Leone (1970), has attempted to estimate the processing load of a variety of cognitive tasks. Case (1978, 1982) has been one of the most eloquent supporters of the position that cognitive development is constrained by the growth of working memory and of central processing capacity. Although it is widely recognized that a construct akin to working memory is essential in a theory of development (Flavell, 1978, 1982), such a concept is not without its difficulties. Reviewing the literature on age differences in basic capacity, Brown et al. (1983) concluded that at this point in time, the evidence is moot, existing data could be explained in terms of change in knowledge or processing strategies, just as readily as changes in underlying capacity (Chi, 1976). And, Flavell (1978) rightly queried "How are we to decide, in a consistent fashion, exactly what constitutes an "item" in working memory for any given problem-solving strategy, and hence, how are we to decide exactly how much memory load use of that strategy imposes?" (p. 100).

More recently, Case and his colleagues (Case, 1982; Case, Kurland, & Goldberg, 1982) have emphasized the importance of "operational efficiency" which, they suggest, controls the growth of processing capacity. In the modified position, total capacity remains constant with performance being determined by a trade-off between storage requirements and the efficiency of mental operations. Decrements in necessary operating space occur as a result of the growing speed, efficiency, and automaticity of basis processes (e.g., storage and retrieval).

Although Case's recent position emphasizes the importance of separating the structural and the processing components of the developing problem-solving system, it does not completely clarify his overall theoretical position. Indeed, Flavell (1978) focused on the main point of difficulty, by asking of Case's view, "Won't it be even harder to decide that a mental operation is 'sufficiently automatized' than to decide how many such operations have to be held in working memory during the execution of a strategy?" (p. 101). Reliance on the concept of changes in working memory capacity to "explain" task-varient effects is to raise rather than to answer the basic question.

Flavell's research on perspective taking skills takes another approach to explaining rather than just demonstrating precocious processing. The perspective taking task has an interesting history in the light of arguments concerning early competence. According to Piagetian researchers, visual or spatial perspective taking is a developmentally advanced accomplishment coinciding with the emergence of logical thinking skills in middle childhood. Piaget and Inhelder (1956) developed the three-mountain problem to assess whether children could predict the perspective of an individual other than oneself. In this task the child has to infer how an array of objects looks to an observer who views the array from a different position to that of the subject. The failure of young children to adopt the perspective of another on the three-mountain task was attributed to egocentrism that is considered to be characteristic of preoperational thinking.

More recently, however, it has been demonstrated that a variety of contextual manipulations affect children's judgments on perspective-taking tasks, casting doubt on the Piagetian claim that young children lack the cognitive structures necessary for perspective taking (Fehr, 1978; Rosser, 1983). For example, if 4-year-olds are allowed to rotate a second array, mounted on a lazy-susan device, they can accurately judge perspective (Borke, 1975), and if they are allowed to view the test array from all possible perspectives, they make fewer errors than if they make perspective judgments without having first viewed all aspects of the array (Eiser, 1974). In addition, Nigl and Fishbein (1974) found that children are better able to coordinate perspectives when three- rather than two-dimensional choice stimuli are used. This is an interesting finding because in the typical perspective-taking tasks two-dimensional photographs are used as judgment stimuli. As a final example of a factor that affects perspective taking skill, Cox (1975) found that children are more likely to make correct responses if they are judging what a human sees rather than a doll. In sum, it seems that children as young as 4 years of age are able to coordinate relatively complex perspectives provided the task setting is conducive, a fairly robust example of the influence of contexts in learning.

This selective summary of some of the task factors that affect the developmental emergence of perspective-taking skill again leaves unanswered the question of why certain task contexts are more conducive than others, and how perspective-taking skills develop. It is to these questions that Flavell and his colleagues have addressed themselves. Their work goes beyond the descriptive and offers analyses over and above simple demonstrations that Piaget must have been wrong.

As Flavell (1977) pointed out, Piaget and Inhelder's three-mountain problem "appears in hindsight to be a rather 'noisy,' insensitive measure of the basic ability it was designed to assess" (p. 45). Flavell argued that one would expect a developmental sequence in the emergence of perspective taking of the following form: (a) the child would first understand that another's experience is different from that of their own without being able to determine the exact nature of the other person's experience, and (b) the child would subsequently become able to infer the other's experience (Flavell, 1977; Flavell, Everett, Croft, & Flavell, 1981; Lempers, Flavell, & Flavell, 1977). In the earlier developing *Level 1* knowledge, children can infer what object a person does or does not see, and are also capable of saying what objects can be seen by them and not by another person. At the later developing *Level 2,* children are aware that an object gives rise to differing images, depending on the point from which it is viewed. This two-stage sequence is not independent of task complexity; Flavell, Botkin, Fry, Wright, and Jarvis (1968) have shown that even adults are unable to infer another's perspective if the task is sufficiently complex. Nevertheless, working with relatively simple stimuli, Flavell has provided supportive data for the two-stage development of perspective-taking skills.

In support of their claim for the Level 1–Level 2 distinction, Flavell et al. (1981) showed that 3-year-old children performed well on tasks that call for Level 1 knowledge but poorly on tasks requiring Level 2 knowledge. The Level 1 task involved presenting children with a card with a picture on each side of it (e.g., a dog on one side and a turtle on the other). The child had to say what picture the experimenter saw. The Level 2 task involved placing a picture on a table (e.g., a picture of a turtle) so that it was either right side up for the experimenter or the child. The task was to indicate which of the two orientations the experimenter saw. Three-year-old children continued to perform poorly even when the task was changed to be more familiar with their everyday experiences and even after training.

A second kind of developmental sequence in perspective-taking is the distinction between *Rules* and *Computation* (Flavell, Omanson, & Latham, 1978; Salatas, & Flavell, 1976). Computation refers to the cognitive processes invoked to solve many perspective-taking problems (e.g., mental rotation). In contrast, Rules refers to knowledge of the general invariant relational properties that hold for all arrays (e.g., if I know that you are examining an array from a different postion to me, I do not have to look at the array to know that your view will be different from mine—it is an invariant rule that is known to be true). The distinction between Rules and Computation is important because if a child fails on a perspective-taking task, the error may be due to inadequate rule knowledge, inappropriate computation strategies or some combination of both (Flavell et al., 1978).

The distinction between Rules and Computation was examined by Flavell et al. (1978) by having first, third, and fifth grade children identify which of two photographs represented an observer's view of an array of three dolls. The amount of prior information given to the children about the positioning of the three dolls was varied so that, in principle, they could identify the correct photograph without seeing the array. In fact, in one condition, children did have to choose which was the correct photograph without seeing the array. The purpose of this manipulation was to determine whether children could apply their rule-based knowledge. In a second condition, however, the children were allowed to see the array after receiving the hints to see whether they would decide which photograph was correct on the basis of computation or on the basis of their knowledge of perspective-taking rules. The results were clear. First, few first-grade children did well on the rule condition. Second, children who understood the perspective rule, as indexed by performance on the rule condition, continued to use that knowledge even when presented with the opportunity to observe the array; that is, they saw no need to confirm by computation what they already knew. Furthermore, Flavell et al. (1978) found that nearly all children who made rule-based decisions, as indicated by their speed of choosing the correct photograph, were able to articulate the nature of the rule. As Flavell et al. noted, for "older subjects . . . such rules . . . become explicit, completely general, semi-necessary truths" (p. 464).

Some a priori distinctions concerning what would make a context simple or difficult, of the type used by Flavell and Case, are clearly needed if we are to avoid the circularity of the arguments often proposed to explain early and partial competence. But in addition, we need to go farther and ask whether the early competence we see is principled, in the sense that under a variety of easy instantitations the child can perform well. For example, if it were possible to reduce the memory load, or processing capacity demands equally for two or three tasks, would the child perform consistently well? And if we then increase the processing load, would the child show less and less competence proportionally? We do not know the answers to these questions and will not come to know them unless we undertake systematic examination of what supportive contexts are.

It is also an interesting question whether the creation of a principled set of task environments, some that tap newly emergent understanding, some partial knowledge, and some complete flexible comprehension of "the explicit, general semi-necessary truths" kind, could serve to create development through learning. This point has not been addressed systematically, although Crisafi and Brown (1983) have shown that it is possible, through analogical transfer, to teach 3-year-olds to perform well on difficult versions of the inferential reasoning tasks in question. Would the provision of a guided tour through a set of ever more complex tasks variants lead to more mature performance in young children on the difficult, process-demanding versions of a particular problem? (i.e., would the child learn to deal with progressively more difficult instantiations? Or is performance totally determined by the processing load factors?). These questions remain to be answered.

A central question for further research is whether early competence is really fleeting, is really of the "now you see it, now you don't" quality or whether its emergence and maintenance is governed by a systematic set of discoverable rules. Also, an important issue is the extent to which early competence is domain specific or domain general. Similarly, we need to consider carefully whether the results of learning in easy-to-hard contexts, in social interactions, and so on, have any generality or stability? In short, the questions concerning the developmental status of precocious thinking, however it is induced, are only now being raised in systematic ways. Demonstrations of early competence that show that Piaget was wrong in his estimate of when competence should emerge are legion. What is needed now is the development of a consistent theoretical rationale of what governs the emergence of competence within and across domains.

CONCLUSION

Learning and development are interwoven in a complex spiral such that none of the four alternatives mentioned in the introduction fully capture the flavor of the relation. As Vygotsky argued, learning in contexts, including the social, creates development that in turn determines the level of learning and teaching for which the child is ripe.

Thus, a main theme of this chapter is that contexts create learning and development. Any estimate of developmental status must depend critically on the environment in which it is revealed. Important environmental factors include the social, in which parents, teachers, peers, and experimenters provide degrees of contextual support for learning, sometimes deliberately and sometimes without conscious intent to do so. These interactional accomplishments are an important driving force of cognitive development. But in addition, we should not overlook the fact that a great deal of development is instigated by the enquiring mind of the child herself. Developmental status cannot be assessed in a vacuum and the contexts used to reveal or disguise competence must come to figure more prominently in theories of cognitive development. Supporting environments are the things to be understood, not an explanation of development.

The second main theme of this chapter was the emphasis on microgenetic analysis, the method of observing development taking place in children "right before one's eyes." Much of the picture of development described in this chapter came from a consideration of short-term changes in children, developing and learning, with or without the help of others. We argued that the concept of bandwidths of competence through which the child navigates over time and across settings is a more fruitful metaphor for cognitive development than the legacy of a poorly understood stage theory, i.e., a reliance on static snapshot descriptions of developmental status frozen in time and welded to a particular task environment.

We believe that a main agenda for developmental psychologists is to expand their theories to account for environments in which learning and development occur. As developmental psychologists, if we can come to understand: (a) self-directed learning, (b) sensitive methods of assessing readiness for change, (c) the dynamics of social situations that are successful in inducing change, and (d) supportive experimental contexts, we will have gone a long way in unraveling the complex interactions of learning and development. This agenda is the one set by Vygotsky, a pioneer in the development analysis of human cognition.

ACKNOWLEDGMENTS

The preparation of this manuscript was supported by Grants HD05951, 06864, and 15808 from the National Institute of Child Health and Human Development. The authors wish to thank the following colleagues for their cooperation at various stages in the project: Nancy Bryant, Joseph Campione, Maria Crisafi, Judy DeLoache, Robbi Ferrara, Lucia French, Roberta Jones, Mary Jo Kane, Carolyn Long, Annemarie Palincsar, Esther Steinberg, and Susan Sugarman.

REFERENCES

Au, K. H., & Kawakami, A. J. (1984). Vygotskian perspectives on discussion processes in small group reading lessons. In L. C. Wilkinson, P. L. Peterson, & M. Hallinan (Eds.), *Social contexts of instruction: Group organization and group process* (Educational Psychology) (pp. 209–224). New York: Academic Press.

Baer, D. M. (1970). An age-irrelevant concept of development. *Merrill-Palmer Quarterly, 16*(3), 238–245.

Bales, R. F. (1950). *Interaction process analysis: A method for the study of small groups.* Cambridge, MA: Addison-Wesley.

Binet, A. (1909). *Les idees modernes sur les infants.* Paris: Ernest Flammarion.

Borke, H. (1975). Piaget's mountains revisited: Changes in the egocentric landscape. *Developmental Psychology, 11*(2), 240–243.

Brown, A. L. (1975). The development of memory: Knowing, knowing about knowing, and knowing how to know. In H. W. Reese (Ed.), *Advances in child development and behavior* (Vol. 10, pp. 103–152). New York: Academic Press.

Brown, A. L. (1982). Learning and development: The problem of compatibility, access and induction. *Human Development, 25,* 89–115.

Brown, A. L. (1985). Mental orthopedics, the training of cognitive skills: An interview with Alfred Binet. In S. Chipman, J. Segal, & R. Glaser (Eds.), *Thinking and learning skills: Current research and open questions* (Vol. 2, pp. 319–338). Hillsdale, NJ: Lawrence Erlbaum Associates.

Brown, A. L. (in press). Analogical learning and transfer. What develops? In S. Vosniadou & A. Ortony (Eds.), *Similarity and analogical reasoning.* New York: Cambridge University Press.

Brown, A. L., Bransford, J. D., Ferrara, R. A., & Campione, J. C. (1983). Learning, remembering, and understanding. In J. H. Flavell & E. M. Markman (Eds.), *Handbook of child psychology* (4th ed.). *Cognitive development* (Vol. 3, pp. 515–529). New York: Wiley.

Brown, A. L., & Campione, J. C. (1984). Three faces of transfer: Implications for early competence, individual differences, and instruction. In M. Lamb, A. Brown, & B. Rogoff (Eds.),

Advances in developmental psychology (Vol. 3, pp. 143–192). Hillsdale, NJ: Lawrence Erlbaum Associates.

Brown, A. L., & Day, J. D. (1983). Macrorules for summarizing texts: The development of expertise. *Journal of Verbal Learning and Verbal Behavior, 22,* 1–14.

Brown, A. L., & DeLoache, J. S. (1978). Skills, plans, and self-regulation. In R. Siegler (Ed.), *Children's thinking: What develops?* (pp. 3–35) Hillsdale, NJ: Lawrence Erlbaum Associates.

Brown, A. L., & Ferrara, R. A. (1985). Diagnosing zones of proximal development. In J. V. Wertsch (Ed.), *Culture, communication and cognition: Vygotskian perspectives* (pp. 273–305). Cambridge, MA: Cambridge University Press.

Brown, A. L., & French, L. A. (1979). The zones of potential development: Implications for intelligence testing in the year 2000. *Intelligence, 3,* 255–277.

Brown, A. L., & Palincsar, A. S. (1982). Inducing strategic learning from texts by means of informed, self-control training. *Topics in Learning and Learning Disabilities, 2*(1), 1–17.

Brown, A. L., & Palincsar, A. S. (in press). Reciprocal teaching of comprehension strategies: A natural history of one program for enhancing learning. In J. Borkowski & J. D. Day (Eds.), *Intelligence and cognition in special children: Comparative studies of giftedness, mental retardation, and learning disabilities.* Norwood, NJ: Ablex.

Brown, A. L., Palincsar, A. S., & Purcell, L. (1986). Poor readers: Teach, don't label. In U. Neisser (Ed.), *The school achievement of minority children* (pp. 105–144). Hillsdale, NJ: Lawrence Erlbaum Associates.

Brown, A. L., & Scott, M. S. (1972). Transfer between the oddity and relative size concepts: Reversal and extradimensional shifts. *Journal of Experimental Child Psychology, 13,* 350–367.

Bryant, N. R., Brown, A. L., & Campione, J. C. (1983, April). *Preschool children's learning and transfer of matrices problems: Potential for improvement.* Paper presented at the Society for Research in Child Development meetings, Detroit.

Budoff, M. (1974). *Learning potential and educability among the educable mentally retarded.* Final Report Project No. 312312. Cambridge, MA: Research Institute for Educational Problems, Cambridge Mental Health Association.

Campione, J. C., Brown, A. L., & Bryant, N. R. (1985). Individual differences in learning and memory. In R. J. Sternberg (Ed.), *Human abilities: An information processing approach* (pp. 103–126). San Francisco: Freeman.

Campione, J. C., Brown, A. L., Ferrara, R. A., & Bryant, N. R. (1984). The zone of proximal development: Implications for individual differences and learning. In B. Rogoff & J. Wertsch (Eds.), *New directions for cognitive development: The zone of proximal development* (pp. 77–91). San Francisco: Jossey-Bass.

Campione, J. C., Brown, A. L., Ferrara, R. A., Jones, R. S., & Steinberg, E. (1985). Differences between retarded and nonretarded children in transfer following equivalent learning performance: Breakdowns in flexible use of information. *Intelligence, 9,* 297–315.

Carey, S. (1985). *Conceptual change in childhood.* Cambridge, MA: Bradford Press.

Case, R. (1978, Summer). A developmentally based theory and technology of instruction. *Review of Educational Research, 48,* 439–463.

Case, R. (1982). General developmental influences on the acquisition of elementary concepts and algorithms in arithmetic. In T. P. Carpenter, J. M. Moser, & T. A. Romberg (Eds.), *Addition and subtraction: A cognitive perspective* (pp. 156–170). Hillsdale, NJ: Lawrence Erlbaum Associates.

Case, R. (1985). *Intellectual development: A systematic reinterpretation.* New York: Academic Press.

Case, R., Kurland, D. M., & Goldberg, J. (1982). Operational efficiency and the growth of short term memory span. *Journal of Experimental Child Psychology, 33*(3), 386–404.

Chi, M. T. H. (1976). Short-term memory limitations in children: Capacity or processing deficits? *Memory and Cognition, 4,* 559–572.

Cole, M., & Bruner, J. S. (1971). Cultural differences and inferences about psychological processes. *American Psychologist, 26,* 867–876.

Cole, M., Gay, J., Glick, J. A., & Sharp, D. W. (1971). *The cultural context of learning and thinking: An exploration in experimental anthropology.* New York: Basic Books.

Cole, M., & Scribner, S. (1975). Theorizing about socialization of cognition. *Ethos, 3,* 249–268.

Cox, M. V. (1975). The other observer in a perspectives task. *British Journal of Educational Psychology, 45,* 83–85.

Crisafi, M. A. (1980). *The inferential abilities of two-year-old children.* Unpublished master's thesis, University of Illinois.

Crisafi, M. A., & Brown, A. L. (1983, April). *Flexible use of an inferential reasoning rule by very young children.* Paper presented at the Society for Research in Child Development meetings, Detroit.

Dashiell, J. R. (1935). Experimental studies of the influence of social situations on the behavior of individual human adults. In C. Murchison (Ed.), *Handbook of social psychology* (Vol. 2, pp. 1097–1158). Worchester: Clark University Press.

Dean, A. L., Chabaud, S., & Bridges, E. (1981). Classes, collections, and distinctive features: Alternative strategies for solving inclusion problems. *Cognitive Psychology, 13,* 84–112.

DeLoache, J. S. (1980). Naturalistic studies of memory for object location in very young children. *New Directions for Child Development, 10,* 17–32.

DeLoache, J. S. (1984). What's this? Maternal questions in joint picture book reading. *The Quarterly Newsletter of the Laboratory of Comparative Human Cognition, 6,* 87–95.

DeLoache, J. S., Sugarman, S., & Brown, A. L. (1985). The development of error correction strategies in young children's manipulative play. *Child Development, 56,* 928–939.

Doise, W., Mugny, G., & Perret-Clermont, A. N. (1975). Social interaction and the development of cognitive operations. *European Journal of Social Psychology, 5,* 367–383.

Egorova, T. V. (1973). *Peculiarities of memory and thinking in developmentally backward school children.* Moscow: Moscow University Press.

Eiser, C. (1974). Recognition and inference in the coordination of perspectives. *British Journal of Educational Psychology, 44,* 309–312.

Fehr, L. A. (1978). Methodological inconsistencies in the measurement of spatial perspective taking ability: A case for concern. *Human Development, 21,* 302–315.

Ferrara, R. A., Brown, A. L., & Campione, J. C. (1981, April).*Children's learning and transfer of inductive reasoning rules: A study of proximal development.* Paper presented at the Society for Research in Child Development meetings, Boston.

Feuerstein, R. (1979). *The dynamic assessment of retarded performers: The learning potential assessment device, theory, instruments, and techniques.* Baltimore: University Park Press.

Feuerstein, R. (1980). *Instrumental enrichment: An intervention program for cognitive modifiability.* Baltimore: University Park Press.

Feuerstein, R., & Richelle, M. (1963). Children of the Melah. Socio-cultural deprivation and its educational significance. *The North American Jewish Child.* Jerusalem: The Szold Foundation for Child and Youth Welfare.

Fischer, K. W. (1980). A theory of cognitive development: Control and construction of hierarchies of skills. *Psychological Review, 87,* 477–531.

Flavell, J. H. (1977). *Cognitive development.* Englewood Cliffs, NJ: Prentice-Hall.

Flavell, J. H. (1978). Metacognitive development. In J. M. Scandura & C. J. Brainerd (Eds.), *Structural-process theories of complex human behavior* (pp. 213–245). The Netherlands: Sijthoff & Noordoff.

Flavell, J. H. (1982). On cognitive development. *Child Development, 53*(1), 1–10.

Flavell, J. H., Botkin, P. T., Fry, C. L., Wright, J. W., & Jarvis, P. E. (1968). *The development of role-taking and communication skills in children.* New York: Wiley.

Flavell, J. H., Everett, V. A., Croft, K., & Flavell, E. R. (1981). Young children's knowledge about visual perception: Further evidence for the Level 1 - Level 2 distinction. *Developmental Psychology, 17*(1), 99–103.

Flavell, J. H., Omanson, R. C., & Latham, C. (1978). Solving perspective-taking problems by rule versus computation: A developmental study. *Developmental Psychology, 14*(5), 462–473.

Forman, G. E. (1982). A search for the origins of equivalence concepts through a microgenetic analysis of block play. In G. E. Forman (Ed.), *Action and thought: From sensorimotor schemes to symbolic operations* (pp. 97–135). New York: Academic Press.

Gagné, R. M. (1962). The acquisition of knowledge. *Psychological Review, 4,* 355–365.

Gelman, R. (1978). Cognitive development. *Annual Review of Psychology, 29,* 297–332.

Gelman, R. (1983). Recent trends in cognitive development. In J. Schierer & A. Rogers (Eds.), *The G. Stanley Hall Lecture Series* (Vol. 3, pp. 141–175). Washington, DC: American Psychological Association.

Gelman, R., & Baillargeon, R. (1983). A review of some Piagetian concepts. In J. H. Flavell & E. M. Markman (Eds.), *Handbook of child psychology (4th. ed.). Cognitive development* (Vol. 3, 167–230). New York: Wiley.

Gelman, R., & Brown, A. L. (1986). Changing views of cognitive competence in the young. In N. J. Smelser & D. R. Gerstein (Eds.), *Behavioral and social science: Fifty years of discovery.* Washington, DC: National Academy Press.

Gelman, R., & Gallistel, C. R. (1978). *The child's understanding of number.* Cambridge, MA: Harvard University Press.

Greenfield, P. M. (1980). Toward an operational and logical analysis of intentionality: The use of discourse in early child language. In D. R. Olson (Ed.), *The social foundations of language and thought.* New York: Norton.

Greenfield, P. M. (1984). A theory of the teacher in the learning activities of everyday life. In B. Rogoff & J. Lave (Eds.), *Everyday cognition: Its development in social context* (pp. 117–138). Cambridge, MA: Harvard University Press.

Hull, C. L. (1952). *A behavior system.* New Haven: Yale University Press.

Inhelder, B., Sinclair, H., & Bovet, M. (1974). *Learning and the development of cognition.* Cambridge, MA: Harvard University Press.

Karmiloff-Smith, A. (1979a). Micro- and macro-developmental changes in language acquisition and other representational systems. *Cognitive Science, 3,* 91–118.

Karmiloff-Smith, A. (1979b). Problem solving construction and representations of closed railway circuits. *Archives of Psychology, 47,* 37–59.

Karmiloff-Smith, A. (1984). Children's problem solving. In M. Lamb, A. L. Brown, & B. Rogoff (Eds.), *Advances in developmental psychology* (Vol. 3, pp. 39–90). Hillsdale, NJ: Lawrence Erlbaum Associates.

Karmiloff-Smith, A., & Inhelder, B. (1974–1975). If you want to get ahead, get a theory. *Cognition, 3,* 195–212.

Kelley, H. H., & Thibaut, J. W. (1954). Experimental studies of group problem solving and process. In G. Lindzey (Ed.), *Handbook of social psychology* (Vol. 2, pp. 735–785). Reading, MA: Addison-Wesley.

Kendler, H. H., & Kendler, T. S. (1962). Vertical and horizontal processes in problem solving. *Psychological Review, 69,* 1–16.

Kendler, T. S., & Kendler, H. H. (1967). Experimental analysis of inferential behavior in children. In L. P. Lipsitt & C. C. Spiker (Eds.), *Advances in child development and behavior* (Vol. 3, pp. 157–190). New York: Academic Press.

Kuenne, M. R. (1946). Experimental investigation of the relation of language to transposition behavior in young children. *Journal of Experimental Psychology, 36,* 471–490.

Laboratory of Comparative Human Cognition. (1983). Culture and cognitive development. In P. H. Mussen (Ed.), *Handbook of child psychology (Vol. 1): History, theory, and methods* (pp. 295–356). New York: Wiley.

Lave, J. (1977). Tailor-made experiences in evaluating the intellectual consequences of apprenticeship training. *Quarterly Newsletter of Institute for Comparative Human Development, 1,* 1–3.

Lave, J., Murtaugh, M., & de la Rocha, O. (1984). The dialectic of arithmetic in grocery shopping. In B. Rogoff & J. Lave (Eds.), *Everyday cognition: Its development in social context* (pp. 67–94). Cambridge, MA: Harvard University Press.

Lempers, J. D., Flavell, E. R., & Flavell, J. H. (1977). The development in very young children of tacit knowledge concerning visual perception. *Genetic Psychology Monographs, 95,* 3–53.

Maier, N. R. F. (1936). Reasoning in children. *Journal of Comparative Psychology, 21,* 357–366.

McNamee, G. D. (1981, April). *Social origins of narrative skills.* Paper presented at the meetings of the Society for Research in Child Development, Boston.

Nigl, A. J., & Fishbein, H. D. (1974). Perception and conception in coordination of perspectives. *Developmental Psychology, 10*(6), 858–866.

Ninio, A., & Bruner, J. S. (1978). The achievement and antecedents of labelling. *Journal of Child Language, 5,* 1–15.

Palincsar, A. S., & Brown, A. L. (1984). Reciprocal teaching of comprehension-fostering and monitoring activities. *Cognition and Instruction, 1*(2), 117–175.

Pascual-Leone, J. (1970). A mathematical model for the transition rule in Piaget's development stages. *Acta Psychologica, 63,* 301–345.

Perlmutter, M., & Myers, N. A. (1979). Development of recall in two- to four-year-old children. *Developmental Psychology, 15,* 73–83.

Piaget, J. (1926). *The language and thought of the child.* London: Routledge & Kegan Paul.

Piaget, J. (1928). *Judgement and reasoning in the child.* New York: Harcourt.

Piaget, J. (1959). *The language and thought of the child.* (3rd ed.). London: Routledge & Kegan Paul.

Piaget, J., & Inhelder, B. (1956). *The child's conception of space.* London: Routledge & Kegan Paul.

Raven, J. C. (1938). *Progressive matrices: A perceptual test of intelligence.* London: Lewis.

Reese, H. W. (1968). *The perception of stimulus relations: Discrimination learning and transposition.* New York: Academic Press.

Reeve, R. A., & Brown, A. L. (1985). Metacognition reconsidered: Implications for educational practices. *Journal of Abnormal Child Psychology, 13*(3), 343–356.

Rogoff, B. (1982). Integrating context and cognitive development. In M. E. Lamb & A. L. Brown (Eds.), *Advances in developmental psychology* (Vol. 2, pp. 125–170). Hillsdale, NJ: Lawrence Erlbaum Associates.

Rogoff, B., & Gardner, W. (1984). Adult guidance of cognitive development. In B. Rogoff & J. Lave (Eds.), *Everyday cognition: Its development in social context* (pp. 95–116). Cambridge, MA: Harvard University Press.

Rogoff, B., Malkin, C., & Gilbride, K. (1984). Interaction with babies as guidance in development. In B. Rogoff & J. V. Wertsch (Eds.), *Children's learning in the ''zone of proximal development''* (pp. 31–44). San Francisco: Jossey-Bass.

Rogoff, B., & Wertsch, J. V. (Eds.). (1984). *Children's learning in the ''zone of proximal development''.* San Francisco: Jossey-Bass.

Rosser, R. A. (1983). The emergence of spatial perspective taking: An information-processing alternative to eogcentrism. *Child Development, 54,* 660–668.

Salatas, H., & Flavell, J. H. (1976). Perspective-taking: The development of two components of knowledge. *Child Development, 47,* 103–109.

Saxe, G. B., Gearhart, M., & Guberman, S. R. (1984). The social organization of early number development. In J. Wertsch & B. Rogoff (Eds.), *Children's learning in the ''zone of proximal development''* (pp. 19–30). San Francisco: Jossey-Bass.

Scollon, R. (1976). *Conversations with a one-year-old.* Honolulu: University Press of Hawaii.

Shatz, M. (1977). The relationships between cognitive processes and the development of communication skills. In B. Keasey (Ed.), *Nebraska symposium on motivation* (pp. 1–42). Lincoln: University of Nebraska Press.

Shatz, M., & Gelman, R. (1973). The development of communication skills: Modifications in the speech of young children as a function of listener. *Monographs of the Society for Research in Child Development, 38*(5, Serial No. 152).

Shaw, M. E. (1932). A comparison of individual and small groups in the rational solution of complex problems. *American Journal of Psychology, 44,* 491–504.

Simon, H. A., & Kotovsky, K. (1963). Human acquisition of concepts for sequential patterns. *Psychological Review, 70,* 534–546.

Sophian, C. (1986). Developing search skills in infancy and early childhood. In C. Sophian (Ed.), *Origins of cognitive skills.* Hillsdale, NJ: Lawrence Erlbaum Associates.

Stevenson, H. W. (1970). Learning in children. In P. H. Mussen (Ed.), *Carmichael's manual of child psychology* (Vol. 1, pp. 849–938). New York: Wiley.

Tharp, R. G., Jordan, C., Speidel, G. E., Au, K. H., Klein, T. W., Calkins, R. P., Sloat, K. C. M., & Gallimore, R. (1984). Product and process in applied developmental research: Education and the children of a minority. In M. E. Lamb, A. L. Brown, & B. Rogoff (Eds.), *Advances in developmental psychology* (Vol. 3, pp. 91–141). Hillsdale, NJ: Lawrence Erlbaum Associates.

Thornton, S. (1982). Challenging "early competence": A process oriented analysis of children's classifying. *Cognitive Science, 6,* 77–100.

Vlasova, T. A. (1972). New advances in Soviet defectology. *Soviet Education, 14,* 20–39.

Vygotsky, L. S. (1962). *Thought and language.* Cambridge, MA: MIT Press.

Vygotsky, L. S. (1978). *Mind in society: The development of higher psychological processes.* (M. Cole, V. John-Steiner, S. Scribner, & E. Souberman, Eds.). Cambridge, MA: Harvard University Press.

Wellman, H. M., Ritter, K., & Flavell, J. H. (1975). Deliberate memory behavior in the delayed reactions of very young children. *Developmental Psychology, 11,* 780–787.

Wellman, H. M., & Somerville, S. C. (1982). The development of human search ability. In M. E. Lamb & A. L. Brown (Eds.), *Advances in developmental psychology* (Vol. 2, pp. 41–84). Hillsdale, NJ: Lawrence Erlbaum Associates.

Wertsch, J. V. (1979). From social interaction to higher psychological processes: A clarification and application of Vygotsky's theory. *Human Development, 22,* 1–22.

Wertsch, J. V. (1984). The zone of proximal development: Some conceptual issues. In B. Rogoff & J. Wertsch (Eds.), *Children's learning in the "zone of proximal development"* (pp. 7–18). San Francisco: Jossey-Bass.

Wertsch, J. V., & Stone, C. A. (1979, February). *A social interactional analysis of learning disabilities remediation.* Paper presented at the International Conference of the Association for Children with Learning Disabilities. San Francisco.

White, S. H. (1965). Evidence for a hierarchical arrangement of learning processes. In L. P. Lipsitt & C. C. Spiker (Eds.), *Advances in child development and behavior* (Vol. 2, pp. 187–220). New York: Academic Press.

White, S. H. (1970). The learning theory tradition for child psychology. In P. H. Mussen (Ed.), *Carmichael's manual of child psychology* (Vol. 1, pp. 657–701). New York: Wiley.

Wood, D. J. (1980). Teaching the young child: Some relationships between social interaction, language, and thought. In D. R. Olson (Ed.), *The social foundations of language and thought* New York: Norton.

Wood, D., & Middleton, D. (1975). A study of assisted problem-solving. *British Journal of Psychology, 66,* 181–191.

Wozniak, R. H. (1975). Psychology and education of the learning disabled child in the Soviet

Union. In W. Craikshank & D. P. Halahan (Eds.), *Research and theory in minimal cerebral dysfunction and learning disability* (pp. 407–479). Syracuse, NY: Syracuse University Press.

Zabramna, S. D. (Ed.). (1971). *The selection of children for schools for the mentally retarded.* Moscow: Prosveshchenie.

Zeaman, D., & House, B. J. (1963). An attention theory of retardate discrimination learning. In N. R. Ellis (Ed.), *Handbook of mental deficiency* (pp. 159–223). New York: McGraw-Hill.

9 Developmental Method, Zones of Development, and Theories of the Environment

Robert H. Wozniak
Bryn Mawr College

In a cogent discussion of the role of supportive context in learning and development, Brown and Reeve (chapter 8) develop a series of arguments clustered around three basic themes. The first of these themes is that cognition is best studied in change. Citing Piaget's "methode clinique," Vygotsky's "zone of proximal development," and their own research as instances, Brown and Reeve make a persuasive case for the need to employ time varying methods in the study of microgenetic development. In addition, they succeed in illustrating quite clearly that the microgenetic approach has considerable potential for clarifying the nature of the mechanisms involved in children's acquisition of novel competence.

The second of the Brown and Reeve themes is more complex, constructed as it is around two variations. The first such variation is an extended argument for the interpolation of Vygotsky's concept of zone of proximal development into the mainstream of developmental psychology not only as microgenetic method but as the framework for a theory of the development–learning relationship. As Vygotsky (1978) described it, the zone of proximal development "is the distance between the actual developmental level as determined by independent problem solving and the level of potential development as determined through problem solving under adult guidance, or in collaboration with more capable peers" (p. 86). Supported by the teaching–learning context of social interaction, children are able to elaborate what Brown and Reeve term a "bandwidth of competence" in advance of their completed developmental level. Within the bandwidth, with expert support, children learn to develop. They acquire functions in cooperative activity that eventually become internalized as their own "independent developmental achievement" (Vygotsky, 1978, p. 90).

The second variation is actually a caution on the first. Arguing from their own work and from that of Karmiloff-Smith and Inhelder (1974/1975) among others, the authors use the results of microgenetic analyses of children working alone to suggest that "children create and extend their own zones of competence without aid from others" (p. 198). Indeed, they point out, "it would be a mistake to overemphasize the conception of the child as other-directed, i.e., always guided in his learning by outside forces" (p. 198).

Third and finally, Brown and Reeve ask the critical question, "What does it mean to call a context supportive?" (p. 211). Referring to research on the induction of early competence through contextual manipulation and to research on variations in contextual difficulty, the authors call for a theory that would allow prior specification of what makes a context simple or difficult, that is, a theory of the microenvironment.

All three of these themes entail claims with which I have considerable sympathy. The as yet largely untapped potential of microgenetic analysis to enhance our understanding of acquisition mechanisms, the theoretical fertility of the notion of a "zone of proximal development," particularly as applied to the problem of the relationship between learning and development, the importance of understanding the child's capacity for self-development, and the need for a theory of the microenvironment are all points that must be made, and Brown and Reeve have made them well.

Yet because these three themes involve issues that are exceedingly complex, I believe that they can benefit from even further elaboration. Such elaboration constitutes the substance of this chapter. Taking each of the themes in turn, I first argue that although Piaget's "methode clinique" and Vygotsky's "zone of proximal development" are, indeed, methods for studying cognition in change, they are much more than that. They are methods for studying cognition in *inter*change.

Second, I suggest that although the concept of a "zone of proximal development" is a most important one for Vygotsky, it is secondary to, derived from, and must be understood in terms of Vygotsky's broader theory of thought. In this theory, Vygotsky founds abstract conceptual knowing on the internalization of a historically derived, socially held, semiotic system and it is from the fact of internalization that "zones of proximal development" follow.

Third, I indicate the direction in which I think the eventual specification of a theory of the microenvironment may lie. This is a direction already indicated by Gibson (1979) through his elaboration of the concept of "information," a concept that is at the heart of the ecological approach to perception.

In conclusion, I touch directly on a question implicit in much of what I have said already, but one that Brown and Reeve have (probably wisely) chosen to ignore. This is the question of the relations that exist between the respective views of Piaget, Vygotsky, and Gibson. To what extent, if at all, does it make sense to try to accommodate one to the other in pursuing an overall framework for understanding learning and development? Surprisingly perhaps, I argue that Piaget and Vygotsky, despite many important and obvious points of convergence, are fundamentally at variance and that Piaget (at least Piaget when he was concerned with sensorimotor intelligence) and Gibson, despite being at variance in many and obvious ways, are fundamentally compatible.

TIME VARYING METHOD

Cognition should, as Brown and Reeve suggest, be studied in change; but to this, one might add that cognition and, for that matter, learning are even more profitably studied in *inter*change. It is not simply a question of Piaget's "methode clinique" or Vygotsky's "zone of proximal development" going beyond the static, independent test to measure change, but of their also transcending another—and in many ways more serious—limitation of the static situation: its supposed objectivity.

The static experimental method was imported into psychology in the 19th century in emulation of natural science. To achieve scientific objectivity, psychologists were urged to employ experimental method. Experiments were to consist of the systematic manipulation of an independent variable under standard and unvarying conditions and the measurement (or, in the case of introspection, the report) of a dependent variable allowed to vary freely. By utilizing this method, the psychologists/scientists could, it was argued, in effect remove themselves and their own subjectivity as a source of bias from the scientific knowing equation.

Unfortunately, however, the static experimental method is one that has severe limitations when applied to many of the problems of interest to psychologists. These limitations stem primarily from the fact that psychology's subject matter is just that—*subject* matter. The objects of study in psychology are not, as they are in physics, objects—but knowing, thinking, feeling subjects who study the psychologist while the psychologist is studying them.

Psychologists must, therefore, take this subjectivity, their own and their subjects', into account and turn it to good use. Piaget and Vygotsky were both well aware of this. Indeed, it was certainly one reason that they eschewed the pseudo hypothetico-deductive procedures ubiquitous in American psychology in favor of the "methode clinique" and "zone of proximal development", respectively. These methods, as it has been noted (Wozniak, 1983), depart in very significant ways from the canons by which the experimental method is supposed to guarantee objectivity.

First, the independent variable is not and cannot be set at predefined levels independent of the subject. On the contrary, the values that the independent variable or variables assume depend on the subject's initial level of development.

Second, manipulation of the independent variable is not systematic. Rather, questions, prompts, and actions-on-objects are only quasi-systematically organized to take advantage of the subject's and the experimenter's changing levels of understanding; and, third, the dependent variables are not, as a rule, quantified observations, but action–object statement complexes generating protocols which stand in need of interpretation—more reminiscent of discursive text than of physical measurement.

The "methode clinique" and the "zone of proximal development" are, in other words, methods that might be characterized as being neither "objective" nor "subjective," but quintessentially *inter*subjective. They involve the social co-construction of knowledge between the psychologist-as-subject and the subject-as-subject. As the subject comes to understand the task at hand, to make sense of it as best he or she can, the psychologist comes to understand the subject as a sense maker. That is to say that the psychologist-as-subject uses the methode clinique or the zone of proximal development as method to explore the subjectivity of the subject-as-subject to penetrate to the deep structures of mind.

ZONE OF PROXIMAL DEVELOPMENT

Clearly, as Brown and Reeve suggest, the "zone of proximal development" is an idea whose time has come. In the study of cognitive development, the swing away from a focus on the child as an isolated problem solver and toward recognition of the critical importance of the social environment, the return to a concern, now cognitively motivated, with mechanisms of learning, and widespread dissatisfaction with psychometric techniques that have hardly changed in the past 70 years have prepared us well for a notion of this sort. Yet there is more to Vygotsky's idea than meets the eye, and I am not certain that we are still quite far enough along to take full cognizance of the implications of this concept.

To make this point, let me briefly situate the notion of "zone of proximal development" within the broader "sociohistorical" theory of development of which it is a part. Vygotsky conceived of human consciousness as having a structure provided by the system of interrelations that obtains among psychological functions such as attention, perception, language, and thought. In the course of the child's development, he believed, the "primary" or biologically given system of relations becomes realigned (i.e., consciousness becomes restructured) as functions at first present only in external social activity (most notably those involved in communicative speech between child and adult) are internalized as the inner psychological functions of the child.

When this occurs, the primary system of functional relations yields to a secondary, historically derived system in which functions like attention or perception take on a mediated, self-controlled (or, as Vygotsky might have put it "properly human") form. This is, then, the zone of proximal development—a zone of potential restructuration of consciousness through the internalization of forms of regulation acquired in the social context of learning—instruction.

Taken by itself, this is at face an interesting view, and it is the view with which psychologists most readily associate Vygotsky. But Vygotsky's sociohistorical theory is, in my opinion, a great deal more subtle and sophisticated even than this; and an appreciation of this subtlety demands that careful attention be paid to Vygotsky's concept of speech and the role played by speech in developing the child's intersubjectivity.

For Vygotsky, the internalization of social forms of regulation is much more than the acquisition of self-control through inner speech. As the child experiences the world, he or she experiences it in the context of communicative speech. The child encountering a cup here and a cup there is told: "Here's a cup," "There's milk in the cup," "Don't drop the cup," "The cup is glass," "The cup is empty," or "Give Mommy the cup." In Vygotsky's view, this common lexical item serves as a nexus around which the child abstracts and generalizes experience with the characteristics of sets of objects in the world. The development of abstract, categorical concepts, in other words—in fact the very transition from the sensorimotor thought of the infant to the properly conceptual thought of the preschooler—occurs, for Vygotsky, in and through the internalization of speech.

More importantly, as Vygotsky constantly stressed, the lexical items that facilitate the child's synthesis of experience themselves already pre-exist the child in a wide-ranging, socially developed system of significances, a system of meanings, held by the society into which the child grows. Thus the transition from sensorimotor to abstract thought is also the internalization of a social semiotic system (an already evolved system of socially and historically derived meanings) and, for Vygotsky, sociality and historicity are, as a consequence, embedded in the very core of human conceptualization. Human thought, from his perspective, is, in the deepest sense, social and historical.

This view seems to have many implications and suggests numerous questions for both theory and research. Here, however, I consider only three of the implications, those most relevant to the Brown and Reeve discussion, and these only rather briefly. First, it should be noted that Brown and Reeve's caution that it would be a mistake to overemphasize the "child-as-other-directed" is a caution that would as readily have been urged by Vygotsky himself. For Vygotsky, the inherent sociality of every thought the thinker thinks comes neither from the presence of an implicit other or from constant other-direction, but from the fact that conceptual thought, as abstract and general, is formed in the process of internalizing a social system of intersubjective speech acts. As that system is mastered, the child internalizes the capability of altering the environment on his or her own in such a way as to provide the occasion for independent self-development. The child, in other words, does, in Vygotsky's view, create and extend his or her own zones of proximal development but does so through self-regulated functioning made possible through the operation of thought structures developed through the internalization of a system of socially derived significances.

Second, the social context that serves, for Vygotsky, such an important function in the zone of proximal development should not be seen merely as the context of a social group. Granted, it is a social group and the properties of interaction and executive regulation of the individual that can exist in the group are worthy of attention; but the defining characteristic of sociality, for Vygotsky, is intersubjectivity. The critical function of the social context is to provide the child with an opportunity to master the intersubjectively held social semiotic system on the basis of which the child becomes acculturated, acquiring the shared knowledge, beliefs, and attitudes common to members of his or her own society.

Finally, given this last point, it is striking that in most current work in cognitive development, even that which has been partially motivated by Vygotsky's ideas, there still seems to be a relative lack of appreciation for the developmental function of communicative language interaction. Students of *language* development, of course, have for some years been heavily concerned with the cognitive prerequisites of language, but students of *cognitive* development do not seem, in their turn, to have been nearly as concerned with the possible functions that language might play in the development of thought. One suspects that this reflects the continuing influence of Piaget, whose concern with the development of logico-mathematical structures led him to adopt a rather extreme position regarding the priority of logic over language. But even if Piaget was right with respect to logic and language, there is much more to cognition than logic, and an understanding of the full implications of Vygotsky's "zone of proximal development" for theories of cognitive development requires that careful attention be paid to the function of language in that process.

THEORY OF THE ENVIRONMENT

Finally, as Brown and Reeve have indicated, developmental psychology badly needs a theory of the microenvironment. Developmental psychologists simply have no principled idea of how our manipulations of context affect the child. We have focused exclusively on the structures and processes of the mind while ignoring the structure and process of the environment, where by "environment" I mean psychologically effective physical and social reality.

We give lip service to interactionism. We agree that experience, symbolic discourse, and action are constructed between mind and world; but our explanations make reference only to mind. To experience a camera as something which can take a picture, we say that we must *know* something about light, lenses and film; or to understand spoken English, we must *know* the syntactic rules that govern spoken English; or to tie a shoe, that we must *know* how to move our fingers in relationship to the laces. But what about the structure of the camera, the sound stream, and the laces? How are we to take them into consideration? The answer may lie in something like Gibson's "ecological" approach, but combined with a cognitivism which he rejected. For Gibson, to experience a camera as affording picture-taking, we must, over time, detect the higher order invariant structures in the light to the eye which bear a regular (and hence informative) relation to certain properties of the camera, properties that themselves reflect the structure of the camera. To understand spoken English, we must, over time, extract the higher order patterns informative about certain symbols that have been coded into the sound stream by the speaker. To tie a shoe, we must detect properties of laces such as their flexibility, their solidity, and their small diameter in relation to that of the fingers, properties that will support that action.

Stated simply, physical and social structures support properties of physical and social objects and events. These properties are in turn broadcast in the higher order invariant relationships over time that exist in patterned energy to the receptor and, when detected in relationship to what the organism knows, they are experienced by the organism as objects and events affording certain actions and not others.

Combining this view with the constructivism of a Piaget or a Vygotsky leads one to argue that theories of the environment must compliment our theories of the developing mind. The psychologically relevant properties of physical and social structures and the actions they afford must be as central to our explanation of developing human experience, symbolic discourse, and action as are the structures of knowing with which developmental psychologists have so far been almost exclusively concerned.

CONCLUSION

This leads directly to the final issue discussed in this chapter. To what extent does it or does it not make sense to combine the ecological approach of Gibson with the constructivism of Piaget or, for that matter, to combine the constructivism of Piaget with the socio-historicism of Vygotsky? The form that might be taken by a general answer to this question, one which is well beyond the scope of this chapter, has been at least tentatively sketched in other places (Wozniak, 1975, 1985).

There are, however, two more narrow aspects of this broad question which, given the previous discussion, can and should be addressed here. The first has to do with the nature of the respective views of Piaget and Vygotsky on the question of the role of language in the genesis of the transition from sensorimotor to conceptual intelligence. The second has to do with the nature of the respective views of Piaget and Gibson on the nature of the organism–environment relationship. As was earlier suggested, a careful look at these issues suggests that despite substantial commonality of method and metatheory, Piaget and Vygotsky are further apart, and despite sharp divergences in method and espoused metatheory, Piaget and Gibson are closer together than has often been thought.

Piaget and Vygotsky on Language and Conceptual Thought

As argued in some detail elsewhere (Wozniak, 1975), the general constructivist metatheory underlying Piaget's genetic epistemology shares many important features with the Marxist dialectical metatheory underlying Vygotsky's socio-historical approach to psychological development. There is, however, one fundamental point on which Piaget and Vygotsky are in profound disagreement, a point so fundamental that disagreement on this issue leads to much of that which is seen to be at variance in their respective theories.

The point at issue is the nature of the psychological relationship between language and the genesis of abstract conceptual thought. For Vygotsky, as earlier noted, words acquired and used in social interaction (i.e., in discourse) provide the consistent core which allows the child to abstract from and generalize over widely varying experiences with objects, events and people. Words, that is, are at the heart of the child's emerging concepts. Because words are embedded in communally held systems of meanings which pre-exist the child, sociality and historicity are internalized, as concepts are elaborated. Abstract human thought is, consequently, inherently social.

For Piaget, on the other hand, abstract thought structures are derived not from language but from action. Conceptual thought has its origins in the sensorimotor schemes of the infant which, in the emergence of the semiotic function, are detached from action, abstracted, and generalized as the basis for conceptual thought. Conceptual thought rather than being derived from the internalization of a social semiotic system and dependent on the acquisition of language is derived from schemes that are prior to language and upon which language depends.

Although the general effect of the emergence of language for Piaget may be to liberate thought from the immediate present and allow it simultaneous representation of chains of action or elements of organized structures, language does not in itself bring about the fundamental alteration in the basic nature of the child's thought that occurs in the transition from the sensorimotor to the preoperational period. Rather, language only provides the newly emerging abstract thought structures with tools necessary to the fulfillment of their own potential. As Piaget and Inhelder (1969) phrase it, "language . . . contains a notation for an entire system of cognitive instruments (relationships, classifications, etc.) for use in the service of thought" (p. 87). Language, in other words, is secondary to and its meanings are derived from the child's thought, thought which is not, therefore, inherently social but which must be socialized during the course of experience with other human beings.

Piaget and Gibson on the Organism–Environment Relationship

Piaget was concerned with the genesis of internal mental structures while Gibson, arguing for a theory of "direct perception," completely eschewed the concept of mental representation. Gibson focused on the pick up of information about the environment while Piaget, in emphasizing the development of logico-mathematical thought structures, largely ignored the environment. For these reasons, it has been suggested (Goldfield, 1983) that the constructivist program of Piaget and the ecological program of Gibson are fundamentally at odds and that a Gibsonian account of the structure of the microenvironment cannot, therefore, be made to supplement a Piagetian account of the development of knowledge.

In my view, this is a mistake, founded either on a failure to compare the Piagetian and Gibsonian accounts at the level of sensorimotor intelligence where they ought properly to be compared, or on a "representational" misreading of Piaget's theory of sensorimotor intelligence. To make this case, I turn first to Piaget's view of sensorimotor intelligence. Figure 9.1 presents a diagrammatic representation of the sensorimotor scheme–action–object relation as I believe Piaget envisioned it.

Notice first that, as represented in Fig. 9.1 the scheme is not the act. The scheme is an internal mental (or psychological) structure that acts as a general organizing principle with respect to external physical action. As Piaget (1969) put it, "the scheme is the structure or organization of actions as they are . . . generalized by repetition in similar or analogous circumstances" (p. 4).

Notice next that the action, therefore, is a realization of the possibilities inherent in the scheme. When the baby grasps the rattle, the baby is realizing the possibility of grasping. In Piaget's terminology, the baby is also *assimilating* the rattle to the grasping scheme. Thus—and this is often not well understood—at

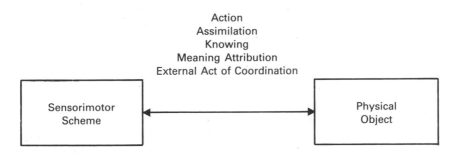

FIGURE 9.1   Scheme/action/object Relation in Piaget's sensorimotor theory.

233

the sensorimotor level, assimilation *is* action and action *is* assimilation. For the baby to assimilate the rattle to its grasping scheme is for the baby to grasp the rattle.

Furthermore, because for Piaget the only way in which the sensorimotor infant may know or attribute meaning to the world is by acting on it, when the baby grasps the rattle, the baby is also knowing the rattle as a graspable object or, put another way, he or she is attributing meaning to the rattle as a graspable object. Thus, although they differ connotatively, action, assimilation, external coordination, knowing, and meaning attribution at (but only at) the sensorimotor level, all refer extensionally for Piaget to the same physical action.

But what about the object? Here we have something that seems to be even less well understood about Piaget. In an equilibrated act, the realization of the sensorimotor scheme is as much a function of the specific characteristics of the object being acted on (accommodation) as it is of the general coordination of the scheme (assimilation). This is to say that the scheme as organizational principle is necessary but by no means sufficient for the specification of the particular action. On the contrary, the realization of the scheme in a particular act requires information about the object in the environment. Action is, put another way, a joint function of scheme and object—agent and environment in a transactional relation.

Furthermore (and this is perhaps least well understood), at the sensorimotor level, the agent–environment relation is, for Piaget, a direct one, unmediated by mental representation. This is so because the scheme is in no sense to be taken as a type of mental representation. The scheme, which is highly general, an ''action procedure'' but not an ''action program'' (Mounoud, 1986), provides only the very broad organizational *constraints* on the form that the action may take. The action takes the specific form it does only in relation to directly perceived information specifying the characteristics of the object to be acted upon.

The model one suspects Piaget had in mind here, is the biological model of gene regulation in which genetic structures (genotypes) constrain but do not preprogram phenotypic development. The phenotype is one particular realization of the constrained possibilities inherent in the genes, particularized as it develops in relation to constantly available and constantly changing environmental information.

This is not to say that Piaget paid any attention to the characteristics of the object or that he cared in any way about formulating a theory of particular acts. As Mounoud and Haubert (1982) have correctly pointed out, ''Piaget has . . . passed over the whole problem of the specification of these general action coordination plans as far as situation dimensions or particular characteristics are concerned'' (p. 12).

But Piaget never claimed to be a psychologist (in fact, he disavowed it). He was an epistemologist, concerned with the growth of logic from the logic of action through the logics of order and class to the propositional logic and hypothetico-deductive thinking characteristic of the adult scientist. At the sensorimotor level, therefore, it was the development of forms, changes in the intercoordinations among schemes, or, as he called it, the "logic of action" that captured Piaget's attention. Nonetheless, it can be suggested that in his view of sensorimotor action, Piaget is much closer to Gibson than either he or Gibson or any of their respective students would have been or would be willing to admit.

REFERENCES

Gibson, J. (1979). *The ecological approach to visual perception*. Boston: Houghton-Mifflin.

Goldfield, E. (1983). The ecological approach to perceiving as a foundation for understanding the development of knowing in infancy. *Developmental Review, 3*, 371–404.

Karmiloff-Smith, A., & Inhelder, B. (1974/1975). If you want to get ahead, get a theory. *Cognition, 3*, 195–212.

Mounoud, P., & Haubert, C. (1982). Development of sensorimotor organization in young children: Grasping and lifting objects. In G. E. Forman (Ed.), *Action and thought* (pp. 3–35). New York: Academic Press.

Mounoud, P. (1986, November). *Action and representation*. Paper presented at the Motor Development Conference, Columbia University Teacher College, New York.

Piaget, J., & Inhelder, B. (1969). *The psychology of the child*. New York: Basic Books.

Vygotsky, L. S. (1978). *Mind in society*. Cambridge, MA: Harvard University Press.

Wozniak, R. H. (1975). Dialecticism and structuralism: The Philosophical foundations of Soviet psychology and Piagetian cognitive developmental theory. In K. F. Riegel & G. C. Rosenwald (Eds.), *Structure and transformation: Developmental and historical aspects* (pp. 15–45). New York: Wiley.

Wozniak, R. H. (1983). Is a genetic epistemology of psychology possible? *Cahiers de la fondation archives Jean Piaget, 4*, 323–347.

Wozniak, R. H. (1985). Notes toward a co-constructive theory of the emotion/cognition relationship. In D. Bearison & H. Zimiles (Eds.), *Thought and emotion: Developmental issues* (pp. 39–64). Hillsdale, NJ: Lawrence Erlbaum Associates.

10

EPILOGUE
Approaches to Development and Learning: Conflict *and* Congruence

Lynn S. Liben
The Pennsylvania State University

In establishing the theme of the 14th Annual Symposium of the Jean Piaget Society from which this volume is drawn, the terms *conflict* and *congruence* were used to focus attention on whether two sets of ideas—the first, development and learning, and the second, Piagetian and information-processing approaches—should be understood as competing or complementary. The terms *conflict* and *congruence* are now used to organize closing comments about the book as a whole, but here the focus is on conflict and congruence among the contributors to the volume itself.

The chapter begins with a brief discussion of two points of agreement, first, that culture plays an important role in cognitive development; and second, that the assessment of cognitive development must be dynamic in nature. The remainder of the chapter addresses some of the conflicting positions that arise in the course of defining and contrasting the terms *development* and *learning;* in distinguishing between Piagetian theory and information-processing approaches; and in searching for conflict itself.

CAUTIOUS CONSENSUS

The Role of Culture.   One of the themes emerging from this volume is that culture plays a critical role in cognitive progress. The role of culture is implicit in contributors' discussions of elementary- and middle-school curricula, because decisions about what material is included in school and how it is taught are culturally influenced. The role of culture is explicitly acknowledged as well. Resnick, for example, contrasts patterns of mathematical constructions observed

237

in the United States, France, and Israel versus those observed by Scribner in unschooled cultures. Brown and Reeve discuss the impact of a variety of cross-cultural and cross-situational learning contexts and contents. Feldman conceptualizes his universal-to-unique continuum as culturally driven, not only because cultural domains of knowledge vary from group to group, but also because even discipline-based and idiosyncratic domains are affected by what is available to individuals in a particular society.

Given the context of a Symposium and book produced under the auspices of the Jean Piaget Society, however, perhaps the most dramatic indication of attention to culture is that many contributors draw heavily on Vygotsky (see especially Strauss; Brown & Reeve; Wozniak), a theorist who is correctly understood as placing social forces at the core of his theory. He views social interaction as primary because it allows linguistic communication, which in turn makes possible the internalization of culture, and the reflection and elaboration of experience.

For a number of reasons, social interaction in Piagetian theory is often seen as unimportant. Piaget (1964) downplayed the importance of the social transmission of isolated facts that must be learned, but that have little cognitive importance; he has warned that the social context can *hinder* cognitive progression by providing premature adult solutions that dissipate children's disequilibrium, thereby reducing the motivation for change. At the same time, however, there is much in Piagetian theory to support the assertion that sociocultural variables are important. Variables such as culture, schooling, and social class moderate the expression of cognitive development (see Neimark, De Lisi, & Newman, 1985). Even more importantly, it is social interactions—especially among peers—that press children to appreciate perspectives other than their own (Piaget, 1965). Thus, even if the two theorists suggest a somewhat different balance of externally versus internally driven forces, they agree—as do the contributors to this volume—that sociocultural factors play an important role in cognitive development.

Dynamic Assessment.   A second theme of congruence that emerges in the contributions to this volume is a belief that significant observations about children's cognitive development are best made when one observes the child in the *process* of developing or applying some skill or structure. A commitment to dynamic assessment is not simply a recognition that valid measurement requires multiple sampling of behaviors. More importantly, it reflects a belief that a central aspect of the child's cognitive capacities is its dynamic quality, that is, its ability to modify itself under changing situations and experiences.

The study of microgenetic changes in algorithms and strategies in the work of Resnick and Siegler offers one means of examining cognition in transition. A second approach is again through a Vygotskian construct—the Zone of Proximal Development—which directly acknowledges and records both independent and socially supported performance (see especially chapters by Brown & Reeve; Strauss; and Wozniak).

Piaget, too, placed a heavy emphasis on dynamic assessment. The clinical method—with its exploratory questions, requests for justifications, inclusion of many and varied examples, and use of suggestion and countersuggestion—is strikingly like the dynamic, collaborative, interactive methods of assessment of the Vygotskian tradition. For Piaget, like Vygotsky, it is not simply how a child initially answers a particular question that allows for developmental classification, but also how the child then uses information or demonstrations presented by the examiner.

For Piaget, however, the purpose of the clinical method is to test the boundaries of the child's current level of understanding. Although some cognitive progress may take place in the course of this assessment, cognitive advance is not the *goal* of the assessment procedure. When the goal is cognitive advance, either in the form of "training" studies within experimental research settings (e.g., Inhelder, Sinclair, & Bovet, 1974) or in the form of ongoing educational curricula (e.g., Kamii & DeVries, 1978), procedures comparable to those of the clinical method are likewise used. But the assessment itself need not result in cognitive progress. Thus, although the procedures for clinical assessment and teaching both challenge the limits of understanding, and although the outcomes *may* be the same (i.e., cognitive progress), the goal of the former is primarily to assess the child's extant structure, whereas the goal of the latter is primarily to *advance* structure. For Vygotsky, the goal of the assessment method includes advancement as well.

In short, although the emphases and vocabulary used by Piaget, Vygotsky, and the contributors to this volume undeniably vary, they vary within a shared belief system that cognition is dynamic rather than static, and must be assessed as such. More profound disagreements do emerge, however, in the course of defining and relating development and learning. These disagreements are the focus of the remainder of the chapter.

DEFINITIONAL DIVERSITY

Each of the contributors was specifically asked to address the relationship between the concepts of development and learning. Some consistency among contributors may be found insofar as the basis for differentiation generally concerns the *derivation* of knowledge labeled as *development* versus *learning*. That is, knowledge called *learning* is generally described as having different origins from knowledge called *development,* rather than, for example, different substantive content or different organization. Beyond this, however, the chapters eloquently demonstrate that there is no simple, universally accepted means of defining and contrasting these two terms. Three derivational criteria that arise in differentiating development from learning are considered here, specifically, distinctions based on the temporal nature of cognitive change; on the context in which knowledge is acquired; and on the degree to which knowledge is self- rather than other-constructed.

Temporal Criteria.   One basis suggested for distinguishing between learning and development is the *time span* over which cognitive change occurs. Siegler and Shipley, for example, suggest that when knowledge (cognitive progress) is the result of a short-term experience, it may be considered learning, whereas when it is the result of long-term experience it may be considered development. Strauss, too, uses temporal criteria, arguing that his "middle-level approach" is concerned with changes over days, weeks, and months, and thus differs from ontogenetic development of the kind studied by Piaget that occurs over years, and from learning studied by experimental psychologists that occurs over minutes.

Although the temporal span during which the cognitive change occurs may well be a good marker variable (such that changes occurring over different time spans are likely to be differentiated on other theoretically significant dimensions as well), particular examples establish that temporal distinctions alone are neither necessary nor sufficient to distinguish development from learning. Acquisition of vocabulary or spelling, for example, takes years, but would be seen by most scholars (if they make a distinction between development and learning at all) as exemplars of learning not development. Similarly, a child might come to re-structure cognitive schemes during a short period, either with or without guidance from others. Numerous examples of significant restructuring of knowledge in the course of short time spans may be found in this volume, ranging from the description of Genevan learning experiments (Inhelder et al., 1974; see Sinclair, this volume) to the descriptions of conceptual growth through interactions in educational contexts (see especially Brown & Reeve; Strauss, this volume).

Contextual Criteria.   A second criterion concerning the origins of knowledge that has been suggested as a means of distinguishing development from learning is the *environmental context* in which knowledge originates. This distinction is expressed in a variety of ways, including, for example, a distinction between knowledge derived from schooled versus spontaneous processes (see Strauss). The setting per se, however, cannot be the defining criterion. This point may be documented by reference to the data reviewed by Brown and Reeve (this volume). Comparable teaching functions that lead to the internalization of executive control may be observed in settings ranging from mother–child dyads working on block puzzles, to groups of experts and novices working together on weaving, to classrooms explicitly constituted to develop reading skills (see especially pp. 179–194).

Constructivism.   A third possible criterion for discriminating development from learning concerns the *self-constructed nature of the knowledge.* Here the issue is whether the knower has derived the knowledge on his or her own (development), or has instead been given the knowledge by an external source (learning). Like most seemingly straight-forward distinctions, however, a number of issues arise on closer examination.

First, *does the distinction rest in the properties of the substantive domain or in the actions of the knower?* That is, should the distinction be made with respect to whether or not the knower *could* have self-constructed the knowledge or whether the knower *did* self-construct the knowledge? For example, consider the acquisition of the knowledge that "1 + 1 = 2." The child *could* construct this knowledge just as Raggedy Ann did when she used twin dolls to represent this addition problem. Alternatively, a child could memorize it by heeding her mother, her teacher, or Bert and Ernie on *"Sesame Street,"* but without necessarily understanding the quantities and relations that the equation represents.

Although the acquisition of some kinds of knowledge (such as addition facts) might or might not be self-constructed, acquisition of other kinds of knowledge (e.g., knowing that the capital of Idaho is Boise) cannot be self-derived. This raises a second issue: *is information of this kind, information that must be "strictly learned," very important?* Such information may, of course, be important for a particular action (e.g., addressing a letter to the governor of Idaho). At a more general level, it may be useful as grist for some cognitive self-construction (e.g., as in understanding hierarchical relationships such as those contained in the concepts of town, county, state, and nation; see Daggs, 1986). But when viewed as grist (or in Piagetian language, "aliment") for the intellectual mill, the particular factual knowledge is secondary and subservient to the more important and general cognitive structure that uses that knowledge.

This raises a third issue with respect to the criterion of self-construction: *Can we ever separate externally provided knowledge from self-constructed knowledge?* That is, is other-provided knowledge *necessarily* incorporated by the individual within the context of the individual's cognitive structure? Such a question, of course, begs for a Piagetian response citing assimilation and accommodation in the *construction* of knowledge. It is not surprising, then, that Sinclair and others sympathetic to Piagetian theory describe the constructive acquisition of knowledge in just such a manner.

But Resnick, not typically associated with a Piagetian perspective, likewise endorses the concept of constructivism, even suggesting that we all now stand united in a commitment to constructivism. "Constructivism, a central tenet of Piagetian theory, in the past sharply divided Piagetians from learning theorists. Today, cognitive scientists generally share the assumption that knowledge is constructed by learners" (Resnick, this volume, p. 19).

It is instructive, however, to look closely at the particular illustrations of constructive processes—both drawn from the domain of number—given by

Sinclair and Resnick. Sinclair discusses Katya's self-directed actions. Katya arranges and re-arranges the swans, fish, and ducks in problems "of her own making" so that, "in the end, to all appearances, she has successfully dissociated logical class, equality or inequality of number, and the space taken up" (Sinclair, this volume, p. 9).

Resnick illustrates her position that "even when all that is *apparently* happening is rehearsal and practice of a performance, people are actually engaged in a process of transforming their knowledge" (p. 20) by reference to the arithmetic shortcuts that young children invent in addition. Resnick reports that regardless of how children are taught to add two numbers, they often "set a 'mental counter' to the larger of the two numbers stated, and then count in the smaller number by ones" (p. 20). An artificial intelligence program has been written such that at the onset it:

> has only the inefficient algorithm of counting all the objects, but in the course of performing this algorithm transforms its procedure into the more efficient one. The program does this by inspecting its own performance on trial after trial and applying a small set of procedure-modifying heuristics. The program serves as one theory of how humans might be "learning" the efficient procedure. (p. 20)

Although Sinclair and Resnick are ostensibly discussing the same concept—constructivism—they create rather different pictures of the "active knower." Katya is posing for herself and solving problems about the very fundamental meaning of quantity. She *transforms* the environmental aliment to something that is known by acting upon it in various ways—by classifying, re-classifying.

The child (modeled by the computer program) in Resnick's example, too, "inspect[s] its own performance," but here the inspection is not aimed at understanding and at discovering alternative ways to contrast the representation of quantity with other logical systems (e.g., groupings based on spatial arrangements, or on class membership), but instead is aimed at discovering repeated outcomes. There are *transformations* here too: the child (program) "transforms its procedure into the more efficient one." It substitutes one rule for another in an attempt to achieve greater efficiency in reaching the correct answer, not necessarily in understanding the *meaning* of combining quantities. (Indeed, as Resnick specifically notes, the model ignores the issue of quantity entirely.) The means of becoming more efficient is through the application of "a small set of procedure-modifying heuristics." Although these are unspecified here, they have been described in more detail by others doing comparable work. Klahr (1980), for example, states:

> We postulate a kernel of innate productions that includes a set of self-modification productions. One general principle governs the operation of the self-modifica-

tion productions. The principle is a least-effort or "processing-economy" principle. . . The system achieves this goal of efficient processing through three major procedures: consistency detection, redundancy elimination, and global orientation. (p. 130)

Thus, there is an ever present drive to achieve greater efficiency, accomplished through the application of innately given procedures.

In summary, in the course of suggesting criteria for distinguishing between development and learning, some important disagreements emerge among the contributors to this volume. Some of these disagreements are obvious because they are specifically raised in one chapter and then explicitly challenged in another. But others (as in the role of constructivism), are more subtle because meanings are not necessarily identical, even though terminologies may be.

It is important to consider whether the disagreements just discussed arise simply as a by-product of trying to create a distinction between two terms—*development* and *learning*—that are perhaps better off left undifferentiated. Some theorists, for example, acknowledge the importance of only one of the two concepts, arguing either that learning is development or development is learning. Although positions of this kind (e.g., the strict behaviorist position taken by Baer, 1970, see Brown & Reeve, this volume, pp. 173–174) *dismiss* the relevance of one or another of the concepts, they do, by implication, acknowledge a conceptual distinction between the two. Other theorists take a different stance about this differentiation. Resnick, for example, suggests that because both so-called learning and so-called development are actually both equivalent constructive processes (in the manner just discussed), "focusing on distinctions between learning and development seems to me an unlikely way to make progress in understanding the nature of knowledge acquisition" (p. 48). Differing opinions about the value of trying to distinguish between development and learning may well reflect yet more fundamental differences in contributors' world views. These are considered next.

DEEP DIVERGENCE

World Views: Information Processing Versus Piaget. At least since the publication almost 2 decades ago of a series of papers on developmental psychology and world views (Overton & Reese, 1973; Reese & Overton, 1970), developmental psychologists have generally recognized that different interpretations of constructs (such as constructivism) are to be expected when the constructs are approached by scholars with different theoretical perspectives or world views. What remains difficult in the context of the present volume, however, is determining who shares which world views.

Ideally, one would want to ask: Can the work reported and described by those who are "information-processing types" be understood/interpreted as congruent with the world view held by those who are "Piagetian types." Indeed, it was essentially this question that was posed to speakers when they were initially invited to participate in the Symposium (see Preface).

The major difficulty in answering the question posed this way is that whereas there is unquestionably a Piagetian theory, there is no single information-processing theory. Indeed, despite the fact that information processing takes its place next to Piaget, Freud, and Social Learning in most contemporary presentations of "developmental theories" (e.g., see Miller, 1983), it is not obvious that information processing is a theory at all, or if instead it is a technique. This issue is raised in passing by Sinclair when she discusses the meaning of self-directed activities of Nicolas (in mastering an object-concept) and of Katya (in mastering a number concept): "By contrast, I fail to see how learning theory or the information processing approach (*if the latter is seen as a theory of cognition rather than as a technique that can elucidate particular phenomena*) can account for the examples I have cited" (p. 11, italics added).

Some consistencies among information-processing proponents may be noted. Those who are identified with information processing usually draw boxes and flow charts, often use computer structure or software as models of cognition, and typically focus on narrowly restricted substantive domains. But the nature of an information-processing perspective varies dramatically depending on (among other factors) what goes into the "executive" (e.g., associative links vs. schemata); on whether there is simultaneous versus sequential application (arrows) of isolated versus interactive constructs (boxes); and on how the knower gets information (e.g., entry of environmental stimulus "as is" vs. construction of knowledge through the application of organismic variables to environmental stimulation). Indeed, with the appropriate combination of declarative knowledge (structures d'ensemble), procedures (operations; assimilation and accommodation), and goals (dynamic equilibrium), it would be quite possible to present Piagetian theory in information-processing terms.

Interestingly, this statement is reminiscent of Piaget's (1964) discussion of Berlyne's translation of Piagetian theory into learning theory. Piaget acknowledged that Berlyne's translation was successful because it included "transformation responses," which Piaget saw as equivalent to operations, and "internal reinforcements," which Piaget saw as equivalent to equilibration: "So you see that it is indeed a stimulus-response theory, if you will, but first you add operations and then you add equilibrium. That's all we want!" (Piaget, 1964, p. 19). It is similarly true that using information-processing language per se is not the defining criterion for identifying a theorist's world view. Thus, one must look more deeply at contributors' positions on a number of fundamental issues. Two critical issues are considered here: the *goals of explanation* and the *mechanisms* used to explain cognitive change.

Explanatory Goals.   The contributors to this volume reveal some significant differences in the goals of their conceptual and empirical work. One major difference concerns the scope of the endeavor. For some, the major goal is to model children's cognition by producing and testing a general cognitive structure. The particular format of that structure (e.g., hierarchical; linear) is not at issue here. What is critical, instead, is whether or not the structure is broadly applicable to a wide variety of behaviors, and thus whether or not it illuminates the interconnectedness of behaviors across many different domains.

Within the present volume, the most direct endorsement of this kind of goal is made by Murray in asserting what is developmentally interesting about children's progressing arithemetic skills:

> The developmental mechanism, however it is specified, is that which provides coherence to all the algorithms, procedures, and notational systems; it is the glue, so to speak, that holds the notational system to the quantities and allows the notations and procedures to form a system. From the Genevan perspective, it is a system of algorithms that has the well-known operational features of reversibility, compensation, and so on . . .
>
> What develops, in other words, is the notion of mathematical necessity . . . The development of necessity requires the invention of a system in which otherwise separate events are connected together on some common dimension. (p. 53)

Murray directly contrasts these kinds of goals—which characterize the Genevan research program—against Resnick's research program that is focused on the much narrower domain of manipulation of number symbols per se. A similar contrast may be drawn between the scope of the Genevan tradition and the work of Siegler and Shipley (Liben, this volume). Thus, in the latter kind of approach, what is examined and modeled is a series of domain-specific rules and procedures. What appears to be generalizable across domains is a *method of study,* that is, the way in which the knower's representations and procedures for manipulating information are modeled. In contrast, what is generalizable in the broadly framed Genevan work is the underlying structure that the knower "has."

This difference means that empirical data will of necessity be used differently in the two approaches. In one approach, empirical data form the basis on which to build a highly specific model (e.g., a computer program) of the knower's declarative and procedural knowledge, a model that is useful (and tested) for that highly specific domain only. As noted earlier (see Liben, this volume; Overton, 1984), such models have the advantage of being highly accurate with respect to prediction, but the disadvantages of being circular with respect to their derivation (having been derived and tested within the same domain), and of being highly restricted with respect to their application (being relevant to that domain only).

In the Genevan approach, empirical data are examined for consistency with the cognitive model at a much more general level. As Murray notes, for example, the kinds of arithmetic errors that Resnick finds in young children:

are completely consistent with the typical pre-operational responses that are so familiar to researchers working in the Genevan tradition. The competence, for example, to simultaneously treat two or more aspects of the same thing is a hard-won developmental achievement . . . . Thus, we expect place value notation to be difficult for the pre-operational pupil. . . . (p. 52)

There is, admittedly, a larger leap in going from a structural model of pre-operational thinking to children's performance on place-notation tasks than there is in going from a computer model of a place-notational system to children's performance on place-notation tasks. But while bridges between the model of pre-operational thought and empirical data may therefore be more difficult to build than those between the computer simulation and the child's protocol, the conceptual landscape spanned by the former is more diverse and inclusive than that covered by the latter.

Scope is not, however, the only important difference that distinguishes among the goals of the contributors to this volume. A second difference concerns *what aspects of the child's behavior are the focus for explanation*. There need not be a difference in the general topic or substantive domain of the inquiry. Sinclair, Resnick, Siegler, and Murray, for example, all focus on number. But what is it about the child's numerical progress that is to be explained?

Sinclair is concerned with how children come to raise and answer their own questions about number concepts. Children are therefore at their most interesting when they are showing themselves as "problem seekers or raisers," not as "problem solvers." Murray, as another representative of the Genevan approach, is concerned with children's developing notion of mathematical necessity, not with their increasing ability to find correct answers to problems.

The slant of Resnick's work is somewhat different. She begins with a focus on children's mastery of arithmetic algorithms, with learning and applying externally given rules for a range of mathmetical operations. The malrules observed demonstrate the inadequacy of having children apply procedures without a true understanding of what makes these procedures work. Interestingly, the malrules found by Resnick are *absent* in cultures in which children manipulate quantity *without* formal instruction in these arithmetic algorithms (Scribner, 1984; see Resnick, this volume, p. 48). It would appear that children's buggy algorithms arise because children must manipulate number symbols without first understanding how quantity is mapped into the notational system.

Assuming that our society wishes to continue teaching arithmetic rules, it is important to know how children's acquisition and application of these rules is moderated by their incomplete understanding of the relation between the notational system and quantity. To accomplish this, we must study not only the child's understanding of quantity that arises through self-generated processes, but also the child's attempt to make sense of externally provided rule systems. Ideally, one would want to link these two forces in devising instruction, a point made elsewhere by Resnick (1982). Although both kinds of research endeavors are thus vital from the perspective of education, the thrusts of Sinclair's and Resnick's work do differ in subtle but important ways.

Like Resnick, Siegler and Shipley also focus on children's skills for manipulating numbers in arithmetic problems, rather than on children's growing understanding of quantity itself. In describing the strengths of their distributions of associations model, Siegler and Shipley note that:

> Finally . . . the model suggested how development might occur. As children's distributions of associations become increasingly peaked, they rely increasingly on retrieval, advance the correct answer more often, and answer more quickly. In short, their performance becomes increasingly adultlike. (p. 89)

The focus is thus on adultlike performance in the sense of speed and accuracy in producing responses, rather than in the sense of an *understanding* of the mathematical relationships expressed in a particular arithmetic expression.

Mechanisms of Change.   A key dimension that distinguishes among different families of developmental theories concerns the mechanisms invoked as responsible for developmental change. Three major mechanisms may be identified: one dealing with biological, inherited processes; a second with environmental, experiential processes; and a third with interactive processes. Importantly, the latter may be interpreted in two ways. One, a *weak* form of interaction (statistical interaction) simply acknowledges the joint contributions of biological and environmental processes. Interpreted in this manner, an interactive perspective would be endorsed by virtually all contemporary developmentalists. The second, a *strong* form of interaction (dynamic interaction; reciprocal interaction), is much more radical since it holds that organismic and environmental forces can never be separated from one another (see, for example, Kitchener, 1978; Lerner, 1978; Overton, 1973; Sameroff, 1975). It is in this strong sense of interaction that the Piagetian concept of constructivism must be understood.

The contributors to this volume invoke these three mechanisms differentially. As noted earlier, some contributors use biological programming to account for the presence of certain cognitive equipment. Siegler and Shipley, for example, appeal to biology explicitly in explaining the origins of the ability to retrieve information from memory, and implicitly in accounting for the organization of strategies (see Liben, this volume, p. 120). Similarly, Resnick's appeal to "procedure modifying heuristics" implicitly suggests species-given equipment, at least insofar as alternative origins are not specified, and insofar as these heuristics are said by others to be "a kernel of innate productions" (Klahr, 1980, p. 130; see quotation pp. 242–243).

It is not necessarily antithetical to constructivism to assert that the organism is biologically endowed with certain physical and psychological properties. The key question is whether biology is seen as the *cause* of development in and of itself, or alternatively, is viewed as the *raw material* with which the individual works. Piaget endowed the organism with an important general goal (equilibrium), but very little in the way of specific behaviors or strategies (i.e., only basic reflexes). Others, such as Gelman (1986), have given the human organism much more to work with. But both leave to the individual's self-controlled activity the work of *constructing* meaning, strategies, and so on by *using* this endowment. Thus in either of these instances, the biological mechanisms are not primary.

Experiential factors may be analyzed in an analogous fashion. In one interpretation, that consistent with classic associationist theories, environmental contingencies *determine* the developmental outcome. As argued earlier (Liben, this volume), Siegler and Shipley's formulation may be interpreted in this manner. The alternative is to view experiential influences (be they through the general cultural context or specific instructional curriculum, see especially in this volume, Brown & Reeve; Feldman; Strauss) as grist for self-directed constructive processes. Thus, in this view, experiences do not in and of themselves control outcome. What is critical is how the individual selects from and uses these resources.

In short, the contributors to this book reflect different positions with respect to which mechanisms are seen as *causal* for development. The depth of such differences is often masked because the same term is used for different processes (see especially the earlier discussion of alternative views of constructivism, pp. 241–243) and because the impact of the same factors (biological endowment; environmental experience) may be understood in radically different ways (see also Liben, 1981).

CONFLICT ABOUT CONFLICT

In addition to the conflicts that arise in the course of differentiating development from learning and with respect to core theoretical issues, a perhaps even more fundamental conflict is contained within these chapters: Should we be searching for conflict at all? The evaluation of the role of conflict may be considered at two levels: one concerns conflict as a mechanism for fostering developmental progress in the individual; the second concerns conflict as a mechanism for fostering progress in the realm of scholarly inquiry.

From the perspective of Piagetian theory, conflict is an essential component of development. It is the inability of existing cognitive structure to assimilate perturbations—be they externally or internally induced—that calls up the cognitively progressive equilibration process. Thus, conflict is a critical process for explaining spontaneous (uninstructed) developmental progress, as well as for informing educational experiences that induce cognitive growth.

The Genevan literature overflows with examples of conflicts that yield cognitive development, be they conflicts that arise in the course of spontaneous play (as in Katya's struggle with number and spatial correspondence, see Sinclair, this volume, pp. 8–10); in laboratory-posed problems (as in the balance problem studied by Karmiloff-Smith & Inhelder, 1974/1975, see Brown & Reeve, this volume, pp. 202–205); or in training studies (e.g., see Inhelder et al., 1974; Murray, 1972; Strauss, 1972). Furthermore, educational curricula rooted in Piagetian theory (e.g., the instructional program on heat and temperature described by Strauss, this volume; or general educational programs such as those of Forman & Kuschner, 1978; Furth & Wachs, 1974; Kamii & DeVries, 1978) specifically capitalize on instructionally induced conflict.

The use of conflict for analyzing cognitive progress and for formulating instructional curricula is not limited to contributors working within a Piagetian orientation. Brown and Reeve, for example, cite numerous and diverse examples of both spontaneous and instructional instances of conflict-induced cognitive progress (see especially pp. 199–205).

Not all contributors, however, appear to place internal conflict at the center of instruction. In discussing the ideal relationship between instructed and constructed knowledge, for example, Resnick endorses "the design of interventions that aim to place learners in situations *where the constructions that they will inevitably make will be powerful and correct ones,* constrained by the principles that govern a domain" (p. 47, italics added).

This differential endorsement of conflict for producing cognitive development in the child is mirrored by a differential endorsement of conflict for producing development in scholarship as well. Some contributors to this volume explicitly urge us to focus on our differences:

> If it is true that progress in knowledge stems from disequilibria of which contradictions (and, in the interpersonal domain, argumentation amongst peers in a situation of collaboration, as Piaget himself adds) are an essential mechanism, then we should rather look for profound oppositions than for eclectic conciliations. Thus, as collaborators in a common cause, we should look for and highlight our differences; our agreements and common principles will look after themselves. (Sinclair, pp. 15–16)

Yet others emphasize the points of agreement:

> We are in the midst of a major convergence of psychological theories. Functionalists and structuralists, learning theorists and developmental psychologists, information-processing psychologists and Piagetians are finding common ground in today's research on cognition. (Resnick, p. 19).

That there is conflict about conflict itself is not surprising in view of the differential role contributors assign to internal versus external forces in promoting developmental progress.

QUALIFIED QUESTIONS

It should be recognized that despite an earlier warning concerning the risks of contrasting information processing and Piagetian approaches, the preceding discussion of contributors' differences seems to divide contributors precisely along these lines. This is largely because the contributors to this volume who are viewed as prototypical information-processing researchers (i.e., Resnick; Siegler) generally fall on one side of the theoretical issues discussed, while those who are viewed as prototypical Piagetians (i.e., Sinclair; Murray) generally fall on the other.

Although a division along these lines typically occurs when comparing information-processing researchers to Piagetians (see Beilin, in press; Liben, this volume), this does not mean that one *cannot* use information-processing techniques in conjunction with fundamentally structural, constructive theories (Case, 1986). It is important to note, however, that the existence of scholars who might be described as doing so (e.g., Robbie Case and Annette Karmiloff-Smith; perhaps Ann Brown and Rochel Gelman), does *not* mean that *all* researchers associated with information processing are working from theories that are fundamentally compatible with Piagetian theory. To determine theoretical compatibility, one must look at core theoretical assumptions and the intentions or goals of the research programs, not at superficial methodological techniques and vocabulary.

In view of the preceding analysis, one might justifiably argue that inviting contributors (see Preface) to consider how "questions generated within the framework of structural cognitive-developmental theories such as Piaget's have been analyzed from the perspective of a task analytic, information-processing approach" was a badly conceived request. It presupposes that we are all asking the same questions. The thrust of the argument given in the present chapter is, of course, that we are not. Although the volume cannot, therefore, offer universally acceptable answers to the questions raised in the Preface, perhaps it can help us to formulate better questions for our future dialogues.

ACKNOWLEDGMENTS

An earlier draft of this Epilogue was read by Robbie Case, Roger Downs, Rochel Gelman, and Frank Murray. On the basis of their insightful comments, I have modified some of my earlier points, and, while leaving others unchanged, have prepared myself for some of the conflict that the chapter is likely to engender. I am grateful to each of them for their generous help.

REFERENCES

Baer, D. M. (1970). An age-irrelevant concept of development. *Merrill-Palmer Quarterly, 16,* 238–245.

Beilin, H. (in press). Current trends in cognitive development research: Towards a new synthesis. In B. Inhelder, D. deCaprona, & A. Cornu-Wells (Eds.), *Piaget today*. Hillsdale, NJ: Lawrence Erlbaum Associates.

Case, R. (1986). The new stage theories in intellectual development: Why we need them, what they assert. In M. Perlmutter (Ed.), *Perspectives on intellectual development. Minnesota Symposium on Child Development* (Vol. 19, pp. 57–91). Hillsdale, NJ: Lawrence Erlbaum Associates.

Daggs, D. G. (1986). *Children's understanding of geographic hierarchies*. Paper presented at the 16th Annual Symposium of the Jean Piaget Society, Philadelphia.

Forman, G., & Kuschner, D. (1978). *The child's construction of knowledge*. Monterey: Brooks Cole.

Furth, H. G., & Wachs, H. (1974). *Thinking goes to school: Piaget's theory in practice*. New York: Oxford University Press.

Gelman, R. (1986). *First principles for structuring acquisition*. Presidential Address, Division 7, presented at the 94th Annual Convention of the American Psychological Association. Washington, D.C.

Inhelder, B., Sinclair, H., & Bovet, M. (1974). *Learning and the development of cognition*. Cambridge, MA: Harvard University Press.

Kamii, C., & DeVries, R. (1978). *Physical knowledge in preschool education*. Englewood Cliffs, NJ: Prentice-Hall.

Karmiloff-Smith, A., & Inhelder, B. (1974/1975). If you want to get ahead, get a theory. *Cognition, 3,* 195–212.

Kitchener, R. F. (1978). Epigenesis: The role of biological models in developmental psychology. *Human Development, 21,* 141–160.

Klahr, D. (1980). Information-processing models of intellectual development. In R. Kluwe & H. Spada (Eds.), *Developmental models of thinking* (pp. 127–162). New York: Academic Press.

Lerner, R. M. (1978). Nature, nurture, and dynamic interactionism. *Human Development, 21,* 1–20.

Liben, L. S. (1981). Contributions of individuals to their development during childhood: A Piagetian perspective. In R. M. Lerner & N. A. Busch-Rossnagel (Eds.), *Individuals as producers of their development: A life-span perspective* (pp. 117–153). New York: Academic Press.

Miller, P. H. (1983). *Theories of developmental psychology*. San Francisco: Freeman.

Murray, F. B. (1972). Acquisition of conservation through social interaction. *Developmental Psychology, 6,* 1–6.

Neimark, E. D., De Lisi, R., & Newman, J. L. (Eds.). (1985). *Moderators of competence*. Hillsdale, NJ: Lawrence Erlbaum Associates.

Overton, W. F. (1973). On the assumptive base of the nature-nurture controversy: Additive versus interactive conceptions. *Human Development, 16,* 74–89.

Overton, W. F. (1984). World views and their influence on psychological theory and research: Kuhn-Lakatos-Laudan. In H. W. Reese (Ed.), *Advances in child development and behavior* (Vol. 18, pp. 191–226). New York: Academic Press.

Overton, W. F., & Reese, H. W. (1973). Models of development: Methodological implications. In J. R. Nesselroade & H. W. Reese (Eds.), *Life-span developmental psychology: Methodological issues* (pp. 65–86). New York: Academic Press.

Piaget, J. (1964). Development and learning. In R. Ripple & V. Rockcastle (Eds.), *Piaget rediscovered* (pp. 7–19). Ithaca: Cornell University Press.

Piaget, J. (1965). *The moral judgment of the child*. New York: The Free Press.

Reese, H. W., & Overton, W. F. (1970). Models of development and theories of development. In L. R. Goulet & P. B. Baltes (Eds.), *Life-span developmental psychology: Research and theory* (pp. 116–145). New York: Academic Press.

Resnick, L. B. (1982). Syntax and semantics in learning to subtract. In T. P. Carpenter, J. M. Moser, & T. A. Romberg (Eds)., *Addition and subtraction: A cognitive perspective* (pp. 136–155). Hillsdale, NJ: Lawrence Erlbaum Associates.

Sameroff, A. J. (1975). Early influences on development: Fact or fancy? *Merrill-Palmer Quarterly, 21,* 267–294.

Scribner, S. (1984). Studying working intelligence. In B. Rogoff & J. Lave (Eds.), *Everyday cognition: Its development in social context* (pp. 9–40). Cambridge, MA: Harvard University Press.

Strauss, S. (1972). Inducing cognitive development and learning: A review of short-term training experiments. *Cognition, 1,* 329–357.

Author Index

Subject Index